D0554496

Bridge Across Broken Time

Bridge Across Broken Time

Chinese and Jewish Cultural Memory

Vera Schwarcz

Yale University Press

New Haven and London

Copyright © 1998 by Yale University.

All rights reserved.

This book may not be reproduced, in whole or in part, including illustrations, in any form (beyond that copying permitted by Sections 107 and 108 of the U.S. Copyright Law and except by reviewers for the public press), without written permission from the publishers.

Designed by Rebecca Gibb. Set in Joanna type by G & S Typesetters, Inc.

Printed in the United States of America by BookCrafters, Inc., Chelsea, Michigan.

Library of Congress Cataloging-in-Publication Data

Schwarcz, Vera, 1947–

Bridge across broken time : Chinese and Jewish cultural memory / Vera Shwarcz.

p.   cm.

Includes bibliographical references and index.

ISBN 0-300-06614-7 (cl. : alk. paper)

1. Jews—Civilization—Cross-cultural studies.   2. China—Civilization—Cross-cultural studies.

3. Memory—Religious aspects—Judaism.   4. Memory in literature.   I. Title.

DS113.S377   1998   97-40057

305.892′4—dc21   CIP

A catalogue record for this book is available from the British Library.

The paper in this book meets the guidelines for permanence and durability of the Committee on Production Guidelines for Book Longevity of the Council on Library Resources.

10 9 8 7 6 5 4 3 2

Contents

CONCORDIA UNIVERSITY LIBRARY
PORTLAND, OR 97211

Preface

The very idea of a bridge, of course, is a form peculiarly
dependent on such spiritual convictions. It is an act of
faith besides being a communication.

HART CRANE, "LETTER TO WALDO FRANK"

The two oldest, continuous civilizations on earth have yet to be brought into the same semantic universe. Chinese and Jewish traditions have distinctive histories, each with a highly nuanced vocabulary for the transmission of cultural remembrance. Other ancient civilizations, such as Egypt and India, also had deep memory roots, but these withered over time. Chinese and Jewish traditions, by contrast, have endured uninterrupted over millennia. This continuity is not the result of historical or geographical accident. Rather, the fact that Chinese and Jews today can look back upon the past with familiarity—literally recognizing the ancients' words in their own speech today—underscores a fierce attachment to remembrance. To understand this connection requires an effort that is by no means abstract or simply intellectual.

My work has been guided by a personal engagement with the question of cultural memory. I could not have sustained this attempt at bridge building between two very different cultural traditions without the spiritual convictions that Hart Crane talks about in his letter to Waldo Frank; for me, as for Crane, the bridge is "an act of faith" and "an act of communication." [1] Crane's act of faith is rooted in his background as an American poet, mine in the unique combination of circumstances that led me to Chinese studies.

I was born in Cluj, Transylvania, a cacophonous site that nurtured curiosity about different memorial traditions. The city is called Cluj in Romanian, Kolosvar in Hungarian, and Klausenburg in German. In our family we spoke all three languages, because no single tongue could convey the remembrances of my parents, who were Jewish survivors of the Holocaust. My father hired a Hebrew tutor for the home and sent us to Romanian schools. Under the Communist regime in Romania, we were also taught Russian and French. Naturally enough, I learned to listen to what was expressed between words, or more often wordlessly.

These listening skills served me well when I began my work in Chinese studies. I entered this field in the early 1970s, before the formal opening of relations between the United States and China. My initial interest in Chinese history centered on the abstract ideas of renaissance and revolution. Then in 1979 I became one of the first Americans to live and study on the Chinese mainland. There, I gained firsthand access to the recollections of Chinese intellectuals recovering from the trauma of the Cultural Revolution. I listened and recorded their oral histories with an ear attuned to the dilemma of survivors. The result was three books on Chinese intellectual history.

This book developed later, when I had time to absorb and analyze the resonances between the narratives of my Chinese friends and the halting tales of my parents. I became, in effect, an instrument transmuting different cultural sounds and symbols. What I heard and saw in China acquired new significance when placed in the context of Jewish concern with the transmission of cultural memory. In October 1979, for example, the closure of the Democracy Wall in downtown Beijing coincided with Yom Kippur, the Day of Awe, that began the Jewish year 5749. I spent that day reading Elie Wiesel's memoir, *Les Chants des morts*, while fasting in my dormitory room at Beijing University. Wiesel's plea on behalf of memory allowed me to hear more acutely the silences and omissions that punctuated Chinese pleas for freedom of thought after the Cultural Revolution.

By 1989, this concern with the intricacies of memorial language had developed into what a Chinese friend called zhi yin—the sound of two hearts listening to mutually appreciated music. This was an odd phrase to use during the crackdown that followed the student movement in Tiananmen Square. Yet I realized that it was an apt reckoning with older Chinese intellectuals who managed to survive one more round of persecution. On the day the government was preparing to crush the democracy movement and forbid all public recollections of it, my friend tried to piece together a truthful account of his life. He told me he felt understood by me because I was Jewish, because I was familiar with the ravage of history, and because my people had also learned how to endure. Although we came from vastly different worlds, we shared a concern with the scattered remains of broken lives. He was an aged Chinese intellectual; I was a younger woman, the daughter of Holocaust survivors. On the same day, in the same place, we both heard memory whisper: you cannot bring back what is lost, you can only mark the place where absence reigns.

In the aftermath of 1989, I again traveled to China, Israel, and Romania to delve deeper into both Chinese and Jewish traditions. From an initial interest in how survivors use cultural remembrance to deal with the problem of historical trauma, I developed a broader concern with language and memory. Finally, in April 1993, in Cluj, I was able to place this project in proper perspective. On a warm morning, I walked first to our old house and then to the Jewish cemetery that has a memorial for those who were deported to the death camps. In the afternoon, I gave a lecture on the Chinese and Jewish commitment to historical memory. Scenes first glimpsed in China in 1979 had now become real as the result of my research into the texts and rituals that transmit remembrance in these two distinctive cultural traditions. After my lecture, a young woman from the local Hungarian radio station came to interview me about this work on comparative memorial practices. In response to her questions, I found the words to summarize the circuitous germination of this book:

> The project started with the problem of memory and trauma during the Holocaust and the Cultural Revolution. But then, I decided to go back in time and look at what has kept Chinese and Jewish culture alive from ancient times to the present. . . . So much has been destroyed in Romanian and in Jewish and in Chinese history. So much has been lost. But through memory something endures. Memory is linked to loss. To remember is to acknowledge that time has been broken. I am not the same person who was born and raised in Cluj. Memory is the link I forge today, when I go out to walk in my hometown, when I look for "home."
>
> Memory does not sew the past back to the present. Or the present back to the past. Experiential time is all broken up. Memory is an acknowledgment of that fragmentation. It is the knowledge that an absence has to be bridged with words.[2]

During the years spent creating this bridge between Chinese and Jewish memories, I have received encouragement and inspiration from many different people. Foremost among them is my husband, Jason Wolfe. Early on, when I was overwhelmed by the linguistic and religious differences between Chinese and Jewish culture, he urged me to go on. In the past decade, Jason's support for this daunting effort has remained unflagging, and so this book is gratefully dedicated to him.

My parents, Katherine and Elmer Savin, provided the raw material for much of this memory work. My father, who lost his first wife in Auschwitz, told me stories about his years in forced labor with passion, and even humor. My mother, who lost her parents, first husband, and one daughter during the war, shared with me the documents used for her German reparations case. This willingness to reveal the details of their experiences made it possible for me to write about historical wounds more concretely. My mother always tried to answer my questions, no matter how painful the subject, no matter how much she would have preferred to bury the terrifying past. It took me a long time to hear all that my parents were willing to tell.

The resistance to asking questions about Jewish memory after the Holocaust is familiar to such friends as Willy Mund, Dr. Dori Laub, Nadine Fresco, and Sarah Glaz. As survivors and children of survivors, they helped me understand my own flight from the subject of this book. At critical points during research and writing, each offered a willing ear, shared a personal story, or suggested some poem or essay that sent me back looking for more. In the field of Chinese studies, I have been similarly blessed with colleagues who encouraged this inquiry into memorial practices. Wu Peiyi, Yu Yingshi, Tu Weiming, Arthur Kleinman, Albert Dien, and Lynn Struve redirected my focus at different stages. I am grateful for their bibliographic help and insightful comments on early drafts of this project.

In China, I met thoughtful practitioners of the art of memory who shared with me their personal stories. I am especially indebted to Dr. Zhong Youbin, to Professors Zhang Dainian, Tang Yijie, and Yue Daiyun, and to creative writers such as Zhang Jie, Wang Meng, and the young poet Fu Hao. In Israel, Yehuda Amichai, Sidra Ezrahi, Saul Friedlander, Natan Beyrak, Arieh Barnea, and Bozsi and Zoltan Blau greatly helped me in my effort to learn more about the Jewish context of memorial practices. Dov Bloom, a member of Kibbutz Maaleh Gilboa, stands out among my Israeli friends for his remarkable ability to make traditional sources about Jewish memory intelligible to a novice such as myself. His informed, detailed critique of this work has made me more appreciative of the intellectual and spiritual resources beyond the academic community. In Romania, Professor Ladislau Gyemant of the Moshe Carmilly Institute of Jewish Studies and Alma Seulean of the Dao Association proved to be kind hosts and helpful guides during my visit of spring 1993.

At Wesleyan University, I was able to teach four versions of a seminar on the Chinese and Jewish commitments to remembrance. The students in these classes taught me a great deal, and I am especially grateful for the ongoing correspondence with David Fine and Cheryl Pearl Sucher. Jan Willis, Ilyse Kramer, Hsu Hsiao-ch'ing, and Esther Tammuz are foremost among colleagues at Wesleyan who helped in the long evolution of this project. Debbie Sierpinski has once again worked with patience on the word processing challenges of this project—our fifth book together. At Yale University, I received guidance and new sources from Joanne Rudof, archivist at the Fortunoff Video Archive for Holocaust Testimonies. Last, but not least, I want to thank my editors at Yale University Press, Charles Grench and Karen Gangel, who have helped shape this book with their good advice. Although this is not our first collaboration, I continue to learn a great deal from them about the craft of writing.

In this book I employ the pinyin system for the transliteration of Chinese names, which is now standard around the world. References using the older Wade-Giles system, however, have been left unchanged. Unless otherwise indicated, all translations are my own. The Chinese and Hebrew calligraphy for this book come from two artist-friends, Charles Chu and Sima Hilsenrath.

Research and writing time for this study was supported by a Founder's Fellowship from the American Association for University Women, by the Guggenheim Foundation, and by a Meiggs Grant from the Department of History at Wesleyan University. In addition to generous financial aid, I have been privileged to be able to write this book in the lovely natural setting of Kibbutz Maaleh Gilboa. This small, remote, and welcoming community of observant Jews provided the daily inspiration for my effort to bring together the different worlds of Chinese and Jewish guardians of historical memory. It is on Gilboa Mountain that I finally understood how much of a blessing remembrance can be in our daily life. Bracha, the Hebrew word for "blessing," has the same numerical value (227) as the word zakhor, "to remember." Our sages teach us that this equivalence is the outer sign of a deeper connection. I can only hope that this book reveals a bit of the vast blessing that memory can bestow on those who guard it faithfully.

Introduction

Because of Memory, Because of Hope, Because of Distress

If I forget thee, oh Jerusalem
let my right hand forget its strength,
let my tongue cleave to the roof of my mouth
if I do not remember thee.

PSALM 137

Hold with the past, don't lose the past,
If you lose the past, the will easily crumbles,
If you lose the past, the sword also breaks.

MENG JIAO, "AUTUMN MEDITATIONS"

The blessings of memory are rarely voiced in positive terms. Those who try to hold on to remembrance more often see themselves burdened rather than uplifted by the effort. The past is invariably vanishing in front of our eyes. To cling to it is to try to arrest the natural erosion of time. No wonder that recollection was likened by the Russian-Jewish poet Joseph Brodsky to the predicament of "a baby clutching a basketball: one's palms keep sliding off."[1] This sweaty, almost pointless project did not deter Brodsky, nor previous generations of Jewish and Chinese rememberers, from seeking to hold on to the past.

Meng Jiao, a poet of the Tang dynasty (618–907), was intensely mindful of the slippery nature of memory. He knew that his contemporaries found flight from remembrance more convenient than the hard work of attachment to tradition. Nonetheless, he pleaded with them to return to the ancients, to honor the covenant of connectedness to the past. To make his message more urgent, Meng Jiao phrased it as a warning: if you forsake history, you will have no will left for moral action. If you turn your back upon those who came before, the weapons in your hand will break and make dominion over the present impossible. A similar warning is voiced by the Jewish psalmist who addresses himself to the exiles in Babylonia. They, like Meng Jiao's compatriots, may have preferred to forget about the past—which for the Jewish refugees was both a place and a state of mind. Yet they are prevented from taking comfort in amnesia by the poet's terrifying images, made more compelling by being spoken in the first person: If I live as if the loss of the past did not ache daily, I will be paralyzed right here and now. If I do not speak as if history matters, I will be struck dumb and find no words for the glories of the world around me.

Each poet speaks about memory as a cultural and ethical imperative. Each uses distinctive metaphors to call to mind the dangers of forgetfulness as well as the difficulties of recollection. Although the linguistic and religious differences are immense, the Chinese and Jewish poets share a passion for remembrance. This passion inspired my effort to create a dialogue between their disparate traditions. Meng Jiao, as well as the writer of psalms, is a master of his own art. Each one's recollection may be likened to a gem that bears the marks of a skilled cutter: it is unique but also fragile. Connected to the world of other rememberers who cherished the past, individual memory becomes part of the chain of remembrance that has allowed Chinese and Jewish tradition to endure from the ancient times to the present.

Ren, the Chinese ideograph for "endurance"—symbolized by a heart beneath the cutting edge of a knife—captures this emotional commitment to the past. This character suggests a difficult, protracted struggle to maintain fidelity to history in the face of violent disruption.[2] Similarly, masoret, the Hebrew word for "tradition," conveys the effort involved in the passing on of communal memories. Behind the noun one finds the verb "to transmit"—which, in turn, goes back to the Akkadian word musaru, which suggests two ideas: the grasping of an object and the setting free of something.[3] To hand on the past, in this sense, is to lay the foundations of genuine freedom.

This distinctive definition of freedom lies at the heart of both Chinese and Jewish memorial traditions. Both encourage and demand close attention to texts. Only a trained, literate person can pass traditions from generation to generation; only one who remembers (especially classical texts) can become an architect of cultural continuity. That the Chinese characters used today in the People's Daily can be directly linked to inscriptions on oracle bones of the seventh century B.C. is not a freak coincidence of history. That Jewish scientists write about thermonuclear dynamics in the same language in which the Bible first spoke about the creation of the world is no quaint tribute to political Zionism. Rather, both these marvels bear witness to repeated choices enacted in Chinese and Jewish tradition to reaffirm a commitment to the past. Over and over again, as will be shown, freedom became identified with the preservation and transmission of textual wisdom.

The cultivation of memory, however, is by no means the spiritual monopoly of Chinese and Jews. It is a subject that is moving to the center of scientific and historical studies of continuity all over the world.[4] Oliver Sacks, a neurosurgeon and writer, has summarized some of this work: "Memory itself is characteristic of life. And memory brings about a change in the organism, so that it is better adapted, better fitted to meet environmental challenges. The very 'self' of the organism is enlarged by memory." [5] This enlargement of self through attach-ment to the past is intimately familiar to the Jewish and Chinese memorialists discussed in this book. Both traditions placed a high moral value on the trans-mission of remembrance. Yet even in this appreciation of historical memory, Chinese and Jews are only remarkably distinctive, not unique. It was, after all, the Greeks who inserted the word for "witness," istor, into the heart of the his-torian's craft.[6] They also embedded "mindfulness," memor, into the core of any remembering activity.[7] Even with all its attention to history and memory, how-ever, the classical Greek tradition was not conveyed forward from ancient Athens.

Chinese and Jewish traditions, by contrast, endure in our time, making their specific, insistent, and often painful claims on contemporary lives. The warning of Meng Jiao and the psalmist did not fall on deaf ears. Their heirs today remain linked to remembrance, even if they may wish to evade its burdens. Each word they speak or write weaves them back into the fabric of the past. The Israeli poet Yehuda Amichai, for example, composes his verses in the language of the He-brew Bible. Amichai cannot walk the streets of Jerusalem without being accosted by Jewish memory. Even when he is sick and tired of its history, Amichai's at-tachment to it is transparent:

> Let the memorial hill remember instead of me,
> that's what it's here for. Let the park in-memory-of remember,
> let the street that's-named-for remember,
> let the well-known building remember,
> let the synagogue that's named after God remember
> let the rolling Torah scroll remember, let the prayer
> for the memory of the dead remember.
>
> . . . .
>
> Let the beasts of the field and the birds of the heavens
> eat and remember.
> Let all of them remember so that I can rest.[8]

But, of course, there is no rest from memory. Amichai may groan under the memorial burden of his tradition, yet he passes it on all the same. He repeats the word yizkor (memorial) like an incantation that will not leave his ears: "Sheha-yizkor yizkor" (So the memorial may remember). Rather than muffling the call of the past, remembrance only makes it more insistent. The author of Psalm 137 speaks through the voice of Amichai. Like the exiles in Babylonia, the contemporary Israeli finds no repose in history and cannot but take his place in it. In fact, his pen name revives it: Amichai means, literally, "my people lives." The poet seals a memory covenant with the language and the land and the people that give him no rest.

Similarly, the Chinese poet Bei Dao, a former Red Guard who took on the pen name "Northern Island," wants to be done with remembrance. Like Yehuda Amichai, he keeps being accosted by a past embedded in the very language of his flight. He pushes away and clings to memory all at once. In the end, Bei Dao, too, comes to cherish the burden of history:

> Let me tell you world,
> I—do—not—believe!
> If a thousand challengers lie beneath your feet,
> Count me as the number one thousand and one.
> A new juncture and glimmering stars
> Adorn the unobstructed sky.
> They are the thousand-year-old pictographs,
> The staring eyes of future generations.[9]

The Chinese rebel wants to be utterly distinctive in his disbelief. He insists on the uniqueness of his challenge to tradition (in Bei Dao's case, the dogma inherited from the Mao era). He spells out his rebellion by lengthening the intervals between four simple words: "wo bu xiang xin" (I do not believe). Yet the young man who calls himself a lonely island also chooses to draw closer to the ideographs of his ancestors and thereby look into the eyes of future generations. It is as impossible for the Chinese poet to forsake his history-burdened compatriots as it is for Yehuda Amichai to tear away from the remembrance-encrusted city of Jerusalem. The very words that Bei Dao uses link him to Meng Jiao and the Chinese tradition.

Yehuda Amichai and Bei Dao are reluctant rememberers who both heed and transmit memory. Each is embedded in a culture that defines identity in terms of historical precedent. Neither can make sense of himself or be understood by others unless he is read through the eyes of tradition. To open up a dialogue between their traditions, I have had to listen to their distinctive cadences. Consequently, this is not simply a work of comparative history. Rather it is a translation and transmutation of one set of cultural concerns into the language and worldview of another. My goal in placing the Chinese memorial practices I have studied alongside Jewish ones that are my native inheritance is not to dwell on their similarities. It is my hope that through a concrete appreciation of the differences between Chinese and Jewish tradition, we shall discern how memory keeps each more fully alive today.

Worlds Apart

In linking two differing traditions of remembrance, I have had to reckon, most obviously, with the disparity between the monotheism of Jewish tradition and the pervasive organicism of the Chinese worldview. The concept of a world-transcending God is key to all Jewish memorial practice. This source-being is both a model for and a guardian of human remembrance. For Jews, memory is not only a cultural habit but a religious commandment. Chinese cosmology, on the other hand, revolves around the concept of Heaven, which embraces all of nature and becomes synonymous with it over time. The Chinese commitment to remembrance grows out of this organismic conception of the universe and returns it through the rituals of ancestor worship and imperially sponsored historiography.

Although I have been intensely mindful of the gulf between Chinese and Jewish worldviews, David Fine, one of my students, has made an argument for their essential similarity. First in a paper for a course on traditional China, then in a published article, he wrote that Chinese and Jews share a "Judeo-Confucian tradition which has kept the identity of two great peoples over three thousand years." [10] Fine's aim is to counter generalizations about the Judeo-Christian tradition (which often denies the distinctive spiritual insights of the Hebrew Bible). His essay dwells on Chinese and Jewish cultural practices that seem analogous to the point of being identical. From an initial discussion of how tradition was handed down in Chinese and Jewish antiquity, he goes on to emphasize the similarity between the cultural position of the rabbi and the Chinese scholar-official and between Confucian ritual (li) and Jewish law (halakha). It is, perhaps, the gift of the novice to see equivalence where parallels prevail. Fine, a learned student of Jewish texts, is more at home in the world of the Zionist pioneer Ahad Ha-Am (Asher Ginzberg) than in the classical Chinese documents that informed the commitments of Confucian poets such as Meng Jiao. No wonder that he clinches his argument about the importance of cultural memory in Chinese and Jewish tradition with Ahad Ha-Am's plea for attachment to the holiness of the Sabbath: "He who truly feels in his heart a connection with the life of his people throughout the generations will find it quite impossible . . . to picture for himself the existence of the people of Israel without the Queen Sabbath." [11]

I share David Fine's concern with the continuity of the Jewish people and Ha-Am's conviction that it is the Sabbath that has kept us going through the long centuries of turmoil and exile. But I am also mindful that there is nothing in Chinese ritual that is analogous to this constant sanctification of time. The ongoing rootedness of Chinese culture in the heartland of East Asia made the relationship to space at least as important as ruminations about time. Confucian scholar-officials were blessed with a relatively uninterrupted connection to the birthplace of their civilization. Jewish history, by contrast, has been marked by a separation from the birthplaces of Jewish identity. Until the establishment of the state of Israel, religious memory was the main expression of communal identity across many lands.

The transmission of memory, too, was envisaged differently in Chinese and Jewish culture. The Torah was originally handed down by divinely inspired prophets, whereas Confucian ideals grew out of the accumulated wisdom of secularly sanctioned sages. William Theodore de Bary, a senior Western scholar of Confucianism, elaborated this distinction between the Confucian sage and the Jewish prophet in his work *The Trouble with Confucianism*.[12] After several decades of dedicated sinological inquiry into the origins of Confucian ideals, de Bary allowed himself to ask what went wrong in the practice of Confucianism. Interestingly, he did not answer this question on the basis of Chinese sources alone but felt compelled to look at the origins of Judaism as well. Although both sage and prophet, according to de Bary, assumed the role of moral leadership in their communities, Confucian critics of the existing social order lacked a prophetic sense of transcendence.

This limitation became, over time, the main vulnerability of Chinese intellectuals in the face of autocratic regimes. They could and did talk endlessly about cultural ideals and about the moral responsibility of the ruler to the ruled. They could talk to the emperor, they could talk for the wordless masses, but they were unable to overcome the discourse that wove their words back into the imperial system they were seeking to critique. Jewish prophets, however, spoke God's words, and their prophecy was rooted in a concept of transcendence. This idea of righteousness authorized beyond the social and natural universe was, according to de Bary, a distinctively new development in the religious consciousness of the ancient Near East. Because of the prophets' belief in a radically transcendent Being, the whole earthly order (including monarchical institutions) became relativized. Prophets, unlike Confucian sages, could not only plead with rulers but challenge them:

In this way we may speak of a clean break made by the ancient Hebrew prophets with the prevailing institution of cosmological kingship in the Middle East. The Confucian noble men stood in a more ambiguous relationship with the imperial center than the Hebrew prophets did. In the foreground, the belief in inner transcendence and the concomitant ethics of spiritual aspiration clearly pointed to the noble man as an alternative center of meaning and authority that stood in tension with the Son-of-Heaven. In the background, however, the belief in Heaven, with its earthly linkages, often turned into a truncated transcendence.[13]

Chinese guardians of ethical values and cultural memory did not have a concept of God to draw upon in their battles with imperial abuse. Nor did they have the Jewish prophet's certainty that he spoke to a cohesive community—to the people of Israel—with their specific destiny in world transformation. The sage protects the people, speaks for them, whereas the masses, as a collectivity, have no voice.

Yet despite the considerable differences between prophets and sages explored by de Bary, there is a certain similarity of purpose. Both share an enduring concern with cultural memory and the fate of humanity in this world. This similarity was aptly summarized by Benjamin Schwartz, another eminent sinologist fascinated by Chinese-Jewish comparisons, in his masterful study *The World of Thought in Ancient China*. Schwartz wrote: "While Moses and the prophets [when compared to the Confucianists] may be 'god-centered,' they are not theologians, and the diverse revelations which they receive all direct their attention back to the concern with the salvation of man." [14] The central theme of Schwartz's study of the origins of Confucianism is the question of how to become fully human—a concern that grows out of Chinese sources. Moses and the prophets are brought into the discussion to highlight Confucian concerns and to place these in a universal context.

Both Benjamin Schwartz and William Theodore de Bary probe Chinese-Jewish similarities from a distinctively sinological perspective. Unlike David Fine, who is studying to become a rabbi, they are China scholars who have spent decades decoding the complexity of Confucian texts and their usage in imperial and bureaucratic practice. Toward the end of their distinguished careers, each writer ventured guardedly into the realm of comparative historiography. This was not the case with Joseph Levenson, a Chinese historian who died in a boating accident in California in 1969. Although he did not live long enough to fulfill all the promise of his work, Levenson left the field of sinology deeply marked by an insistently comparative perspective. From his first book, *Liang Ch'i-ch'ao and the Mind of Modern China*, to his masterful trilogy, *Confucian China and Its Modern Fate*, Levenson was determined to redraw the parameters of Chinese historiography in light of his own concerns as a Jewish intellectual. He introduced an urgent emphasis upon cultural subjectivity into an academic discipline that prides itself on prolonged mastery of difficult ideographs. Whereas most China specialists have been trained to pay close attention to what is discrete and unique in Chinese tradition, Levenson asked questions that emphasized cross-cultural problems.

The transmission of cultural memory is one such problem. By the time I began to explore it in Chinese and Jewish contexts, I had in front of me Levenson's pioneering work. The third volume of *Confucian China* became for me a kind of manifesto of the historian's creed. In this text, Levenson wrote that one must "take one's own day seriously, retaining the moral need to declare oneself and stand somewhere, not just swim in time." [15] I read the trilogy over and over, searching for Levenson's anchor in the river of time. I found it in the plethora of Chinese-Western comparisons, a testimony to Levenson's cosmopolitan reaching as well as to his insistence that Chinese history must make sense in the same world of meaning that we construct for ourselves in the West.

Levenson's trilogy ends with a Hassidic tale. His last, unfinished manuscript was titled "The Choice of Jewish Identity." [16] To be a Jew—or, more precisely, to attempt the task of becoming a Jew through effortful inquiry into one's inherited traditions—was Levenson's way of declaring where he stood. It was a moral commitment grounded not in the marvelous intricacies of Chinese history but in what he saw as the core meaning of the revelation at Sinai: "Jewish particularity stems from a positive definition of the meaningful life. It does not have—as the exclusiveness of the 'white race' does have—the superiorness, the lack of inner existence, of mere negation." Jewish particularism, according to Levenson, is not a cultural burden but a starting point for critical consciousness. He also knew well that to affirm one's subjectivity so explicitly was bound to be "a scandal to so many open minds with large views, anchored in closed communities and petty selves." [17] Nonetheless, Levenson dared to reclaim his particular inheritance even as he pursued his inquiry into Chinese intellectual history.

Like Levenson, I am interrogating China's past in the light of decisive dilemmas posed by my Jewish inheritance. This refraction can be mistaken for projection. An early critic of Levenson's work phrased his reservations about a Jewishly minded sinology as follows: "Levenson's tools were not the products of Chinese history, but of a mind trained in Western methods and traditions, a cosmopolitan American Jewish intellectual's way of speaking about Chinese intellectuals."[18] This critique stings even today. As I proceed with my inquiry into Chinese and Jewish memorial practices, I ask: Are my analytical tools the products of Chinese history? Can any Westerner—never mind a self-conscious Jewish intellectual like Levenson—grapple with the lives of Chinese intellectuals without taking the vocabulary of his or her own culture into account? Clearly, conventional sinology would answer the latter question in the affirmative. Joseph Levenson, by contrast, put forth a counter argument in an essay titled "Will Sinology Do?" Answering those who would discourage us from bringing outside concerns into the parameters of Chinese studies, Levenson wrote: "We never really know what is without knowing what it is not. Sinology cannot alone fulfill sinology. We have to see darkly through cultures, to see one culture clearly. Only from this nettle, intellectual danger, may we pluck this flower of assurance."[19]

The challenge of seeing darkly is at the heart of this work on Chinese and Jewish memory. To be sure, my Jewish inheritance differs from that of Joseph Levenson. He was the product of an American-Jewish experience and had great faith in the cosmopolitan values of the Diaspora. He could write of nettles and flowers because the dangers of comparison were largely intellectual. Like David Fine, his main quarrel was with the Judeo-Christian tradition, and so he explored Chinese-Jewish similarities with verve and confidence. My own Jewish identity is marked by Eastern European history. After the Holocaust, Romania's state socialism forced Jewish memory into corners far darker than Levenson's metaphors. Public remembrance was an event orchestrated by those who held power. To be sure, they could not contain all its elusive energy. Fragments of personal recollection broke through the official performance. In Cluj, as in Moscow or Prague or Budapest, a forgotten name would be spoken, a repressed event commemorated in a synagogue or church.[20] This danger-filled appreciation of memorial crevices now prevents me from pursuing the problem of recollection in a theoretical framework. Instead, this book is grounded in the voices and visions of those who managed to cultivate remembrance in inimical times. At its core lies what my Chinese friend called *zhi yin* in 1989: a mutual understanding that depends on the will to piece together fragments of broken time.

Abstraction is ill suited to the subject at hand. Remembrance, according to the German-Jewish literary critic Walter Benjamin, does not proceed in the manner of a straightforward narrative but instead "must assay its spade in ever-new places and in the old ones delve to ever deeper levels."[21] Benjamin, like Levenson, was a Jewish intellectual in rebellion against the assumptions of historicism. He, too, sought to argue for the moral need to declare oneself, not just to swim in time. Benjamin's time, however, was arrested in midstream not by a boating accident but by the dread of being captured as a fugitive Jew on the border between France and Spain. A victim of Nazi persecution, Benjamin took his own life in 1944. His "Theses on the Philosophy of History," like Joseph Levenson's *Confucian China and Its Modern Fate*, inspires these explorations into Chinese and Jewish memorial roots. To develop this study, I had to stray further from conventional historiography and closer and closer to what Benjamin called the "construction" of historical truth: "No fact that is a cause is for that reason historical. . . . A historian that takes this as his point of departure stops telling the sequence of events like the beads of a rosary. . . . For every second was the straight gate through which the Messiah might enter."[22]

Walter Benjamin wrote about gates. I prefer the metaphor of the bridge for the task at hand. Both are narrow passageways carved out of a difficult material. The bridge between Chinese and Jewish memory constructed here is not based upon mutual contact or influence, though certain moments of historical convergence are discussed at length. My focus, rather, is upon a shared commitment to the transmission of remembrance. I have tried to let each culture speak in its own voice, embroidered with its distinctive metaphors. Precisely because the Jewish and Chinese cultures are so different, they cannot be simply placed alongside one another. Connections must be conceived with care.

Building Bridges

A bridge, by its very nature, links separate and distinct shores. The Chinese word for "bridge," qiaoliang, is rooted in an ancient ideograph depicting a plank of wood placed across a stream.[23] Out of this plain beginning emerged the elaborate art of Chinese bridge building that so impressed Marco Polo, the Venetian merchant who visited thirteenth-century Hangzhou. After seeing some of the 347 bridges that adorned the capital of the southern Song dynasty, he wrote back about the marvels of a million. Although Marco Polo exaggerated what he had seen in China, he managed to convey the grace and daring that guided Chinese bridge builders. Their skill in designing pierced spandrels, as exemplified by the Great Stone Bridge built in the seventh century, was unique and innovative in its time.[24] Chinese methods of making bridges lighter and longer were not adopted in Western Europe until the eighteenth century.

Chinese bridges arch, indeed almost leap across watery divides. The engineering techniques that gird their beauty from below augment the delight of informed passersby. Those not familiar with the art of bridge building would undoubtedly experience awe mixed with fear if they encountered a narrow structure stretching across a daunting precipice—the type of bridge found in most Chinese landscape painting and in the more remote corners of China. Yang Shen, a sixteenth-century traveler in southwest China, described his emotions upon crossing a gorge on an iron-chain suspension bridge:

> Fearful of step, on the flying ladder I advance.
> Woven of iron, a lonely thread straight through the sky
> In malarious mists the cloud-dragons wander,
> In the abyss below, peacocks drink the river's spume . . .
> China's heartland so far, a myriad miles from here.
> With the ancients' deeds in mind
> How can my heart not fill to overflowing?[25]

This poem captures aptly the emotions of a dangerous crossing. The bridge of seemingly firm iron is nothing more than a fragile ladder threading its way skyward. Malarious mists may be the physical reflection of the hubris discovered within. Like Yang Shen, I am also fearful of step as I build a bridge between Jewish and Chinese memory. I am constantly mindful of the abyss below: the vast cultural differences that are more real than a river's spume. Yet I persist, drawn forward by the possibility that the ancients' deeds—and texts—will guide me across. Remembrance is a particular form of action. If well cultivated, memorial acts may even strengthen the heart in moments of difficult transition.

The Hebrew words related to bridge building are considerably more cautionary than the Chinese. Gesher, the term for "bridge," does not appear in the Hebrew Bible. To fully understand its connotations, one must turn to the Talmud, the great compilation of oral law and commentary codified after the destruction of the Second Temple. This encyclopedic collection of legal decisions, parables, and lengthy debates among rabbinical authorities embodies the process of memory transmission itself. Contradictory interpretation of existing facts and disputes about observable events are all preserved here.[26] To engage the Talmud in study is to enter into a stream of ongoing recollection. The more one learns about its intricacies and disputes the more deeply one becomes inscribed into the fabric of a living past. Talmudic references to gesher, unlike Chinese discussions of bridges, are far from poetic. The Jewish sages are concerned with deciding questions of law and morality. Bridges, by their nature, complicate these matters. For example, should two herds separated by a bridge be considered two different entities for the purpose of taxation? The answer is no, since bridges unite—they make two seemingly separate categories one.[27]

In another passage, the question of the desirability of bridges is considered in light of the Romans, who excelled in building ramps, bathhouses, and marketplaces for trade. The rabbis witnessed all this with a critical eye and put their reservations into the mouth of Shimon bar Yohai, who responded to the boasts of the conquerors: "All that they made they made for themselves; they built market-places, to set harlots in them; baths, to rejuvenate themselves; bridges, to levy tolls for them."[28] Although the Romans were held in contempt, bridges, according to sages of the Talmud, were both necessary and problematic. They were to be used, not praised. Crossings were neither encouraged nor forbidden. Spiritual caution prevailed.

Another, less guarded appreciation of gesher comes through in the Midrash, a compilation of stories woven around the interstices of the Hebrew Bible. In one such tale, Jacob—the patriarch whose name becomes synonymous with the Jewish people—is likened to a bridge: "Asa atsmo k'mo gesher" (He made himself into a bridge).[29] This passage evokes the image of a giant, his feet planted in disparate worlds, ferrying treasures from bank to bank. Jacob, who left his homeland, eventually returned to it much enriched (with wives, children, and property). The land of Israel became greatly strengthened by the man who dared to be like a bridge.

Jacob's descendants continued to meditate upon bridge building with awe. Jediah ben Avraham Bedersi, a Provençal poet of the late thirteenth century, for example, called the whole world "a strong sea while time was but a flimsy bridge built over it."[30] This poetic evocation of earthly existence as a bridge over troubled waters is elaborated in the Hassidic teachings of Rabbi Nachman of Bratslav (1772–1811). This great mystic knew from personal experience the terrors of traversing a dangerous terrain. After a lifetime of warring with depression, sexual urges, and intellectual confusion, he deemed bridge crossing to be the quintessential human endeavor.[31] One of Rabbi Nachman's most famous sayings places the idea of gesher at the heart of the Jewish worldview: "Know this: Man must traverse a very, very narrow bridge, but what is most important is not to be afraid at all."[32] Transformed into a popular Israeli song, this teaching is heard on the lips of children today. Although they do not yet understand the difficulties of spiritual discipline, the image of the world as *gesher tzar meod*—a narrow bridge that can be fearlessly traversed—has enormous appeal.

The metaphor of the narrow bridge links the far-flung worlds of Rabbi Nachman of Bratslav and the Chinese scholar-official Yang Shen. Both knew the dangers awaiting one who ventures across the abyss of earthly existence. For both, a bridge can be as fragile as thread or as strong as the will of the individual who dares to confront inner and outer demons. The cultural crossing attempted in this work has its own "cloud dragons"—the vast cultural differences between Chinese and Jewish traditions. Consequently, caution must govern the first step.

Proceeding with caution, I am mindful of another link in Hebrew etymology: that between *gesher* and *kesher*. The latter word means a "knot," an act of will that binds the disconnected. Without straining cultural uniqueness too much, this book seeks to knot together the disparate worlds of Chinese and Jewish rememberers. Each chapter explores a specific question about the transmission of cultural memory. First, I explore the challenge that embodied memory poses to existing notions of intellectual history. Next, I consider the way in which metaphor becomes a distinctive aid to memory in Chinese and Jewish tradition and how personal memory manages to insert itself into public commemorations in both of these cultural worlds. Finally, this book circles the sore subject of my family's history—the Holocaust in Transylvania—which I approach only after a consideration of the Jewish experience in Shanghai and as a prelude to some reflections on memory and the healing of historical wounds.

The bridge I am constructing here is a rambling structure. It resembles the winding wooden path in a painting by the Ming dynasty scholar Mi Wanzhong. Although this bridge is narrow, like the one traversed by Yang Shen and immortalized in the teachings of Rabbi Nachman of Bratslav, it is not a fear-inspiring structure. Instead, it allows for a leisurely pace, for contemplation of discrete detail. Its twistings and bendings prevent a straight crossing and thereby evoke an alternative narrative strategy. This bridge was designed by Mi Wanzhong during the last years of the Wan Li reign (1612–1624). A famous painter, Mi spent his life close to imperial politics. He was dismissed from office in 1625 after being denounced at court by a powerful eunuch. Like many of the rememberers discussed in this book, Mi Wanzhong took refuge from the murky present in the beauty and complexity of cultural memory. In a village northwest of the capital, he planned and later painted the twisting paths, the clear pools, the strangely accosting rocks, and the inviting pavilions of Spoon Garden (Shao Yuan). There, he could commune with friends as well as with the poet-painters of past generations:

Facing the Western Hills,
Sipping wine relaxed in the moonlight.[33]

Spoon Garden (Shao Yuan), hand scroll painted by Mi Wanzhong, ca. 1625. (Courtesy of Hou Renzhi, Beijing University)

Mi Wanzhong's Shao Yuan stands on the grounds occupied by Peking University today. It has withstood the collapse of two dynasties as well as the tamperings of Westerners ranging from European diplomats to American missionaries. Shao Yuan has outlasted even the murderous decade of the Cultural Revolution. The very endurance of this site reflects the resiliency of cultural memory. In the words of Hou Renzhi, the garden's foremost historian in our time: "If we do not recall the past, we can hardly believe what a painful experience the quiet corner of our campus has undergone. We are sure, the past is not to be forgotten."[34]

Chinese gardens were always meant to be sites that nurture and transmit remembrance. Paths, arcades, and rock formations were supposed to kindle recollection. As a result of careful planning by highly cultured literati like Mi Wanzhong, a walk through the garden becomes a memory stroll embellished by well-placed quotations from previous amblers and cultivators of the art of remembrance.[35] The two gentlemen in Mi's painting have stopped their bridge crossing to admire a willow, perhaps to share some lines of poetry—like the ones that are used throughout this book to make the subject of memory less abstract. Just as Chinese gardeners borrow their surroundings to open up the vistas of memory, I am borrowing Mi Wanzhong's bridge to evoke a link between Chinese and Jewish memory.

This book, however, is not simply a stroll on the bridge of memory. Because it deals with Jewish as well as Chinese rememberers and because the stuff of their recollection is often traumatic, I have had to draw upon less lyrical metaphors as well. Hart Crane's bridge of faith is one such image. When the young poet from Ohio saw the mighty links of the Brooklyn Bridge, he had to call forth within himself something he called "faith," and he sang its praises:

Some motion ever unspent in thy stride—
Implicitly thy freedom staying thee! [36]

These lines mirror a physical structure as well as the poet's determination to balance freedom from the past with the staying power of unspent motion. Crane's bridge links past and future. The poet who contemplates freedom does not shake off the claim of history. It changes and moves with him, through him, as it were.

The paradox of an ever-changing yet firmly anchored past is also at the heart of the Jewish commitment to remembrance. It, too, is based upon a faith. According to the theologian Abraham Joshua Heschel, this unwillingness to sever the cord of memory accounts for the spiritual survival of Jews in our time:

Why did our hearts throughout the ages turn to Erets Israel, to the Holy Land? Because of memory, because of hope, because of distress.

Because of memory. There is a slow and silent stream, a stream not of oblivion but of memory, from which we must constantly drink before entering the realm of faith. To believe is to remember. The substance of our very being is memory, our way of living is retaining reminders, articulating memory. [37]

Heschel seems to be restating here what Oliver Sacks argues is the precondition for survival in all advanced organisms. Both writers assert that memory is the core of life itself. But Heschel is saying this as a Jew, as the self-conscious heir to a long tradition of remembrance. I am part of that tradition. However far Beijing may seem from Jerusalem, my sojourns in these cities demanded an encounter with both Jewish and Chinese tradition. Abstractions about cosmopolitanism no longer sufficed when I came face-to-face with the fragments of a living past.

ONE

How to Make Time Real

From Intellectual History to Embodied Memory

What can you dream to make Time real again?
I have read in a book that dream is the mother of memory,
And if there is no memory . . . —oh, what—is Time?

ROBERT PENN WARREN, "DREAM"

Fragments of a living past accost the historian at every turn, and unlike ideas, they will not stay still or fit neatly into the frameworks we construct. To reconstruct the full meaning of a piece of history requires that we dream time anew. Robert Penn Warren was not a historian but a chronicler of the human spirit. Yet he grasped better than many of us who work on wars and revolutions (with their seemingly solid reference points in the chronology of nations) the urgency of dreaming time anew. He understood that temporality encompasses us and carries us toward understanding—often through pathways far removed from academic rationality.

Warren's question—"if there is no memory . . . what is Time?"—suggests that memory is the raw material that allows us to make time concrete, a bridge we cast backward to connect with those who went before us. Their lives demand our attention not because they were significant but because we must encounter them on intimate terms before our own present and future can assume more humane proportions. The Chinese and Jewish guardians of memory in our time have had their full share of dreaming. Although the metaphor sounds lyrical, the experience of creating a new sense of temporality is not. Historians who would capture that experience in their works have to traverse the same difficult terrain as the subjects they write about. Dislocation is the hallmark of this landscape. Ordinary time suddenly becomes unfamiliar, and one is forced to rethink connections between past and present. Such displacement may be the result of physical exile from one's native place or spiritual distance from the pieties that one's contemporaries use to make sense of daily life. The psalmist and Meng Jiao, as well as Yehuda Amichai and Bei Dao, experienced some kind of dislocation, in that each had to refashion his relationship to time.

This refashioning is anything but orderly or elegant. Instead, it is like the stammer of one who has been forsaken by the mother tongue. Jews, dispersed in many lands, have created their memorial practices out of this shared experience of displacement. The Chinese, who have entered the twentieth century through a series of revolutions that dislodged them from the classical language of Confucianism, also know memory to be a fragile mother tongue. I did not understand the full extent of this vulnerability until I went to live in Beijing and was forced to give up my previous generalizations about Chinese history. In my encounters with contemporary intellectuals, I had to pay attention to what they said as well as to what they could not voice, either psychologically or politically. Silence, laughter, and digression from recollection were all part of the memorial process. As in the reconstruction of my childhood in Romania, history had to be pieced together from surviving fragments, and no one language sufficed to tell what had taken place.

Memory distinguishes the past we inherit from the history we create for ourselves. Robert Penn Warren's fellow Southerner Eudora Welty also grappled with this distinction. Like Warren, she was not a historian, yet her novel *The Optimist's Daughter* captures the vitality that remembrance infuses into the dead fabric of the past better than most history books. Whereas Warren spoke of dreams, Welty's heroine contemplates her father's coffin and fastens onto the tears, the wounds, and the final grace that memory bestows upon the living: "The past is no more open to help or hurt than father in his coffin. The past, like him, is impervious and can never be awakened. It is memory that is the somnambulist. It will come back from its wound calling us by our own name and demanding its rightful tears. . . . Memory can be hurt time and again. But in that may lie its final mercy. As long as it is vulnerable to the living moment, it lives for us." [1] And through us, I would add. Only when we are ready to have memory call out our name, when we respond to the haunting call of the "somnambulist" do we really wake to the promise of living fully in time. Insofar as history comes alive for us, we become more alive in the present as well. For the sake of this vitality we risk the possibility of repeated pain. Time cannot become concrete unless it winds itself around the gritty details of our lives. A historian who, like the optimist's daughter, wants to understand the past must become vulnerable to the living moment. Great ideas and grand themes are no substitute for the coffin, the wound, the tears of daily life.

When I arrived at Stanford University to begin graduate study in Chinese history, the importance of this grounded temporality was not immediately obvious to me. In 1971 the campus was on fire with ideas, especially the concept of student revolution. I was there to do research on the May Fourth Movement of 1919, a seminal moment in the Chinese students' revolution. The combination was heady. Geographical distance from China, on one hand, and proximity to American slogans about the liberating promise of revolution, on the other, allowed me to conflate past and present. For a while, I had no need of memory, because the possibility of contact with Chinese revolutionaries did not exist.

Having experienced China only as an abstraction at that time, I imagined historiography as a dizzying concoction of ideas. I read Jean-Paul Sartre (the guru of the student revolution) and made my way slowly through Lu Xun, the history-seasoned witness of China's social upheavals. My dissertation centered on the ideas of Individualism, Liberalism, Renaissance, Enlightenment and, of course, Revolution. I began to teach Chinese history while the Yellow River and the Yangtze were still no more than intriguing lines on a map. Then, three years after finishing my thesis, I visited China for the first time, as a member of one of the first groups of official exchange scholars. I arrived in Beijing in February 1979, and as I began to meet octogenarian survivors of the May Fourth Movement, the events of 1919 began to lose their capitalized abstraction. It took another decade for me to realize how deadly such abstractions can be—not only because people have been killed in the name of ideas but because abstraction itself desiccates the fabric of history.

Now that I am circling back to the details of Chinese and Jewish memory, I am more mindful of how ideas can dull one's historical sensibility. Long before I began to delve into my parents' experiences during the war, I was aware of how little I understood (or was moved by) writings about the Holocaust. It was too huge a container for the shards I had collected in an attempt to make sense out of my past. I needed something smaller, more intimate, more forgiving of loose ends. And so I began to listen to the voices of Jewish rememberers that had been collected at the Fortunoff Video Archives for Holocaust Testimonies at Yale.[2] The lives of Chinese intellectuals, in turn, became more real for me as I learned more about the fate of men and women who had shared my parents' nightmare.

The Holocaust, as Judith Miller has argued, makes sense only bit by bit—only if we try to encounter it one story, one memory, at a time. Otherwise the numbers and technicalities become so overwhelming that revisionists feel justified in arguing that the Holocaust never took place. Concretely embodied memory, however, is a powerful antidote to Holocaust revisionism. It is also the most effective antidote against a dullness about the past that invades us through abstraction. Singular fragments rescued from the totalizing impulse are the historian's best ammunition. In Chinese as well as in Jewish history, Judith Miller's message carries urgent significance: "Abstraction is memory's most ardent enemy. It kills because it encourages distance, often indifference. We must remind ourselves that the Holocaust was not six million. It was one, plus one, plus one. . . . [Only thus] is the incomprehensible given meaning." [3] How to make time real is therefore not only a poet's question but a historian's imperative. And there is no more meaningful or more difficult place to start than remembrance.

Memory: A Rough-Hewn Mother Tongue

The ancient Greeks envisaged remembrance as the wellspring of all creative life. Mnemosyne, goddess of memory, is considered the mother of the nine Muses, inspiring everything from mathematics to dance, poetry, and drama. The Muses, according to Homer, are nourished by and also provoke remembrance. They pour the spiritual powers of their mother into the heart and mind of the poet. [4] Clio, the Muse of history, is one of Mnemosyne's daughters. She, too, demands attention to memory's call and does not bestow her song except on those who would pay homage to her mother. No Greek historian presumed to arrange facts unless recollection guided the patterning mind. [5]

The force of the Greeks' early insight into the generative powers of memory has been lost over time. Having relinquished the rich vocabulary of memory to the storage capabilities of computers, we now face our past with a constricted vision of Mnemosyne and Clio. The contemporary philosopher Edward Casey has warned repeatedly against the modern flight from memory. His encyclopedic work *Remembering: A Phenomenological Study* suggests that our diminishing appreciation of Mnemosyne is the result of an infatuation with another idol—Reason. According to Casey, from Descartes onward Western thinkers have wanted nothing to do with memory because it is a muse filled with doubt. Neither Mnemosyne nor Clio can give a simple answer to the current question about what is true. [6]

George Allan, a modern heir of Descartes, takes this critique of memory one step further. The problem with recollection, he says, is not merely its uncertainty but the challenge it poses to our perception of the world altogether. The only way to still the voice of doubt is to make the experience of the past analogous to our mastery of the present: "When I remember something I had previously experienced, I am merely having a new present experience. I do not re-experience the prior experience; I have a quite different experience which I claim is a replication, a copy, of the earlier one." [7] If the present is nothing more than a replica of the past, then Clio has nothing to add, no song to waken in the remembering mind. If there is no point to reexperiencing history, then why bother to weep like the optimist's daughter? Why look into the coffin again?

Allan's critique of memory does not consider these questions. It promises mastery over the past without explaining its power to stir and inspire us. Yet Mnemosyne does not spring solely from the mind. She is on intimate terms with the heart, with the shadowy places where longing, dreams, and nightmares commingle with history. No wonder that memory cannot answer the positivist's query: "What precisely happened back then and there?" Instead, she whispers some dark song, closer to a half-forgotten lullaby than to an empirically verifiable fact. Memory, in this sense, bears all the stretch marks of a mother tongue. She is capacious enough to accommodate our questions about the facts of the past and wise enough to remind us that the truth of historical experience lies beyond what can be known through reason alone.

In French, the very word for memory has two aspects: un mémoire is a male, fact-anchored narrative constructed about the past; une mémoire is a recollection, suggesting a feminine perception of events. These two concepts evoke the duality of remembrance: it is both a goal-oriented act and a surrender of mastery over the past. This latter sense of la mémoire is at the core of an essay by Nancy Huston entitled "A Tongue Called Mother," the work of a woman who was raised in an English-speaking world but who chose to become a writer in French. Huston left her mother tongue behind only to come back to it enriched by another cultural experience: What are we able to say more clearly with borrowed words? What are the advantages—and disadvantages—of straying far from the language of our first memories? What gets betrayed and what gets transmuted in moving between two cultural worlds? With an ear trained to listen for the gendered mythology of discourse, she writes: "It's the father's voice that stands for reason. . . . Our mother's voice, our mother's tongue, [is associated with] licking our wounds and tickling our ears and instructing us all at once, so that the word itself has become an inextricable mixture of body and mind, concrete and abstract, the wet pink mass of taste buds." [8]

Huston goes on to play with the dichotomies of body and mind, concrete and abstract, evoking a nurturing image of the mother tongue only to quarrel with it in the end. She refers to licked wounds and linguistic taste buds, yet she cannot hide the ambivalence of a woman who chose to flee the warm embrace of native speech. Only later, after many novels, essays, and poems written in French, does she allow herself to take the risk of returning to the sonorities of early pain. [9]

This is a risk that I, too, know well. My mother tongue was Hungarian. Anya nyelv, the Hungarian expression for native speech, is related to both "beehive" and "womb." [10] It brings with it a coating of honey—a seeming sweetness that belies the dangers, the sting of history, it connoted for me. In this hardly mothering tongue are preserved my earliest questions about family history. When I was about five years old, a neighbor showed me a photograph album about Auschwitz that I was instructed, in Hungarian, never to open. In the meantime, my parents spoke to each other in German about the war, about parents and spouses they had lost. They did not want the children to know any of this, so they retired behind their childhood words and the glass doors of the bedroom. I couldn't help but press my head against that door, trying to decipher the German, in the same way that I itched to open the album. My schooling in Romania's state institutions did nothing to answer or quiet these questions about the past. They were simply put aside, at least for a while, as I learned the new language of socialist optimism.

But the Romanian vocabulary I learned in school did provide mastery over the past. It is the nature of memory to scratch, to disturb the harmony that borrowed words create temporarily. When the Hungarian we spoke at home and the German whispered behind glass doors finally broke through the enforced quiet, I found myself in company of other writers ill at ease with mother tongues. My predicament was in no way unique, however; it was simply distinctive in its setting and in the fragments I had to collect. Memory work, in this context, became a form of linguistic archaeology.

As I come closer to my parents' history, words became less and less adequate for our common inheritance. There is no way to make their past part of my present, except by creating spaces for speechlessness. One must acquire tolerance for memories that cannot show their face in broad daylight. This is also the project of Blaga Dimitrova, a Bulgarian poet who writes from the shores of the Black Sea, which was also part of my home. In a poem titled "Mother Tongue," Dimitrova joins in her mother's silence:

> My mother lost her words.
>   The world grew dumb.
>   And something's dying to be said.
>
> . . . .
> Choking with the effort
>   she must speak
>   or else she'll die.
> Lord, my mother has lost
>   her words in the dark.
>   I am at a loss myself.

Lean on my shoulder, mother;
   we have borne so much; now
   we must silence it out.[11]

Like Dimitrova, I come from a world that grew dumb. I, too, grew up in a family where something was dying to be said. But I did not understand the struggle fully until I went to China and started to listen to the silences of Chinese survivors of war and revolution. There, I recognized the nature of my flight from the confusing details of Jewish memory, my thirst for the abstractions of Chinese history. In China began my long road home. Chinese intellectuals who had withstood the ravages of war and revolution broke down the edifice of theory I had created about history. I learned to listen to lost words.

This education continued in Israel, where I discovered the work of Dan Pagis, a Jewish poet from my native country. Born in 1930 in the Romanian province of Bukovina, Pagis grew up in a German-speaking household, like my parents. After the Holocaust, he made his way to Israel, while they stayed behind in Eastern Europe. Nonetheless, Pagis and my parents shared the loss of family and the feeling of exile from one's mother tongue. When Pagis writes in Hebrew, his new tongue, it is as if he is telling our family story—or rather the history of our struggle—with the muffled voice of memory. His poem "Autobiography" borrows not only the cadences of modern Hebrew but also the voice of Abel, the murdered sibling who begins human history after the expulsion from Eden. This was the garden where words once meant what they seemed to be saying:

If my family is famous
not a little of the credit goes to me.
My brother invented murder,
my parents invented grief,
I invented silence.[12]

"Ani et hashetikah" (And I the silence) states the simple, colloquial Hebrew of the old-world poet. Although Pagis cannot translate himself into his new language—his experiences, his dreams, his nightmares make no sense in it—contemporary Hebrew becomes enlarged by his silence.

A similar enlargement of language and memory occurred in twentieth-century China, when the writer Lu Xun broke the poetic cadence of the classical language with his discordant cries. The Confucian civilization inherited by Lu Xun had no one mother tongue. Its vehicle of transmission was the written language—*wen yan wen*—which had little connection to the many vernacular tongues spoken in the marketplace. China's national *bai hua* (plain talk) was born along with the trauma of its social revolution. Lu Xun's work gave it voice while at the same time perforating it with grief and silence.

Born in 1881, before the political revolution of 1911 and the language revolution of 1917, Lu Xun inherited a broken world. Unlike Dan Pagis, he stayed in the same place—but left it changed by his own quarrel with words. Lu Xun's most famous short story, "Diary of a Madman," borrowed everyday expressions to unmask the pieties that blanketed cultural memory in traditional China. In this allegory, written in 1918, a crazed young man tries to read between the lines of Confucian books and comes up with the terrifying message: "Chi ren" (eat men)![13] Two characters, two words readily understood in the marketplace, launch a war against the edifice of hypocrisy. Lu Xun's tale suggests that "cannibalism" (in this case, the sapping of life from women, the young, and the poor) lies at the heart of much that used to pass for morality in old China.

Although silenced into "normalcy" at the end of the story, the madman never forgets his nightmare. Like Pagis, Lu Xun knew himself to be part of a world that invented murder and grief. So-called sanity was no more of an alternative than the Hebrew poet's silence. In 1921, when Lu Xun wrote the preface to his first collection of short stories (which included "Diary of a Madman"), he made it clear that memory was what kept him from being too "healthy" in his troubling times: "When I was young, I, too, had many dreams. . . . My trouble is that I cannot forget them completely. These stories are the result of what I am unable to erase from my memory."[14]

Here, Lu Xun provides an answer to Robert Penn Warren's question: "What can you dream to make Time real again?" For Warren, the query and the quest for dreams were essentially personal. For the Chinese writer, it became a civic duty as well. Especially in the early 1930s, when the intellectuals' community was being decimated by the White Terror, Lu Xun's voice rang loud with disturbing "dreams." Perceiving himself as "a lone survivor still shouldering my pike beneath the sky," he continued to write bitter essays and poems that recorded the brutality around him.[15] After the murder of one young friend, the writer Wei Suyuan, Lu Xun wrote again about the memories that distressed his nights and days: "I have some memories, but fragmentary in the extreme. They remind me of fish scales scraped off by a knife, some of which stick to the fish while others fall into the water. When the water is stirred a few scales may swirl up, glimmering, but they are streaked with blood."[16]

Bloody fish scales, sticky and seemingly useless, appear to be a far cry from Robert Penn Warren's call for dreaming time anew. Yet this image inspired Lu

Xun's best writing, breaking the cadence of everyday speech. In the silence and stammer that followed, a darker vision took shape.

Doubt, the Hallmark of Experience

Ordinary daytime words cannot encompass the nightmares that are the common inheritance of Chinese and Jews in the twentieth century. Instead, reticence and double-talk come into play where straight narrative is disallowed. This was the case with our family in Transylvania, and this is also what struck me when I arrived in Beijing in 1979. At that time, I still had it in mind to study the central ideas of the May Fourth Movement of 1919. But another story waited to be told on Wang Fu Cang Lane. It was here, off the beaten path, that I conducted a five-year-long oral-history project with Zhang Shenfu (1893–1986), a veteran of the May Fourth Movement. From fall 1979 to spring 1984, I had the opportunity to visit Zhang repeatedly in his home; over this period the layers of China's public memory slowly began to peel away. This oral-history project marked a transition for me: in conversations with Zhang I began to move from the history of ideas to a study of the lives of the thinkers themselves—from what is called in Chinese *sixiang shi* (history of thought) to *ren de sixiang* (history of thinking men and women).

To interview Zhang Shenfu, I first had to wrangle permission from Communist Party officials who controlled access to the aged philosopher. In the winter of 1979, Westerners were still not allowed to visit Chinese intellectuals at will. After obtaining permission, I had to persuade Zhang to allow me to visit him more than once. Then when we began taping in the spring of 1980, I realized the need to move beyond the thrill of access. Many months later, I was able to unravel the meaning of the memories that Zhang Shenfu shared with me. The difference between actual experience and political slogans, between a life distorted by ideology and fragments preserved in personal memory and halting words, became more apparent over time.

This chasm between words and life is also the subject of an interview with the Israeli writer Aharon Appelfeld. Like Dan Pagis, Appelfeld was born in Bukovina, survived the Holocaust as a child, and went on to craft his best works in modern Hebrew in Israel. Reflecting on memory's tenacity, Appelfeld remarked: "If you talk of experience, you don't use slogans. Experience, by nature, is full of questions, of doubts. It is not all-knowing like ideology. Ideology knows exactly what you must do and compels you to do it. Experience is more forgiving, more human, if you will." [17] Appelfeld's words, though far removed from China, helped me develop a more meaningful framework for the memories of

Zhang Shenfu. Doubt, the hallmark of experience, is what infuses genuine remembrance. It is also what makes positivist historians so ill at ease with the
"endurance" of recollection.

Nonetheless, I took the risk of uncertainty and followed Zhang Shenfu's ruminations into the unofficial crevices of China's public history. Zhang had lived
in a world saturated with ideology. Every aspect of his long life has been written
about as if there were no doubts, as if there should not be any doubts.[18] He was,
after all, one of the three founders of the Chinese Communist Party in 1920.
And it was he who introduced Zhou Enlai (China's future premier) into the
party cell in Paris in 1921. But Zhang had also been publicly castigated as a
traitor, first in 1948, then again in 1957, and once more during the Cultural
Revolution of the 1960s. In his public life, Zhang had to learn to withhold
doubts. In our conversations, doubts came to the fore along with his many-sided
contradictions: he was a Communist but also a pioneer of mathematical logic; a
champion of feminism as well as a known womanizer; an ardent follower of
Bertrand Russell and an admirer of Confucius.

To make sense of Zhang's life, I had to uncoil the web of abstractions about
Chinese intellectual history that I had woven at Stanford in the 1970s. The voice
of memory demanded attention to doubts, to second thoughts, to detours from
the main road of revolutionary history that had riveted me earlier. Guiding me
in this process was Zhang Shenfu's laughter, a full-throated chuckle that came
from deep within. He had lived too long, had been attacked too often, and was
too much of an eccentric to care if his story added up to a seamless whole. In
fact, he counted on me to help unravel the grand certainties promulgated around
his activities by official party historians.[19]

Following the circuitous thread of our conversations, I learned the true meaning of zhi yin: Zhang Shenfu and I had a connection that went beyond words, a
mirroring of hearts between a Chinese and Westerner. In fact, our mutual mis-
trust of official language was our strongest bond. This led us to listen to each
other's history closely, lending caring attention to the "music" of omissions,
erasure, and loss. Allowing me rare glimpses of his life, he was able to recall
details like his love of books, women, and fame, which were officially considered petty bourgeois "shortcomings" (quedian), as simply "weakness" (ruodian).[20]
Zhang Shenfu took pleasure in the recognition of traits that endure—without
having to bow to the pressures of political self-condemnation that prevailed outside the walls of his house on Wang Fu Cang Lane.

This zhi yin also characterized the relationship between André Gide and
Zhang Ruoming (unrelated to Zhang Shenfu). One of the first women to join

the Communist group in Paris in 1921, Zhang traveled to France as part of the "Frugal-Study Society" that included Zhou Enlai and Zhang Shenfu's lover, Liu Qingyang. This group of idealistic youths hoped to break down all barriers between workers and thinkers. As Zhang Ruoming put it in an essay written from France in 1921: "We want to . . . combine the personality of the intellectuals and the laborer for everyone; there will be no so-called class, a person who is a laborer, is (also) a laborer with knowledge." [21] By 1927, however, Zhang had drifted away from these Marxist sentiments and became the first woman to pursue a doctoral degree at the University of Lyons. Her excellent mastery of French bore fruit in an insightful thesis on André Gide entitled "L'attitude de André Gide (Essai analyse psychologique)." When Zhang sent a copy of her thesis to Gide in 1930, he wrote back: "It seemed to me that in traversing your pages I gained a consciousness of my own existence. Your chapter five (on narcissisme) in particular delighted me, and I do not think that I have ever felt so well understood. . . . I am so grateful for the light that you have brought on my work! It seems to me as if it is to a friend I write, because, in truth, the 'thank you' that I address to you comes from my heart." [22]

The zhi yin expressed here is initiated by a Westerner who recognized himself afresh in the work of a young woman from China. Gide, who was a well-known writer by 1930, had been judged too often, too politically. Zhang Ruoming held up a different mirror, one that reflected the possibility of a more psychological understanding, even of his most notorious shortcoming, narcissism. Over the years, Gide's work became a mirror of Zhang Ruoming herself. Although she remained sympathetic to the goals of the Chinese Communist Party, she took the liberty of studying literature from a less ideological perspective. Like Zhang Shenfu, she tried to remain an informed and free-minded fellow traveler of the Chinese Revolution. Unfortunately, she succumbed to attacks against her cosmopolitan outlook and committed suicide during the antirightist campaign of 1958. Zhang Shenfu, by contrast, outlived his critics and managed to find a way to tell his story afresh in the 1980s. For both, contact with a Westerner provided a way out of the ideological constraints of a party-dominated universe. Each found a new way to think about both self and world.

Zhang Shenfu was, and knew himself to be, unalterable. He enjoyed his "weaknesses" up until the end of his life. My presence across the small table in his kitchen gave him a chance to reflect on his experiences in the doubt-colored mirror of memory rather than through the rigid framework of party ideology. Away from the glaring light of official historiography, we began to fill in the grays of recollection. Moments of indecision, a limp moral will, all got their due here. Foibles had as much room in our conversations as great ideas. Following the thread of Zhang Shenfu's conversations, I began to rethink my father's recollections about the war in Transylvania.

My father, like Zhang Shenfu, was a man full of contradictions. He also managed to laugh and enjoy the various adventures that befell him in the midst of terrifying events. His memories of suffering in the forced-labor camps were peppered with romantic tales. After coming to the United States, he started to record these stories while resisting the temptation to make them into a morality tale. As Zhang Shenfu skirted the teleological demands of historians who wished to fit his memories into the official history of the Communist Party, so too my father avoided giving a singular meaning to his recollections of wartime Europe.[23] To the end of his life, he insisted that his memoirs be called simply "Encounters Dictated by Fate." Fate was my father's word for the fickle face of his experiences. It sometimes appeared in his stories like a protective mother, sometimes like an imperious mistress who toyed with his desires. No matter the guise, he always enjoyed her surprises and marveled at what was next in store for him.

My father used to talk of fate when he remembered his first lover, Carla, a Gentile with whom he lived in spite of his parents' objection. Fate was also invoked during the rare times he spoke about his first wife, Rozsi Braun, who was deported and killed in Auschwitz. Finally, it was to fate that my father appealed most often when talking about Kathy, my mother. She had been his girlfriend briefly during his bachelor days in Cluj, then was forbidden to see him by her religiously observant parents. He met Kathy again at a public beach in 1945, not yet aware that she had lost her parents, her first husband, and one of two daughters. A search for pleasure—both in the actual experience and in the retelling of them—animated my father's survival stories. They reflected a man who saw himself as both spared and privileged. Fate served to break down conventional notions of "us" and "them," of good and bad. Only such an improbable idea could explain, for example, how my father's life had been spared by an SS trooper in the woods on the Austrian border. This fragment of memory strains the imagination, much like Zhang Shenfu's recollections. My father told this story often, and always with the following highlights:

> We were fugitives from the forced marches of late 1944. I'm hiding with two friends in the snow-covered forest. Sick with diarrhea, we slow down to relieve ourselves every few steps. The SS finally catch up with us. The leader's face is hooded by a ski hat. His voice does not sound familiar until he asks me: "Aren't you the son of Herman Schwarcz, the sculptor?"

Then, suddenly, I recognize the German boy who lived in my parents' house as a favorite apprentice. Out of gratitude to my father, the SS officer sent us toward the Russian lines. He even gave us his supply of sausage and brandy.[24]

Unexpected food, unhoped-for goodwill—these are the details that made up my father's notion of fate. They provide the fulcrum for his reminiscences, enabling him to create a retrospective pattern in a bewildering world. This quest for a pattern that only memory can weave is now part of my own legacy; I pursue its twists and turns from Wang Fu Cang Lane to the memorial halls of Jerusalem. Along the way, I am reminded of Walter Benjamin's warning about not reading a sequence of events like the beads of a rosary. To stop the automatic rolling forward of events, a historian must linger for a while near the disconcerting details of the living past. Only when we are accosted by a tale that does not fit into the narrative do we come close to the heart of our subjects' experience. When Gide read about his narcissism in the work of Zhang Ruoming, when Zhang Shenfu spoke to me about his love of fame, women, and books, when my father recalled the SS officer who gave him sausage and brandy, a door opened to an understanding of history. It is the business of totalitarian institutions like the Communist Party in China to slam this door shut. It is the calling of the historian to open it as wide as possible. But we cannot perform this service unless we are willing to call into question our own assumptions, our own way of seeing the world. Walter Benjamin spoke about each second through which the Messiah may enter. Such attentiveness is, more often than not, the gift of murderous times.

A Name and a Place for Broken Lives

On May 20, 1989, murder was imminent on the streets of Beijing. The Communist government had not yet begun to shoot at student demonstrators in Tiananmen Square, but the order for martial law was already in effect. Yet, on this very morning, a few dozen intellectuals gathered to pay tribute to eighty-year-old Zhang Dainian, a well-known professor of philosophy and the younger brother of Zhang Shenfu, who had died three years earlier. May 20 marked the beginning of the end of the latest movement for reform. The confrontation in Tiananmen Square was the tragic, though not unexpected, outcome of the uneven struggle between youthful idealism and party autocracy.

In spring 1989, the world media remained riveted by what Nietzsche in earlier times had called the "hellish noise" of history.[25] Huge demonstrations, loud sloganeering, and a death march for the sake of democracy dominated world-wide television. While Clio screamed, Mnemosyne's whisper could hardly be heard. She spoke in an altogether different manner from the passionate and impatient youths and from the government walled in behind guns. In May 1989, memory wore the tired look of Zhang Dainian. Many months earlier, Zhang's former students and colleagues had planned a commemorative gathering in honor of this intellectual luminary. That day, in preparation, teas were prepared, and a large auditorium on the campus of Qinghua University (Zhang Dainian's alma mater, where he had begun his philosophy studies in the 1930s, inspired by his older brother) was decorated with banners. A large crowd was expected to arrive by bus from the Social Science Academy, but the sudden onset of martial law prevented many from attending.

Instead of hundreds, only two dozen guests managed to arrive by bicycle to pay tribute to the octogenarian philosopher. The contrast between the loud terror on the streets and the soft-spoken recollections in the room was painfully apparent to all of us. A fragment of the much-persecuted community of Chinese intellectuals represented there tried to retain some fidelity to history. Their collective reanimation of one man's past became a gesture of mutual encouragement and mutual consolation for the difficult months ahead. By naming all the broken places along the lengthy career path of Zhang Dainian, his former students held up memory's mirror to their own lives.

They spoke about Zhang's scrupulous reinterpretations of traditional Chinese philosophy, knowing various party hacks had used these to attack him over and over again. They dwelt on the master's *weiren*, his inner humanity, for which he had been persecuted in the 1950s. Declared a rightist in 1957 (like Zhang Shenfu and Zhang Ruoming), Zhang Dainian had been pushed to the side, ignored, and looked down upon for decades. Now, in the dark hour of another repression, he was honored for his integrity. Each speaker offered some token of appreciation: a classical poem or an ink-brush painting. The unifying theme of these offerings was the rugged pine, a traditional symbol of steadfast moral purpose in an unjust and corrupt world. While guns were being loaded on the streets of Beijing, these intellectuals managed to create a moment of stillness.

I was the only foreigner at that gathering. I knew the guest of honor well, because he had been helping me decipher his brother's work for almost a decade. But on this morning of martial law, I understood afresh my connection to history-battered intellectuals like Zhang Dainian. Our friendship was grounded not only in research and our interest in the history of thought but also in our mutual obsession with the vicissitudes of memory. No grand epic could do justice to this fragile tale. Foreigners' emphasis on the heroism of the student movement could not diminish China's grief in the spring of her betrayal. To be sure, CNN and CBS continued to portray the student demonstrations in grandiose terms. At Zhang Dainian's commemorative gathering, however, a darker music prevailed. It was a sound intimately familiar to survivors of history, Chinese and Jewish alike.

Two years after 1989, I heard the same whispering at the Children's Memorial at Yad Vashem, the site of the official Memorial Authority of the State of Israel. Located on a hill on the outskirts of Jerusalem (near the cemetery for the war dead), Yad Vashem is both a Holocaust museum and a research center, combining the difficult tasks of public commemoration and scholarly inquiry. It is also the place where most survivors go to make some sense of their personal loss. I made my way there, not for the first time, after coming back from China in 1989. With the echoes of Tiananmen still fresh in my mind, I walked the darkened hall of the Children's Memorial more slowly. In the middle of a pitch-black room burns a single candle reflected a million times in mirrors. In this hall, the names, ages, and countries of young victims are read out hour after hour. Visiting this veritable temple of grief, I realized the immensity both of the suffering that could not be commemorated in China after 1989 and of the Nanjing Massacre of 1937 with its countless dead that had yet to become imprinted upon communal memory in Japan and in the United States. I also sensed the magnitude of my own loss that could not be assuaged by the light of a candle, even if it was reflected one million times.

I had come to Yad Vashem to look for my sister, Agnes, my mother's second child. But I do not find her in the Children's Memorial—her name does not come across the loudspeaker. She was less than a year old when she died, so perhaps her age is too tiny a fragment of time for the museum at Yad Vashem. The only shred of evidence remaining from Agnes's life is the yellowed birth certificate in my safe deposit box. It is written in Hungarian, the mother tongue that offered no safety for the infant named therein. The document presents cold facts: the place of birth—Budapest; the date of birth—January 10, 1944; the names and ages of the parents—Lorant Lepot Spitzer, thirty-two, and Katalin David, twenty-four. The only warmth comes from the color in the stamps: royal horses, one turned upside down, perhaps because of the haste of the clerk who registered this birth on April 29, 1944. By that day, all hope had drained out of Jewish life in Budapest. Adolf Eichmann had been installed in the Hungarian capital, and plans for the extinction of Hungarian Jewry were well laid. My sister was just one statistic in this larger scheme. The only clear sign of what was to come can be glimpsed in three small letters—"izr"—that appear after the names of Agnes and her parents. These three letters marked individuals as

Birth certificate of my sister Agnes Spitzer. Born in January 1944, before Eichmann's entry into Budapest, she perished in the bombing of the Jewish ghetto there in the winter of 1944–45. (V. Schwarcz)

"Izraelites"—that is, Jews fit only for gas; this brief notation was therefore the beginning of their death sentence.

My mother and her first child, Marian, escaped the sentence with the help of forged Gentile papers. Lorant Spitzer was taken into forced-labor camps. Agnes, too little to hide quietly, was put in the care of a Jewish family in the Budapest ghetto. Later, much later, I learned that Agnes died in the Allied bombing of the ghetto. None of these "facts" are recorded in the Children's Memorial at Yad Vashem.

So, I walk outside along the line of trees planted to honor righteous Gentiles who helped save Jews. No comfort here. It is only when I sit and watch a cold-blooded lizard on a hot rock that Agnes Spitzer's name comes to me, my sister's name and all the loss buried in it. I start a poem, a dialogue with the dead:

Lizard: I start the day with a warm obelisk:
A good day on baked metal,
More soothing even than skin or stone.

Agnes: Stones, small gray stones
Around the ghetto orphanage in Budapest
Where mother left me because I cried
. . . .
Lizard: Silence is the price of basking
In monumental splendor on Hebrew memories.
They warm my blood.

Agnes: My life trickled away during the bombings . . .
Too thin, too hungry to bleed
I faded, a nameless candle in the night. . . .

I begin the poem in the shade of an olive tree. The lizard beyond my sheltered circle loosened words held back for decades. Away from the memorial for the one million children who were murdered during the Holocaust, I finally converse with the one child who mattered to me, the one child who did not even have a name during my childhood. That infant, birthed by my mother only a couple of months before Eichmann arrived in Budapest, I now call up in a language far from our murderous mother tongue. In English, I fill out a page for the Hall of Testimony. This is a simple room in the Yad Vashem complex where archivists collect single sheets about each person who perished in the Holocaust—called Shoah in Hebrew (literally, "abyss," "ruin," or "disaster"). It is while filling out this form for Agnes that I start paying closer attention to the official motto of Yad Vashem. A fragment from the prophet Isaiah sounds heroic at first: "Even onto them will I give in mine house and within my walls a place and a name . . . that shall not be cut off." In the Hebrew Bible, however, Isaiah speaks with a more modest voice about eunuchs, the most incomplete of men, who are nonetheless given the solace of memory: "Thus says the Lord to the eunuchs that keep my Sabbaths, and choose the things that please me, and take hold of my covenant: And to them I will give them in my house and within my walls a memorial [literally, *yad*, 'a place,' and *shem*, 'a name'] better than sons and daughters. I will give them an everlasting name that shall not be cut off [*lo yikaret*]." [26]

"Lo yikaret" is a promise made to broken men, to those made rootless by history, who yet are sheltered by their fidelity to God's covenant. This dark message is more consoling to me than all the candles reflected in the mirrors of the Children's Memorial. Where absence reigns, stone monuments are too heavy. Carefully crafted glass is redundant where loss lies buried in grief. No amplifier does justice to memory's stammer. Another instrument is needed here—one that cuts through silence yet leaves its density intact. Yehuda Amichai tried to describe such an instrument in his poem "Travels of the Last Benjamin of Tudela." In this work, the Jewish poet's war with words and memory goes on:

> History is a eunuch,
> it's looking for mine too
> to castrate, to cut off with paper pages
> sharper than any knife; to crush
> and to stuff my mouth forever
> with what it cut off,
> as in the mutilation of war-dead,
> so that I won't sing except in a sterile chirp,
> so that I'll learn many languages
> and not one of them mine,
> so that I'll be scattered and dispersed. [27]

Amichai's poem captures the dread of being stuffed up with pages of history. The writer imagines a linguistic diaspora in which his song is stifled by others' words. In this poem, the recorded past is a vengeful eunuch, a jealous, impotent force looking to castrate more vigorous voices. But the single pages in Yad Vashem's Hall of Testimony cut nothing but silence. And even that they pierce with

a weak, singular incision. Nothing much is lost or gained through these fragments—unless it is the right to speak itself.

Amichai could afford to worry about being stuffed up with historical narrative, because he lives and writes his poems in Jerusalem, where there is a surfeit
of memory. Speech is indeed crowded by all the names inscribed in stone. But
what about those who were literally silenced by history? Poets such as Yitzhak
Katznelson, whose voice was stifled in Auschwitz? Was history a eunuch who
threatened their lives? Surely the knife it wielded was more cutting than the
pages of paper feared by Amichai. Hitler's war was no symbolic mutilation. It
came close to inflicting wholesale *karet*—the kind of annihilation that was supposed to be God's prerogative alone. If Hitler lost his battle against Jewish life
and memory, it is partly because paper won out over the knife.

Scattered pages left behind by victim-witnesses such as Katznelson defied
Hitler's cause. Born in 1886 (five years after Lu Xun, who gave voice to the
dread of a cannibalistic past on the other side of the world), Yitzhak Katznelson
started life rather securely. His father was a rabbi and his mother's father a modern educator who translated Heine into Hebrew. Well traveled and well-bred,
Katznelson became an accomplished poet in both Yiddish and Hebrew. Before
the war, he had imagined himself as a medieval bard: "I am back to the old
minstrel with his concertina. She plays music of the Middle Ages, more obscure,
more terrible than the history that is coming toward us, menacing us."[28] This
was written before Katznelson came to understand how literally menacing history could be. In 1942, his wife and two children were caught in the mass
deportations from the Warsaw ghetto. Katznelson himself lived on another year
in the French internment camp at Vittel.[29] There, in September 1943, he began
to compose "The Song of the Murdered Jewish Nation."

This was one man's effort to stuff some pages down the gullet of an all-
devouring history. Katznelson used the cadence of the Book of Lamentations,
though he knew that this text was a "festival song" compared to what he had to
write and that exile in Babylon was a Garden of Eden compared to what Hitler
had accomplished against his family at Treblinka.[30] Yet he put pen to paper—
the gesture of a broken man for whom castration, dispersion, and mutilation
had become all too real. Still, he wrote. A few months before he perished in
Auschwitz, Yitzhak Katznelson managed to give voice to memory. He found the
words to evoke his personal and his community's nightmare:

Take your naked harp and slowly sing!
On its delicate cords cast your coarse fingers,

your broken hearts.
Sing the last song of the last Jew on earth.
How to open the mouth?
How to sing?
I am left alone, so very alone . . .

. . . .

Seek, seek above, seek below,
If there is anyone, sing for Him . . .
the last song of the last Jew who
lived
died
without a grave.[31]

A song from the grave? Not even this ridiculous possibility can comfort the mind of a poet who knew his family had been reduced to ashes. What song from what grave? Katznelson knew that words cannot substitute for the dead. I know this, too. No poem I write can bring back Agnes. No matter what page I deposit in the Hall of Testimony at Yad Vashem, Agnes will remain a black hole in our lives. Yet words like Katznelson's do outline the dark shadow of an enduring absence. More than memorials in stone, more than heroic narratives about the Holocaust, such words allow a dialogue with the dead. This is memory's thankless task: to guide us toward an ever-vanishing interlocutor. We persevere because the alternative is a more dreadful silence.

A historian who would join this pursuit must learn to look beyond the markers of public history. There is nothing heroic in the relationship between memory and historical time, only hard-won fidelity to fragments of the past. This is what Lu Xun called the "bloody fish scales." This is what Yitzhak Katznelson "sings" about after the deportation of his wife and two young children. Here Mnemosyne shows her true face, and she is no young beauty. Not for her the unlined mien of the younger Muses. Rather, if you look closely, you see the haggard look of one accustomed to the ravage of grief.

Old Lady Meng's Soup

In China a person who will not forget the past is described as "one who did not drink Old Lady Meng's soup." Borrowed from Buddhist folklore, Old Lady Meng dispenses the Broth of Oblivion to souls leaving the last realm of the underworld on their way to reincarnation. After drinking her soup, the soul is directed to the Bridge of Pain that spans a river of crimson water. There, two

"Old Lady Meng Who Gives the Broth of
Oblivion," popular twentieth-century folk print.
(From J. Hockin, ed., *Asiatic Mythology*)

demons lie in wait: Life-Is-Not-Long and Death-Is-Near. They hurl the soul into
waters that will lead to a new birth.[32]

Old Lady Meng is more than a quaint antidote for the Greeks' Mnemosyne.
She embodies a psychological understanding about the forces that promote, indeed demand, forgetting for the sake of ongoing life. It is not enough to note
that water is linked with amnesia in Chinese folklore in much the same way that
the river Lethe is associated with forgetting in Greek mythology. The challenge
here is to make sense of the distinctively Chinese attachment to remembrance in
spite of the benefits of Old Lady Meng's soup.

In Jewish tradition, too, the benefits of amnesia were acknowledged along
with the sacred commitment to recollection. There is a midrash, or Torah-based
story, that teaches us a lesson similar to that of Lady Meng: "God granted Adam

and Eve an all-important blessing as they were about to leave the Garden of Eden: I give you, He said, 'the gift of forgetfulness.'"[33] What is so precious about amnesia? Why would God, who demands fidelity to memory, offer this relief from recollection? Perhaps it is because without some ability to forgive and forget we might become bound by grudges and hatred. To remember everything may be immobilizing. To flee from memory, however, leads to an ever more debilitating frenzy.

The Chinese poet Yu Guangzhong has fought against both immobility and frenzy. Because he has not drunk Old Lady Meng's soup, he does not forget, but neither does he harbor grudges forever. He is fiercely faithful to the past even though it causes him great pain. Born in China in 1928, Yu was educated in Taiwan and traveled abroad extensively. Yet, he chooses over and over again to link his fate with the homeland left behind. In his poem "Wang Quan" (The River of Forgetting)—written in 1969, at the height of the Cultural Revolution—he calls upon Greek and Chinese mythology to explain his inability to forget. The river Lethe, which brought amnesia to Western souls, merges here with the Shenzhen River separating Hong Kong from China and with the crimson waters running below the Buddhist Bridge of Pain:

> And whether I go East or West,
> Back against or gaze upon,
> It is always the River of Forgetting,
> Always China on another side of barbed wire—
> A legend, a time-worn rumor
> On some page, what page of my childhood?
> . . . .
> And whether I go North or South
> Fringed lace decorates my terror
> A stranger abroad,
> A prisoner at home.[34]

Twenty years after the "loss of China" (not in the polemical sense used by supporters of Senator McCarthy in the 1950s but in the emotionally charged sense of exile from the center of Chinese cultural origination), Yu Guangzhong cannot erase the memory of homeland. It is there on the other side of barbed wire, a reminder that it is impossible to be Chinese except in some tension-filled relationship to the land of China and to Chinese time. Yu's ambivalent attachment to remembrance cannot be grasped by the constructs of intellectual history alone. This is not a matter of the idea of history, or the idea of revolution, or even the idea of tragedy. Rather, remembrance grows out of Yu Guangzhong's somber realization that he is at once "a stranger abroad" and "a prisoner at home." Memory is no homeland but a painful connection to it, a precarious bridge constructed across time. The poet chooses to cross this bridge even when it would be easier to walk away, to live in a foreign country, to drink Old Lady Meng's soup.

The novelist Zhang Xianliang also refused the Broth of Oblivion. Younger than his Taiwan-educated compatriot, Zhang witnessed each development of the Chinese revolution on the mainland. He was a victim of the antirightist campaign of 1957, like Zhang Dainian, Zhang Shenfu, and Zhang Ruoming. After the death of Mao Zedong in 1976 (when all of China was invited or, more precisely, required to get over the painful memories of the Mao era and to proceed with the bright task of socialist modernization), Zhang Xianliang began to write his most bitter fiction. He began to dig deeper and deeper into the shared memories of his generation—a psychological terrain characterized by powerlessness and despair and feared by the new regime.

In his novel Getting Used to Dying, Zhang Xianliang points out the contemporary incarnations of Old Lady Meng. They are none other than the customs officials who seek to erase all tapes brought from abroad. What is being rubbed out, Zhang tells us, is not only news, or even so-called pornography from other countries, but memory itself. Why bother with Western democracy and crude sex brewed beyond China's borders? the customs officials ask. In response, Zhang Xianliang notes that border guards, and party officials as well, are worried not about sex but about historical remembrance. And this is the very brew to which Zhang Xianliang's protagonist is addicted. He cannot forget the past or get rid of the sound of executions, even executions he did not witness, even deaths he did not die from.

Without reading Robert Penn Warren, Zhang Xianliang knows what he needs to dream to make time more real. The nightmares of his own incarceration during the late 1950s come back to him in vivid detail over and over again. China's public history had canonized the years of Zhang's first imprisonment as the Great Leap Forward. In official stories, Mao Zedong's heroic vision of quick-paced communism prevails. Zhang Xianliang, by contrast, calls the period between 1958 and 1962 by its true name: the Great Famine. With the haggard voice of a man who has gotten used to dying, Zhang's hero recalls what happened in his guts while Mao talked of spiritual victories: "He had lived through China's Great Famine in the labor camps, and he knew well that the secretions of the body were precious. Both urine and saliva had their uses in an emergency. Also, if you did not allow yourself to shit for a long time, you could make believe that there was actually something of substance in your stomach. This allowed you to think that you were fully fed, that you did not need, like others, to drop dead along the road. This was fully in accord with Mao's great dictum: 'Turn spirit into matter.'" [35]

A historian who would reckon with such memories cannot but think about excrement withheld, saliva recycled, laughter twisted out of place. All this demands a different kind of temporality. Abstractions generated without the historian's having any contact with the subject must be broken down. My own journey toward a more embodied kind of time was circuitous. It began with Zhang Shenfu and Zhang Xianliang, Chinese intellectuals who were neither symbols nor simply victims of revolution. Listening to their recollections, in turn, allowed me to hear afresh the voices of Jewish survivors. To be sure, the world of Auschwitz was infinitely darker than the blackest night endured by Zhang Xianliang during the Great Famine. Yet, as I move backward from the familiar terrain of Chinese history to the rougher terrain of Jewish terror, I hear some of the same words. Excrement is one of them. In reckoning with bodily refuse, I begin to fathom memory's depths as well.

Adrienne K. is an Auschwitz survivor who talks about the *Scheiss Kommando* (literally, "shit brigade") in a taped testimony for the Fortunoff Video Archives. She was a medical student when deported from Transylvania in spring 1944. In her testimony, Adrienne K. speaks about what it was like to go on living and working after her family members were taken to the gas chambers: "One of my first jobs at Birkenau—B.III, the last camp to be built inside Auschwitz without any electricity or water, just cramped bunks and a few shared blankets—was in the *Scheiss Kommando*. . . . The Germans were looking specially for doctors to do this job. It was part of their perversity. I was only a first-year medical student, but because of a lack of doctors in our camp, I qualified." [36] Doctors shoveling excrement from a hole that served as a common latrine was the Nazi idea of a cosmic joke. But for Adrienne K. it was more than that, more than a smelly curse: "It was a privilege to clean shit. . . . I did not have to stand in one place. I could miss the terrible long roll call that could go on all day. . . . I could choose a group of ten girls for my commando, including my old French teacher [from Cluj] and Judith, a younger girl half crazed with fear, [and] also get some extra food." [37]

Excrement that was meant to humiliate Jewish doctors, to make them less human, also made it possible for Adrienne K. to survive. For Zhang Xianliang, the same smelly substance prolonged the illusion of a full stomach. In Auschwitz, ordure had been, literally, a way for young women like Adrienne K. to get more food. With the aid of this unrefined word, I make my way across the bridge of memory—though I proceed slowly, very slowly, weighed down by my ignorance of Jewish history. Also, I am frightened by the despair that lies on the other side of the Chinese events that have become a familiar subject.

But there is no turning back, for I am irreversibly beyond the abstract ideas that initially sparked my studies of Chinese history. I have even had to leave behind the nuanced intellectual history of Joseph Levenson, a Jewish-American historian at home in many worlds. In Levenson's studies, Chinese intellectuals were portrayed as torn between emotional attachment to a specific cultural inheritance and intellectual curiosity about the verities of the modern West. The recollections I have to make sense of, however, have to do with lost worlds. This is the realm that Aharon Appelfeld calls in Hebrew the terrain of the omek—of "depths" that are unlovely and unlovable but that produce our most nourishing sights and sounds. Appelfeld knows this thorny country well and has mined the treasures of this omek in his masterful stories. He had to borrow words from one world to probe the sores of another: "For forty years I have lived in Jerusalem. I love Jerusalem. . . . But I have discovered that love and depth are different. It would seem that love and depth should be the same place. But gradually, I have learned that my depths are elsewhere. In a place I may not love. And perhaps even hate. But it is there. . . . Day and night it produces colors and smells that nourish me." [38]

The lilting voice of this sweet-faced gentleman becomes halting with these words. The shift in worlds is palpable in Appelfeld's effort to say in daytime Hebrew why the Bukovina of his parents won't leave him alone at night. Appelfeld speaks with great care, and still, he repeats himself: "It becomes clear to me that love . . . it becomes clear to me that love and depth, these two things are different, it becomes clear that love and depth are not the same thing, they are different." [39]

Ahava (love) and *omek* (depth) are as close and as far from each other as the similar sounding Hebrew words of *shovim* (same) and *shonim* (different). Appelfeld repeats them because in the gulf between the two lies memory itself.

This is a divide I now explore as I move away from the Chinese history that has been my intellectual "home" for decades. My companions in this journey are writers and poets, Chinese and Jews, who have reckoned with the burden of remembrance in their lives. But they are not limited to these two worlds. Robert Penn Warren was neither Chinese nor Jewish, yet he grasped the need to dream time afresh for memory's sake. Lucille Clifton, an African American poet on intimate terms with the nightmares of history, also speaks about the need to cherish remembrance. She knows what it means to stand accused of harboring too much darkness and of making too much out of neglected fragments:

> i am accused of tending to the past
> as if i made it,
> as if i sculpted it
> with my own hands. i did not.
> this past was waiting for me
> when i came,
> a monstrous unnamed baby,
> and i with my mother's itch
> took it to breast
> and named it
> History.
> she is more human now,
> learning language everyday,
> remembering faces, names and dates.
> when she is strong enough to travel
> on her own, beware, she will.[40]

A past that lies in wait, ready to travel, is a dangerous past. No wonder that customs officials in China want it rubbed out. More subtle enemies of memory accuse us of sculpting our subject with our own hands—as if by daring to construct a pattern of meaning we had invented senselessness itself. In this poem, Clifton's skillful words hold up a mirror to the past, rendering history more human and time more real. Yet the poet's words do not merely name the past. By calling attention to the "mother's itch," they reveal the power of metaphor. Were it not for the will to cradle what has been irretrievably lost, we would have no historical narrative at all. Metaphor is the word bridge we cast back over the rubble of the past.

TWO

The Bridge of Words

Memory and Metaphor in Chinese and Jewish Tradition

In this burning country
Words have to be shade.

YEHUDA AMICHAI, "LOVE SONG"

T he rubble of the past is useless unless we find words to name the debris. If these words cannot be located in the mother tongue, metaphors have to be sought abroad. This is what happened in China following the violence in Tiananmen Square. Two years later the crackdown continued in Beijing, and the blood in the square remained unavenged. Families of the dead were not allowed to mourn or even mention those killed in the "pacification." Denied in the mother tongue, Chinese remembrance found its outlet in a distant language: in January 1991, the Chinese journal Foreign Literature published the first translations of Yehuda Amichai's poetry in that country. The translator, a young writer named Fu Hao, was not permitted to speak his mind about recent events. Borrowing Amichai's words, he managed to create some space for memory at home.

While Fu Hao was working on his translations of Israel's most widely read poet, he was also undergoing punishment for his participation in the events of 1989. Most graduate students of the Social Science Academy (where Fu Hao was enrolled in the Foreign Literature Institute) had sympathized with the younger students calling for reform in Tiananmen Square. They had joined some demonstrations to support a dialogue between students and the government. But the dialogue never took place. Instead, on June 4th, tanks rolled over makeshift tents in front of the Great Hall of the People. The casualties included burned young bodies and voices crushed into silence.

In the climate of fear that followed, it was impossible to speak about memory in plain words. The dead could not be commemorated openly, and poems memorializing the ideals and the lives of students were censored. Mnemosyne, no longer welcomed in Tiananmen Square, found a more circuitous entrance in the pages of an innocuous magazine. The government was unlikely to worry about Amichai's "Love Songs"—what would Eros have to do with the blood in the square? One of the love songs opens with a woman on a balcony and continues with the tame wish that she might linger a little while longer:

> Heavy and tired with a woman on a balcony:
> "Stay with me." Roads die like people:
> Quietly or suddenly breaking.
> Stay with me. I want to be you.
> In this burning country
> Words have to be shade.[1]

Although China did not yet officially recognize Israel in 1991, there was little in this fragment to attract the eye of the censor. To be sure, the poem mentions people dying, but not in connection with squares or tanks. Amichai could be read as a poet of love, as one longing simply to fold himself into the memory of his beloved. Nothing in his words openly challenges the suppression of China's public remembrance.

Yet those with informed hearts could readily decode Fu Hao's rendition of the last two lines. Those pained by the silence in Beijing found solace in Amichai's words. In the Chinese translation of this love song, "burning country" becomes "*zhoure de guodu*" (burning capital), hinting at a place recently aflame with protests and gunfire. For the Jewish poet, language had not lost its power to console: words provide shade. In China, by contrast, all speech entailed risk in the harsh months that followed the crackdown. Words needed to be protected from those in charge of official forgetting. So the last line of Amichai's poem is translated into Chinese as follows: "Huayu bixu you yinliang" (Words need the shelter of shade).[2]

After the burning ardor of 1989, poetry and memory both needed a cooler climate. Such "shade" was offered to Chinese readers of *Foreign Literature* through the voice of a desert-scorched Israeli writer. Fu Hao's introduction to that issue makes it clear that Amichai is no stranger to burning countries. Born in 1924, in Wurzburg, Germany, Amichai moved to Palestine just a little ahead of the fire that consumed European Jewry.[3] When a homeland spits out its children—as Germany did in the 1930s, and as China came close to doing in 1989—it becomes difficult to speak in the mother tongue. Words that once seemed nurturing turn sour. In French, the crushing of a dream (*un rêve*) can be compensated for by musing (*une rêverie*); male-oriented memory (*le souvenir*) can be enveloped by soft-spoken recollection (*la souvenance*).[4] But such alchemy was not possible in the bitter mood of China after 1989. Fu Hao knew this when he took refuge in Amichai's poetry. Not only did he become an accomplished translator of Chinese into English, but he also began to compose his own poems in a borrowed language. Politics pushed Fu Hao into linguistic exile.

Eight months after publishing his translations of Amichai, Fu Hao hands me a few of his poems in English. He is on temporary leave from his job as clerk in a village school, to which he was assigned as punishment. Although Fu Hao was a low-profile activist in spring 1989, he was nonetheless fingered, like all graduate students in the Social Science Academy. Unlike other colleagues, however, he enjoyed his demotion, using it to write new work about old themes. We are walking around the lake at Beijing University, once the epicenter of the student movement. In a tongue far removed from Chinese, I read Fu Hao's "Bellows":

> I am a metaphor of ancient wisdom
> Hardly known by the people today.
> I never accumulate nor possess
> But I am always full and rich.
> I receive
> Because I give.
> What I include and what includes me
> Are the same.[5]

This work is a conscious evocation of an old Daoist description of the human body as a bellows animated by the gases of life. In this work, a young Chinese witness to the still-unspeakable events of 1989 turns back to native sources: Daoism and Confucianism. Drawing upon allegorical language, Fu Hao stirs up memories, both personal and cultural. "What I include" embraces the voice of the Jewish poet borrowed from afar. "What includes me" is decidedly Chinese memory, which Fu Hao is not about to renounce, even if official managers of public amnesia demand it. The poem is a manifesto about self-enrichment. No matter how many words and memoirs are uprooted at home, the poet will reconstitute other worlds. What is broken without is healed within through openness to all experience, including pain and loss. Party censors might silence recollection of the recent past, but the bellows of antiquity continue to breathe life into the body and mind of a poet who knows the power of metaphor.

Life-Giving Words

This same paradoxical power embedded in muted words is the subject of Cynthia Ozick's essay "Memory and Metaphor."[6] Like Fu Hao, Ozick refuses to be cut off from ancient wisdom. She continuously mines the Bible for what it might

teach us today, though the lessons are never obvious and are not always com-
forting. Ozick's works arrest us in the midstream of common speech and common thought. Her essay on memory and metaphor is addressed to doctors who
presume to cure us (often without understanding the depths of our pain). It
opens with the question of why healers both need and fear metaphor.

Ozick relates her encounter with a group of American surgeons who invited
her to help sensitize them to the pain of their patients. She did so by presenting
them with a parable about a lascivious planet in which grown-ups are too concerned with themselves to tolerate children, to which the doctors reacted with
bewilderment and belligerence. They had wanted the novelist to open the in-
nermost valve of their imagining heart but were unprepared for the sting of
recognition—for seeing themselves naked: "They were stung by what they
instantly termed 'ambiguity.' They protested, they repudiated the writer's instruments and devices as arcane, oracular, technical. Before the use of metaphors they felt themselves stripped and defenseless: they complained that the
examining tables had been turned on them; that their reasoning authority had
fallen away; that they stood before the parable as a naked laity; that I had sickened them."[7]

And so Ozick had. Like Fu Hao in China, she had sickened the so-called healers with the instrument of metaphorical thinking. But such illness may be salutary. As the American novelist and the Chinese poet both know, metaphors can
heal by their capacity to reconcile us with memory. Although indirect and bent
out of shape by the pressures of exile or imagination, or both, these figures of
speech have significant power.

A well-crafted metaphor strips the dross of habit from our ears and hearts.
It cuts through layers and returns us bluntly to basic speech. With the aid of
such stripped words, we learn to say and see things more truthfully. Metaphors
create a bridge between the daily encrustations of technical language—such
as that used by doctors and computer programmers—and simple words that
"give shade."

Ozick, Fu Hao, and Amichai craft metaphors out of a repository of words that
lie buried in both Chinese and Jewish tradition. Despite the vast theological difference between Chinese organicism and monotheistic Judaism, both traditions
are anchored in a concrete appreciation for the world-creating power of words.
In the last chapter of the Analects, Confucius notes the importance of simple
words: "Bu zhi yan er bu zhi ren ye" (Not to know speech is not to know a
person).[8] In this formulation, zhi means a knowing that comes from deep within
the knower and that takes to heart yan, words that come from the heart. For

Confucius, there is no knowledge of humanity apart from this rootedness in words. Yet yan are more than the basic building blocks of culture. They have the capacity to alert us to what lies beyond: the realm of unsayable yet deeply humanizing memories.

The Daoist classic, Lie Zi, develops this insight further. Although Confucianism and Daoism were opposing schools of thought in ancient China, they shared an appreciation for unvarnished speech. For both schools, the power of words lay in what cannot be said: "One who knows the wherefore of speech does not speak with words. Those who fight over fish get wet, and those who chase beasts run, not that they enjoy doing it. Therefore, ultimate speech gets rid of words, and ultimate action is without action." [9] Here, the Daoist's love of paradox echoes Ozick's affection for parable. Neither is afraid of getting wet from fish or of tiring from running with beasts. Beyond the letters that "say" something, there is an entire vocabulary for the passions and the grief that cannot be encapsulated by speech.

This intense yet paradoxical appreciation of words is also at the heart of the Jewish Bible. The first sentence of Genesis states, "Bereshit bara Elokim et hashamayim v'et ha-aretz" (In the beginning God created the heavens and the earth). What is being created here is not only a universe but a language for that universe—or more precisely, a language that can become a blueprint for the universe. As one contemporary commentator, Benjamin Blech, points out: "Before the word ha-shamayim, the heavens, we find the word et which is left untranslated. It comprises both the first and the last letters of the Hebrew alphabet. Indeed, in the beginning, God created the letters, and through the letters and their respective arrangements, God was able to create the universe." [10] To create, in this sense, means to grasp the core power of words. Each letter is a cosmic building block. The secret of the architect is embedded in a simple, untranslatable compound—two letters left as a trace, an invitation to continue the task of creation. This vision of words that engender worlds is further amplified in Jewish mysticism. According to Rabbi Adin Steinsaltz, each of the Ten Utterances (translated more simplistically as the Ten Commandments) continues to maintain the world. These words not only created meaning in ancient times but continue to breathe life into our experience today: "If the letters of the ten utterances by which the world was created during the six days of creation were to depart from it (but for an instant, God forbid) it would revert to naught and absolute nothing, exactly as before the six days of creation. . . . If Divine speech ceases, the result is a reverting to non-being. The letters of this Divine utterance did not create the things of the world; they are the very substance of things." [11]

Speech, according to Steinsaltz, is utterly necessary for the maintenance of life—even when our words fall short of their mark, short of their origin in God's truly creative words.

With this appreciation for the life-giving power of language in mind, we can better understand the terror of those forbidden to talk, forbidden to remember. Where world-creating words are suppressed, creation is in danger of reverting to naught. This was the nothingness that stared Fu Hao in the face when he turned to the poetry of Yehuda Amichai. This is what Cynthia Ozick wanted doctors to understand when she "sickened" them with her parables. Fortunately for both Fu Hao and Ozick, their cultural traditions had long ago learned how to breathe new life into worn words. Chinese and Jewish tradition alike cherished speech through a careful nurturing of memory metaphors. Although disparately rooted, such expressions cultivated the art of recollection by ensuring that the past not become something inert behind us. Those who would not be dead to the present had to find ways to reanimate the past with living words.

Loving the Ancients: Hao Gu and Zakhor

The emphasis on memory transmission may be likened to the foundation of a bridge. Both Chinese and Jewish tradition demand an anchor in the past, firm abutments in the flow of experiential time. Time, in turn, can be envisaged as a thick soup of mud and sand constantly stirred up by the river of history. Bridge builders call this corrosive power "scouring," because the river bottom grinds against anything that lies in its path. The abutment of a pier has to be planned with special care and protected as much as possible if it is to withstand the force of scouring.[12]

Cultural memory requires a similarly concerted effort if it is to withstand the erosion of constantly shifting events. The guardian of memory is a man or a woman or a community who stubbornly, and with extraordinary care, sinks foundations of identity into the past. This is what Confucius urged when he called for "*hao gu*"—that is, fidelity to the ancients. This is what the Jewish Bible demands over and over again with the injunction *zakhor*, which instructs one "to recall and relive" the Exodus and the Sabbath.

The two traditions that developed on the foundations of the Confucian *Analects* and of the Torah both insist that the wisdom of the ancients can become a cornerstone to a meaningful life in the present. Centuries after Confucius's act of hao gu, his spiritual heirs raised the call of fu *gu*—return to the wisdom of the ancients. Similarly, in daily prayer Jews seek to remember their ancestors and to be mindful of their merits. Our zakhor (effort to recollect) makes us heir to their merit and virtue. As the Talmud puts it: "For the sake [sekhar—in the 'merit'] of righteous women of that generation were the Israelites redeemed from Egypt."[13] This verbal echo between the words sekhar and zakhor is intentional in biblical Hebrew. It underscores the capacity for commitment that marked the Jewish women who insisted on continuing to bear children even in slavery. Their commitment enabled subsequent generations to build on Jewish identity and the memory of the Exodus. The same memory thread that bound Jewish slaves in Egypt to Abraham, Isaac, and Jacob binds us in turn to them. Women, above all, treasured that connection and bequeathed to their descendants a capacity for linkage.

In the Chinese context, Confucius stood for a similar principle. Drawn to the ancients, he sought to bind his contemporaries closer to this living source. An itinerant scribe who lived in the fifth century B.C., Confucius later became canonized as "The Teacher for Ten Thousand Generations." In his lifetime, however, the Sage had difficulty finding official employment and turned to teaching instead. Subsequent generations of cultural rememberers emphasized not his political failure but rather his faithfulness to the past. He became a model of the man who looks to history in order to enlighten the present and the future. Confucius's faith in the light of the ancients is voiced in chapter seven of the Analects. In one of the few truly personal passages, Confucius describes himself: "Wo fei sheng er zhi, hao gu, min yi qiu zhi zhe ye," which may be translated, somewhat more wordily, as "I was not born knowing the past. Rather, I love the ancients and seek earnestly to know their way."[14]

Here Confucius makes it clear that memory is not an inheritance but a quest. To put it metaphorically, it is a commitment to sink solid pillars into the vanishing world of our predecessors. Although posterity attributed to Confucius an inborn gift for historical understanding, the man who speaks in the Analects describes himself simply as one who loves the ancients and seeks to understand their way. Hao gu means nothing more, or less, than a determination to become fully human in the process of wrestling with the moral legacy of previous generations. Confucius, far from portraying himself as the codifier of that legacy, sees himself as a seeker for the past, as someone deeply entangled and affected by the problems of historical judgment and cultural transmission.

In another passage from the Analects, Confucius further develops this self-image of the rememberer-transmitter: "Wo shu er bu zuo, xin er hao gu."[15] Here, too, our modern, ego-laden words do not really convey the simplicity of the classical Chinese, which states: "I follow rather than create anew. I believe that it is possible to know the past by loving the ancients." Hao gu is used by the

Master again to suggest the emotional and moral commitment required for genuine historical understanding. Unlike other philosophers, who imagined themselves at the fountainhead of new wisdom, Confucius looked into the mirror of the past and was content with the picture of himself as a transmitter of memory.

"I follow" (wo shu) stands in marked contrast to "I create" (wo zuo). To make, in this sense, is to produce from scratch, to build as if no builders had existed before. This is the arrogant creativity that Confucius abjured for the sake of cultural memory. But, of course, this proud and thoughtful teacher knew that loving the ancients was, in itself, a powerfully creative gesture. This knowledge was passed down to generations of disciples who continued to persist in hao gu, in being faithful to the past in a critical and self-aware fashion. Consequently, they kept their tradition vibrantly Confucian.[16]

Like the commentators-transmitters of the Talmud, Confucius understood the importance of delving into the rich repository of human experience. The compilers of the Talmud also used the power of precedent in discussions of moral and legal codes. We continue to be nourished by this collection of post-biblical wisdom precisely because layer upon layer of debate is embedded in it. Some might harangue contemporaries about the ideal life in abstract terms, but only followers could be sure that the present would live up to the example of the past. Both the Talmud and the Analects use incidents from the lives of predecessors for moral argument. Both insist that humanity is capable of actualizing the ethical ideals of the past in the present. The Chinese word for "past" (shang) suggests this yearning for historical precedent directly. It is simply synonymous with "up," as in the modern expression shang yue, which means "last month" or, literally, "up month." The past is therefore honored by having been given an exalted position in relationship to the present and the future (by contrast, xia yue—"down month"—is the expression for "next month"). In Hebrew, a similar concern with the effort required to reach back into history is embedded in the word for the "past" (avar), which is also the root of the verb "to cross over" (la'avor). The first time that Abraham is called a Hebrew in the Bible, he is identified as someone who enacts a crossing over. This occurs in chapter 14 of Genesis during the war of the Kings. The climax is reached when Avram haivri learns of the capture of Lot and promptly inaugurates a rescue action. The medieval commentator Rashi points out that the soon-to-be father of the Jewish nation is called ivri because he has already accomplished a crucial task: "He had come from the other side [avar] of the river."[17] To be a Jew, in this sense, is to be prepared for crossing, for an action that is rooted in the past but also points toward the future.

Thus, we can see how in both Chinese and Jewish tradition the past is not something inert or a place long forgotten but an act of recovery. One who loves the ancients in Chinese and Jewish tradition is not a conservative who gazes with melancholy upon the long-lost riches of history. Rather, he or she is a seeker like Confucius, who sought to reanimate cultural memory, and a creator like the commentators of the Talmud, who wrestled with history because it posed concrete questions and offered challenging questions about how to deal with the present. The Talmud's love of ancients is but a continuation of an earlier biblical commitment to remembrance (in much the same way that Chinese historiography became an elaboration of Confucius's effort at scrupulous recollection in the *Spring and Autumn Annals*).[18] In later generations, the rabbis of the Talmud became collectively known as *chazal*, an acronym that means "our sages, may their memory be for a blessing."

The idea that memory is a blessing was not novel. Its origins are found in the three-part consonantal root of zakhor (*zayin, kaf, resh*), which appears in the Bible in Genesis 8:1. Noah has just answered God's call by building the ark. The waters then prevail upon the face of the earth for 150 days. Divine rage overwhelms creation. Noah, though sequestered, has not yet gained his stature as survivor. This happens only after "veyizkhor Elokim et Noah ve et kol hahaya" (And God remembered Noah and every living thing). Noah becomes the progeny of a new world only when God's remembrance is activated. To be human after the flood is to be remembered. After Sinai, it is to become a rememberer in turn.

Surely God did not "forget" Noah during the flood. Yet is it only after the destruction of previously created life that zakhor enters the Bible as a precondition for genuine survival. Long before the Holocaust made "never again" a modern slogan, humankind is shown the saving power of memory. According to the Yale theologian Brevard Childs, after Noah there are 168 references to the root word for memory (derived from zayin, kaf, resh), all of which amplify the biblical commandment to remember.[19] This plethora of memorial injunctions eventually becomes condensed into the Six Remembrances that observant Jews still recite each day: "Remember what Amalek did"; "Remember what your Lord God did to Miriam"; "Remember and do not forget how you angered the Lord your God in the desert"; "Remember the Sabbath day, to sanctify it"; "So that you may remember the day when you left Egypt all the days of your life"; "Only take heed and guard yourself most carefully lest you forget those things that your eyes saw . . . the day you stood before the Lord, your God, in Horeb." [20] The cumulative impact of these Six Remembrances is clear: we are to become a holy people through fidelity to the memory of divine impact on our history and through a careful recollection of our deeds and misdeeds.

The Torah instructs Jews in the practice of remembrance. This is what distinguishes a religious commitment to memory from Confucius's history-motivated love of the ancients. And yet, although the theological starting points are vastly different, the consequences of this attachment to recollection are similar in both Chinese and Jewish tradition. Both demand sacred attention to historical memory, and in both traditions the past is the most meaningful repository of moral judgment. Nowhere is this attachment to history more apparent than in the encounter with Amalek during the flight from Egypt. "Zakhor et asher asa lecka Amalek" (Remember what Amalek did to you), we are commanded. We are to remember how he accosted us on the way and how he attacked the faint and weary who straggled far behind. This assault upon the helpless becomes inscribed not only in the daily Six Remembrances but also in Sabbath Zakhor (the Sabbath of Remembrance), which precedes the annual celebration of Purim.

In referring to Amalek's attack upon the Jewish remnant, the Torah uses an unusual phrase: *asher karekha baderech* (how he met you on the way). One interpretation of *karekha* is "cooled you off." In the words of a modern commentator, Amalek sought to dampen the spiritual ardor of Jews who had just witnessed the miracle at the Red Sea. Whereas the inhabitants of Philistia, the chiefs of Edom, and the mighty men of Moab had all been stricken with fear, "only Amalek remained stubborn and unmoved in the face of this cataclysmic event." [21]

The danger of becoming insensitive to one's history is therefore one dimension of the threat of Amalek. Although later identified with all enemies of the Jewish people (including Hitler and Stalin), Amalek remains encoded in daily memory in a unique fashion. Not only are we commanded to remember what Amalek did (how he sought to curb the vision of the Jews after the Red Sea), but we are directed toward a protracted struggle with his role in our history: "You shall blot out the remembrance of Amalek from under heaven, you shall not forget!" (Deuteronomy 25:19). Remember to blot out memory. Do not forget. What are we to make of this paradox? Memory here seems to be simply a prelude to amnesia. But how could this be? We know from Noah onward that whole worlds are created through remembrance alone. We know that Jews were to be especially mindful of memory in their spiritual practice of Sabbath. So the passage about Amalek cannot be understood simply as an invitation to forget. It is a paradox that by its nature deepens our understanding. It represents consciousness of two opposite commitments. We are not allowed to forget the painful past, yet we must erase its scars lest life in the present become overwhelmed by resentment. Bitterness carried to the point of revenge also keeps the past alive in the present.[22] But it is an exhausting, and often pointless, way of memorializing painful events. Remembering and forgetting Amalek at once holds out a different possibility—that of becoming more fully human through a tension-filled relationship to history.

Another side of the attachment to history is embodied in the commandment to remember on Passover. This is a celebration of freedom that every Jew is enjoined to reenact personally. "I left Egypt," the phrase that is the center of the Seder ritual and of the Haggadah, the story we tell, is oriented toward the present. Then, as we raise the matzah, we recite, "Ha lachma anya. This is the bread of affliction our ancestors ate in the land of Egypt." Both the words and the gesture are meant to awaken memory. They help us cross over the gulf between past and present. In Yemen, as part of the Passover Seder, Jews put the matzah in a sack and, slinging it over their shoulders, walk around the Seder table, reexperiencing the Exodus from Egypt. When we sit at the Seder table, we are not looking back, we are there again. Recollection is, in this sense, nothing less than a reactualization of history.[23]

The purpose of memory here is not only to exalt the heart but to expand its sympathies as well. Passover can signal liberation precisely because it reminds us so forcefully of what it was to be a slave in Egypt. Cynthia Ozick, in her essay "Memory and Metaphor," takes this historical experience as the core of her argument about the capacity of well-chosen words to create empathy for the other. She turns to a key passage in Leviticus in which Jews are reminded: "The stranger that sojourns with you shall be unto you as the homeborn among you, and you shall love him as yourself, because you were strangers in Egypt."[24] According to Ozick, memory of Egypt—when translated into metaphor (understanding and loving the stranger among us)—becomes a compelling and enduring force: "Without the metaphor of memory and history, we cannot imagine the life of the Other. We cannot imagine what it is to be someone else. Metaphor is the reciprocal agent, the universalizing force: it makes it possible to envision the stranger's heart."[25]

Metaphor's Universalizing Force: Dream Traces and Lebanon Wine
Metaphor ferries memory across time. It allows us to enter worlds of imagination and feeling that might otherwise be closed to us despite Confucius's urging

to love the ancients and Leviticus's injunction to love the stranger. It's one thing to know that the past matters as a repository of moral judgment but quite another to take it to heart, to live with the past on intimate terms. In this undertaking, the words of sages are not enough. We also need the unique gifts of the poet. Chinese and Jewish traditions of cherishing history might have dried up were it not for the ongoing revival of recollection through what Ozick calls the universalizing force of metaphor. To be an educated person in Chinese tradition required mastery of old texts as well as of the living brush. The arts of poetry, calligraphy, and painting were an integral part of the literati ideal. Similarly, no Jew could become a member of the adult community unless and until he could read the Torah. Familiarity with texts became a broad-based prerequisite for Jewish identity. Without acts of speech that really matter, both hao gu and zakhor might have been difficult to sustain. Without metaphor, however, cultural memory might have become a discarded shard among the ancients.

In China, this ongoing reanimation of memory through metaphor was made easier by the fact that most scholar-officials were also poets. The same men who spent their days memorizing and codifying the public past used their evenings and their retirement years to enliven history with the force of personal emotion. They were Confucians by day and Daoists at night—serious about history but also playful about its seeming rigidities. Metaphors bridged this gulf between day and night. One of the most suggestive expressions for memory that grew out of the literati's struggle with recollection was meng hen—"dream traces." Long before Freud became interested in dreams as a source of recollection, Chinese poets valorized their potential for memorial revelation. Centuries before the experimental psychologist Karl Lashley came up with the concept of "memory engrams" to describe the imprints of remembrance that linger in the brain, Chinese scholar-officials described the simultaneous endurance and fragility of memory in terms of traces of a spring dream.

Lashley's investigations in the 1940s involved the neurological units in the brain that encode remembrance in a personally meaningful fashion.[26] What was at stake for the Western scientist was the individual's capacity to record and recall bits of memorable experience. For Chinese rememberers, the object was similar, but the model different. They sought to capture in vivid words fragments of the once-real yet ever-vanishing past. Dreams were at the heart of this effort. The Ming dynasty artist Tang Yin (1470–1524), for example, developed a distinctive style of commemorative painting. The inheritor of a long tradition that disdained crude claims to originality, Tang Yin modeled his landscapes upon the precedent of Song dynasty painters. He was a follower like Confucius, but he dreamed with ink and brush. The scale of his painting was small, sometimes in miniature, "reminding us that they were always addressed to a limited audience, and were shown in the hand, by appointment only; never placed on a wall for permanent exhibition. . . . The middle-Ming patron wanted a humanistic image, a symbol of the history and values of his own life, restrained in tone, but explicit in its immediate meaning." [27]

For Tang Yin, the challenge was to tame the monumental past with the intimacy of his brush, to bring history into the framework of dreams. But at times, Chinese history shattered the dreamer's world. Then, memory took up the task of painful reconstruction—always mindful of the intimacy of scale. This concern with both history and dreams—or more precisely, with history through dreams—is poignantly evoked in the memoir literature of Song China. In 1127, for example, when Jurchen warriors captured Kaifeng (the capital of northern Song), many of its inhabitants fled to the south. There, they ceaselessly reevoked their lost city in poems, essays, and painting. These intimate fragments turned out to be more durable (in the heart at least) than architectural monuments that memorialized the burden of loss.

Meng Yuanlao was one of the refugees from the north who had found sanctuary in the scenic city of Hangzhou. There, in 1147, exactly twenty years after the traumatic loss of Kaifeng, he wrote his *Tong zhi meng hua lu* (Records of the Dreams of the Eastern Capital's Splendor). The preface to this work described the circumstances of intimate recollection: "As I was gradually entering old age, I felt dejected. I could not but regret and lament when I recalled the happiness of those years, the wonderful festivities and the humane and congenial citizens. Recently, I met relatives and old friends and we talked about the old days. What we said was often greeted with wanton incredulity by the young generation. I was afraid that before long people would have few facts as a basis for their discussion of the customs (of Kaifeng). Therefore I wrote down what I recollected." [28]

Meng's *Dreams* was meant to be a bulwark against forgetting. They represented one man's effort to stem the tide of loss in a setting in which the amnesia of youth compounded the pain of military defeat. He accomplished this by resorting to metaphorical language. According to Professor Pei-yi Wu, a scholar of Kaifeng memoirs, the word *hua* in Meng's title once referred to flowers and flowering but later gained the meaning of "splendor" and "glory." Meng Yuanlao's use of *meng hua* (dreams of splendor) alludes to both memory and loss in a way that is quite different from the English usage of dreams: "In modern English usage, dreams are often projected into the future: they stand for hopes and wishes. In China, dreams are frequently used as figures for the past. Although dreams and events of the past belong to different orders of reality, they are alike in their inaccessibility and in being lodged in Chinese history. Events of this world are so transitory and contingent that their reality is hardly more substantial than that of dreams. If real events are all but illusory, memories of them cannot be more real than dreams."[29] *Dreams of Splendor*, in this sense, may appear to be nothing more than a mirage. But are Meng's memoirs merely a fragile mirror of illusionary events? No. The very depth of his attachment to dreams gives them an existential weight. They matter because the past reevoked in recollection matters. Precisely because the past is broken, fragile, and slippery, holding on to it becomes a consuming spiritual challenge.

The thin boundary between memory and dreams is also explored in the work of the most famous poet of Northern Song, Su Shi (1037–1101). Writing half a century before Meng Yuanlao (in an environment in which the threat of the Jurchen nomads was still somewhat vague), Su Shi elaborated the personal meanings of memory a bit more playfully. Su (also known as Su Dongpo) knew the complexities of attachment to historical memory firsthand. Born into a family of modest means, he managed to pass the highest level of the examination system under the personal supervision of Ouyang Xiu, one of the giants of historical writing in his time. Living according to the moral mandates of history, however, turned out to be a thorny challenge for Su Shi. Because of his opposition to the reform policies of the government, he was exiled from the capital no fewer than twelve times, once to the most distant corner of the realm (Hainan Island, in the south).[30]

Through all these adversities, Su Shi continued to write poetry, to excel in painting and calligraphy, and to deepen his philosophical understanding of Daoism and Chan Buddhism. Out of this experience of suffering and art came his distinctive understanding of memory's relationship to traces of a dream. Su Shi developed his psychological metaphor for remembrance not in abstract terms but in the context of a reunion with old friends. In one poem about friendship, he praises his comrades' fidelity to the past. They gather year after year in the same spot in the woods near a lake. Yet just when the past seems most near, the poet allows himself to see its essential slipperiness as well:

The east wind waits before East Gate,
While we ride horses seeking the old glen.

Men, like wild geese, keep the promise of return,
While the past, like a spring dream, leaves no trace.
. . . .
Since we have vowed to meet year after year,
Why go on calling the spirits of the dead?[31]

Su Shi's metaphor of the spring dream was not new in Chinese literature, but it did crystallize for subsequent generations the wistfulness at the heart of humans' relationship to the past. According to Su Shi, people are not so different from wild geese: both are marked by the urge to retrace past wanderings. What makes us different, however, is the mindfulness that accompanies the tenacity to return. We not only have a past, but we dream of it constantly. Robert Penn Warren understood this need to dream as well. In a different cultural context he, too, affirmed the fertility of night thoughts. Memory is the truth that leads us back to the past. It is the inspiration for Su Shi and his friends to return to the woods year after year. Their fidelity matters more than the spirits of the dead. Like Confucius (who did not pretend to know history but rather sought it through hao gu), Su Shi cherishes the will to reach backward in time.

Following the ancients' model, the Song poet also insists that the "past" (rendered here simply as shi, "things") is not a place but a delicate thread frequently frayed by the passage of events. Spring dreams are full of the promise and the sweetness of rebirth. Yet upon waking, memory has little more to hang on to than a few attenuated traces. What matters is the vow to return. This link between remembrance and the traces of a spring dream endures in Chinese literature long after Su Shi. It colors the poetry of mourning and of friendship with the brush of philosophical doubt. To liken the act of remembering to traces of a spring dream is to reckon with a fragility at its core. It is also to acknowledge that one who remembers is inevitably marked by the act of recollection itself.

It is no accident that the Chinese ideograph heng means not only "trace" but also "scar." Thus, at the very heart of the whimsical dream is a scarring of the self through its encounter with the past. This vision of an individual rememberer crisscrossed by the traces of history also colors the writings of the Qing dynasty scholar-official Wang Huizu (1731–1807). When he sat down to write his recollections, this scrupulous historian returned to Su Shi's metaphor of meng hen. Titling his autobiography Dream Traces from a Sickbed, Wang wrote: "Having been paralyzed in old age, I think about the past all the time. Everything is still very clear in my mind, so I started to dictate this history to my two sons. . . . Su Shi said that 'things vanish like a spring dream that leaves no traces.' But I don't care to see life as a dream. Perhaps dreams are unreal. But traces of recollection are not. Therefore I have tried to record my life as honestly as I can." [32] In this passage, there is no doubt that memory matters. Although dreams may be fragile, the brush that inks them for posterity is not. Wang Huizu was determined to record his personal history in spite of being ill. The urge to leave a trace, to say something instructive about his life to his descendants, led him to endow recollection with more solidity than Su Shi was willing to grant it seven centuries earlier. Wang, like Confucius, knew that the veracity of memory is a longed-for goal, not something assured by the past itself. It requires passion, commitment, honesty, and plenty of reminders. Without something concrete— like a date, a name, a painting, or a text—to prompt the recollecting mind, memory suffers the fate of a vanishing spring dream.

The prophet-poet Hosea also understood the power of reminders. Writing out of the Jewish predicament of exile, of displacement from the geographical center of religious memory, he embraces recollection with even more fervor than Su Shi. Aware that men, like wild geese, keep the promise of return, the Chinese poet was assured of his annual reunion with friends. Hosea, by contrast, had reason to doubt. After the destruction of the Temple of Solomon and exile to Babylon, all that was left him was a fierce longing to return. Jews, in Hosea's time, were scattered from the land that had sustained collective recollection. Some were exiled to Babylonia, others to Assyria. The prophet pointed to this predicament and wondered aloud about the fate of memory. Who would be left to remember the covenant? How were exiles to reconstruct for themselves the world left behind? How was the land of their ancestors to live inside of them, like a memorial flame? What could reanimate a past that seemed forever lost? The very longing to return was Hosea's answer. Out of that longing the poet-prophet weaves a dense fabric of reassuring metaphors. One of them involves a word play on the "scent of memory":

> They that dwell in his shadow
> Shall return, they should revive like corn
> and blossom like the vine,
> And their memory-scent will be as Lebanon wine. [33]

"Scent" here is literally identical with "remembrance" and suggests that the Jewish people themselves can yet become a reminder to God in proportion to what they remember about the ways of Torah. One medieval commentator develops this allegorical translation of Hosea and points out how the use of *zichro* recalls the blasts of the trumpet that accompanied the song of the Levites during the wine libation at the temple. Another, a prominent Hebrew lexicographer from the twelfth century, adds that the Israelites themselves are likened to the scent of Lebanon wine, because it was known to be the best wine in the world.[34] Lebanon wine marks their longing as well as their attachment to memory. The exiles who return to Torah will be returned to the land. Those for whom the distant fragrance of recollection becomes more real than the allure of the present will blossom like grapevines. Simply put, those who cherish the past are cherished in turn.

This bond of memory is also at the heart of the Rosh Hashanah liturgy—a holy day known in Hebrew as Yom Hazikaron (Day of Remembrance). On this occasion, which marks the beginning of the Jewish New Year and recalls the birth of the world at the same time, we sound the shofar in order to inspire the full range of emotions associated with memory. The ram's horn reminds us that we are a people anchored in recollection, because we face an interlocutor who is the embodiment of memory itself. After each blast of the shofar, we remember and ask to be remembered in turn: "You remember the deeds [performed] in the world and recall all that was created in the days of yore. . . . You remember the entire work [of creation] and no creature is hidden from you. . . . For You bring the set time of remembrance that every soul and being shall be recalled, that the numerous deeds and myriad creatures without limit shall be remembered."[35] This is the prayer that we repeat after each sound of the shofar, whose shrill, ancient vibrations are meant to rouse our forgetting hearts. The words that follow remind us that we stand in the face of the ultimate Rememberer who created us and our capacity for recollection. On Rosh Hashanah, we remember Noah, Abraham, Isaac, and Jacob. With memory-laden prayers, we sound the shofar in the hope that it may evoke favorable remembrance from above once again. On this day, the covenant is reaffirmed, and the people of the book become a nation of remembrance (am hazikaron).

The Rosh Hashanah theme of memory and return is further embroidered in the poetry of Jewish exiles who were inspired by prophets such as Hosea and Jeremiah. Judah Halevi (1075–1141), a poet of the golden age in Spain, was one of the most celebrated voices of the many who struggled to keep alive the vision of the Jewish homeland. Although he emigrated to the Holy Land toward the end of his life, his greatest poems describe the longing to reanimate the past in the hearts of those remaining in exile. Far from the site of the Holy Temple,

Judah Halevi refused to forget its mission: to sanctify the material world with light drawn down from the Creator of all worlds.

Jews, he reminded his contemporaries, were not placed on earth only to savor the enjoyments of cultural grandeur. However golden Spain may be, their covenant is with another land, with the Ruler of another kind of time. Always intensely personal, this poet's work echoes the questioning of time found in the poetry of Su Shi (who died on the other side of the globe only forty years before Judah Halevi). But whereas the Song dynasty scholar-official was heir to a long philosophical quarrel with the reality of dreams and time, Halevi inherited centuries of ritualized remembrance centering around Jerusalem. Consequently, when he turns to the past, he is more certain than Su Shi to find some saving anchor—though he realizes full well the ephemerality of times gone by:

> I have roused the slumber of my thoughts
> To lull the longings of my soul and eyes.
> The vicissitudes of the past [vekholefot z'man] are
> doubled in my heart,
> Causing the future to ring in my ears. . . .
> My bones are kindled by a light from His glory.
> It illuminates for me the ways of my sages.
> This light that sparkled in my youth
> Shines brighter in old age.[36]

The poet's heart doubles the vicissitudes of history, yet the soul and the eyes crave to know the past, to complete the arc of return. The ears are blessed with news of the future, because the poet does not give up the struggle with memory. He cleaves to the past, to the wisdom of the ancients, from which streams the guiding light of faith.[37]

In contrast to this positive affirmation of the power of recall, Chinese poets claim a doubt-riddled terrain. Perhaps because Chinese culture has been so stably anchored in the Yellow and Yangtze river valleys, its heirs could afford to question the tenacity of the past in the imagination. With the ruins of ancient structures at hand, remembrance did not have to perform the salvaging operation required of those who longed for Zion with the fervor of Judah Halevi. Su Shi, for example, could contemplate the vanishing traces of the past with a detachment that comes close to that of a Buddhist monk. Even in a poem that celebrates "cherishing old times in the company of my brother," there is a note of wistful self-distancing from the past:

Mortal men run everywhere, seeking what?
Like the wild goose ambling on snowy mud
Leaving it criss-crossed by the footprints of chance
. . . .
Worried if we recall the past or not?
The road is long.
The man is weary.
The lame beast sighs.[38]

Memory's journey is likened here to a twisting road traveled by tired humans and crippled beasts. The pace is slow and painful, because nothing is gained by running around like the wild goose. What matters instead is paying attention to chance, taking time to notice the pattern of webbed footprints in the snow. Hong zhao (wild-goose prints) become another metaphor in Chinese tradition for traces of past events.[39] Like meng hen (dream traces), this image evokes the fleeting quality of all memorial activity—so unlike Judah Halevi's image of a powerful longing that causes the future to ring and the light of the sages to shine ever more brightly.

Yet despite these differences, both Chinese and Jewish poets face the same dilemma: how to grasp through memory what is essentially ungraspable. The Chinese ideograph zhao can be read to mean "claw marks" as well as "wounds." To recall is to risk being injured by a past that has only momentary existence in the material world. Snow, like stone, can be scratched by willful claws. But the heart? To inscribe memory in this landscape requires different tools. Fragile words have to be endowed with toughness for this purpose.

THREE

Burning Snow

Naming the Broken Fragments of Time

Autumn bled all away, Mother, snow burned me through:
I sought out my heart so it might weep, I found—oh the
summer's breath,
it was like you.

PAUL CELAN, "BLACK FLAKES"

Seemingly fragile words have become resilient tools in the hands of Chinese and Jewish rememberers. They fashion the tale that is to be carried forward in time and mend the gap left when the present becomes severed from the past. In classical texts, metaphors perform these operations with the artful grace of wine and dreams. In the wake of twentieth-century trauma, however, metaphorical language is in danger of becoming obscene, unless, of course, it can reveal the impotence of speech itself. The Jewish poet Paul Celan understood the powerlessness of speech. Born in Czernowitz, Romania, in 1920, Celan, like Dan Pagis and Aharon Appelfeld grew up in a German-speaking household. Although German became the language of his mother's murderers, the poet who was called Paul Antschel in his childhood never gave up his difficult mastery of the tools of his youth. German words once had a lyrical power in the mouth of his mother, who sang him German folk songs and helped him memorize the poetry of Goethe and Schiller. During the Holocaust, however, after his parents' deportation to Transnistria, the mother tongue lost its lyricism. In fall 1942 Celan's father died of typhus, and that winter his mother was declared unfit for work and shot to death.[1] The son, then doing forced labor in Transylvania, was far from the wintry Ukrainian landscape in which his parents died. Yet for the rest of his life, Celan remained riveted by the snow that blanketed his homeland while life drained out of those he loved.

The Jewish survivor who continued to write in the *Muttersprache* of his childhood could not resort to naturalistic metaphors like Su Shi's goose prints in the snow. He had to mark an uglier, more recalcitrant terrain. So Celan wrote about snows that burn. In a poem titled "Black Flakes," he imagines his mother asking her child for protection. Alone, shivering with the news of the father's death, the woman who gave birth to the poet asks for the shelter of a shawl. If the world had stayed sane, if words could have gone on saying what they meant, it would have been the mother, or at least the mother's speech, that would have protected the boy. Instead, out of the wreck of history he is left to face, Celan must fashion his own word tools. "Black Flakes," according to John Felstiner— one of Celan's most perceptive interpreters—uses memory to frame an unspeakable experience: "The advent of tears balances the weaving of the shawl, the unmasking force of grief meets the poem's own making: 'Then came my tears. I wove the shawl.' Answering loss with language, this poem weaves a text against winter. . . . We hear his mother ask for a shawl: he writes a poem, restoring to her something, at least, in the mother tongue." [2]

To fully grasp the rupture embodied in the wintry shawl of Celan, we must recall how great was memory's promise in classical Jewish texts: it could transform a vague longing for connectedness to the past into a solid memorial that withstood the erosion of time. Although both Chinese and Jewish tradition acknowledged the fickleness of the human heart, both also held out the possibility of fidelity and return. It was this possibility that was burned out of Celan's life and, to a lesser degree, out of the lives of the Chinese who survived the atrocities of the Mao era.

Those who continued to weave words into shawls had to make do with a more fragile sense of language and remembrance, to redefine memory and words in a way that strained their traditions. In biblical Hebrew, there was a close link between the verb *zakhor* (to remember) and the noun *zikaron* (memorial)—a marker erected in human time to serve as a reminder of what happened in the ever-vanishing past. [3] A memorial was something that stimulated divine remembrance and human attachment to memory all at the same time. Memorials were supposed to engrave the heart, to transform the very fabric of Jewish life. This active meaning of zikaron accounts for the "memory covenant" between Abraham and God, between the Jewish people and their redeemer at Mount Sinai. The expression *likrot brit* (to engrave a covenant) refers at times to memorials carved in stone, such as the pillar erected by Jacob after his encounters with divinity. But the human body can also be the site of a memorial—as in the case of *brit mila*, the circumcision of Jewish males. Chinese tradition had a similar appreciation for the inscriptive power of memory. It, too, insisted that volatile feelings can become durable where remembrance is concerned. The common expression *ming gan*, "to recall with gratitude," suggests something that grows out of one's sinews, bones, blood, and heart. The word *ming* also denotes an inscription carved in stone—perhaps a tablet erected in honor of parents or worthy rulers. In both cases, memory and memorial are closely linked.

Even when the passage of time erased material traces of the past, Chinese and

Jewish tradition assumed that the human heart retained the capacity for affectionate recollection. Pierre Ryckmans, a keen observer of Chinese culture, noted that the emphasis on memory in China stands in marked contrast to a certain disregard for the material remains of history: "From a very early stage—well before Confucius—the Chinese evolved the notion that there can be one form of immortality: the immortality of history . . . which means, in practical terms, in the memory of posterity, through the medium of the written word. . . . Continuity is not ensured by the immobility of inanimate objects, it is achieved through the fluidity of the successive generations."[4] Physical memorials could be (and were) discarded, because literary texts were assumed to be more durable. The past, in both Chinese and Jewish tradition, was made up of words that proved to be more resilient than stone.

Words and Stones

A tension between words and stones is glimpsed in the last of the five books of Moses. Deuteronomy is called Devarim in Hebrew after the second phrase that appears in the book: "Ze ha devarim asher diber Moshe" (These are the words which Moses spoke). *Devarim* means at once "words," "things," and "events." In light of the repeated emphasis given to memory in this portion of the Hebrew Bible, it may be most appropriately translated as "eventful words."[5] Speaking to a people become fainthearted at times, Moses seeks to reaffirm a connection to history. His goal is to engrave in their hearts the memory of communal events, which they in turn will have to retell their children. The remembrance of Sinai must not slip into some vague past. If it is too solid, however, it will break under the pressure of time; if it is merely text, it may be recited and set aside, to be forgotten. Memory would then lose its capacity to guide the people in their everyday lives. To keep the edge of Jewish memory sharp, Moses taught the people of Israel that they must respond to God's speech acts at Sinai with their own acts of devarim. They, too, must create living words. They must become a source of life-sustaining action by observing the commandments.

The rememberer, in this sense, is a person who defies the natural laws of decay, one who makes of the heart a more hospitable ground for traces of the past than stone could ever be. The rememberer might also be a lonely rebel against the passage of time. To resist the erasures occasioned by this passage, memories have to be written down. This was the urgent message of the Tang dynasty scholar-official Han Yu, who raised the call of returning to the ancients. He became a pathbreaker by his very insistence on the language and values of predecessors who had long passed from public favor. As part of a cosmopolitan-

minded Buddhist court, Han Yu became the epitome of the cranky Confucian.
His brilliant essays and poems set the tone for a whole generation of fu gu pai (the
"running-back-to-the-ancients faction," as they were derisively known). This
group included Meng Jiao, the mournful poet who wrote "Autumn Meditations." Unlike Meng, however, Han Yu was a prominent figure in the political
battles of his times. In 819, he was exiled for a fiercely worded memorial pro-
testing the adulation of Buddhist relics. A year later, Han Yu was recalled and
given a post at the Imperial Academy.[6] There, he continued to nurse his sense of
injured memory through finely crafted works such as "Autumn Winds." This
poem reflects the moodiness of an aging man who will not give up his quest for
a return to the ancients:

> Home again I scan through texts,
> (words ocean-like and limitless)
> Who searches the ancient traces but me
> A humble pleasure that makes no precious gift.[7]

"Ancient traces" appear here as a consolation to Han Yu alone. No one else
seeks the humble pleasures of recovering the past. The poet uses his solitude to
enter into a dialogue with ancient texts, undertaking the lonely challenge of
matching words and things. Han Yu's call for fu gu went largely unheeded,
however. A few close friends understood that going back to the ancients meant
to freshen one's voice with their simplicity. Some poets did take up the challenge
of writing in a language that recalled the vitality of Han dynasty texts. Most
preferred the ornate tongue of the day.

Surrounded by works of antiquity, Han Yu nursed his loneliness in poems
full of personal feeling. Although the landscape of Tang China was dotted with
memorials carved in massive stone, his remembering heart made a valiant effort
to cherish something older, more fragile:

> Ancient annals strewn left and right
> Poetry and History placed front and back,
> How do I differ from a bookworm,
> From birth to death encased in words?
> The ancient way dulls and stultifies
> ancient words cage and fetter.
> Modern times differ indeed from antiquity,
> Who today can share such pleasures?[8]

Again, the poet laments the paucity of comrades who share his pleasures. He sits propped up by poetry and history, seemingly a worm encased by words.

This ability to see himself through the eyes of others was one of Han Yu's poetic gifts. He could voice his contemporaries' contempt for bookworms, granting them the insight that modern times differ from antiquity. He even confessed that the ancient way may seem to dull and stultify the mind. But Han Yu stood his ground in the "cage of words." Although ancient words might fetter the mind, his poetry proved that they freed the heart. The ancient way—or rather, an attachment to what he felt to be the power of the ancients' way—enabled Han Yu to craft works of great passion. His contemporaries ended up sharing his pleasures not necessarily because they loved ancient Confucians but because the remembering poet's words became a compelling inspiration.

Solomon Ibn Gabirol, a Jewish poet who lived in eleventh-century Spain (1022–1155), also knew the loneliness of memory and also found ways to compel the attention of his contemporaries and of subsequent generations as well. Born two hundred years after Han Yu, Ibn Gabirol lived most of his life in Saragossa and wrote his major theological work, The Source of Life, in Arabic. His poetry, much like Han Yu's, demanded a return to the ways of the ancients. Ibn Gabirol, too, pared his words down with care. Yet he also felt misunderstood by those who were deaf to the memory-covenant with history. In a poem about leaving his hometown, Solomon Ibn Gabirol decries the predicament of a rememberer, with all the bitterness yet none of the self-irony of Han Yu:

> My throat is parched with crying, my
> tongue clings to my palate. . . .
> I am buried, but not in
> a graveyard: my house is my coffin!
> They are like giants in their own eyes,
> but like grasshoppers in mine. When I
> utter my sayings, they chide me as if I
> were a Greek. Speak an intelligible
> language, so that we may understand,
> for this is gibberish. . . .[9]

Here the outcast chooses to speak differently from his contemporaries. They demand an "intelligible language" (sfat am—literally, "a tongue of the folk," a language that the folk can roll around on their lips in comfort), and Ibn Gabirol gives them odd words—words that do not simply match the shape of things.

The folk think there is a difference between home and the coffin. Yet for the poet they are the same: wooden containers of desiccated words. He speaks gibberish but in a way they are bound to hear, even if they don't understand. Ibn Gabirol is intentional in his usage of the Bible when he tells the folk that they are like "giants in their own eyes." This metaphor recalls the sin of the spies whom Moses sent to report on the Promised Land. These spies had described the inhabitants as giants and themselves as grasshoppers in their own eyes. For Solomon Ibn Gabirol, his contemporaries are neither giants nor grasshoppers but simply boors. Nonetheless, they can wound the poet by augmenting his loneliness and by making his parched throat even more sore.

Regardless of his isolation, Ibn Gabirol continued to write poems addressed "To the Fools" and, like Han Yu, continued his war with the language of his contemporaries. His most lasting contribution was to come in poems that expressed a longing for the higher source of the human soul and for a living bond with the wellsprings of Jewish imagination. These poems call to the Creator with the force of simple, fresh words:

> God Almighty, You who listen to the
> wretched and grant their desire, how
> long will You remain far from me and
> hidden. Night and day I entreat You,
> I cry out with a confident heart.[10]

Here, the social loneliness of the poet gives way to humility. Away from the skirmishes with fools, Ibn Gabirol cries out with confidence, though the object of his entreaty remains hidden. Unlike the poem about leaving home, this work does not complain of a tongue that clings to the palate. Instead, the poet has reached the hard-won fluency of one whose longing to remember unleashes the power of speech. The metaphor of the hand that withers and the tongue that sticks has haunted all Jewish poets who wrote after the author of Psalm 137. They know that to be able to speak at all they must cleave to memory. This fierce faith in words and memory defies the burden of exile. Psalm 137 was the song of prisoners who refused to sing the songs of Zion for the delectation of their Babylonian masters. Instead, by the rivers of Babylon, far from Jerusalem, words were used to counter both distance and defeat.

The words of Psalm 137 remain alive today. More durable than stone, they are intoned softly at Jewish weddings, right after the breaking of the glass, which is a physical reminder of the destruction of the Temple. Before the festivities begin, before the groom can take open delight in the bride, before the guests turn to the personal joy so compelling in the present, the past must have its due: "Al naharot Bavel . . . im eshkaheh Yerushalaim" (By the rivers of Babylon . . . if I forget you O Jerusalem).[11] To forget Jerusalem is, in the words of the contemporary American poet David Rosenberg, not only a religious transgression but also a risk that takes life out of words:

> If I forget thee
> sweet Jerusalem
> let my writing hand wither
>
> my tongue freeze to ice
> sealing up my voice
> mind numb as rock
>
> If I forget
> your kiss
> Jerusalem on my lips. . . .[12]

Rosenberg appears, at first glance, to merely rephrase the old psalm—until we hear a more urgent fear: a frozen voice, a mind grown numb as rock. Again, words stand in contrast to stone. Only words watered by memory remain fresh; only the poet who keeps Jerusalem in mind—in the heart, that is, where words become action—can remain fully alive. David Rosenberg, Solomon Ibn Gabirol, and Han Yu all sought the source spring of living words. They sought to invigorate speech through active remembrance. And they came face-to-face with the limitation of words. Rocklike but more fragile, words can be stretched to accommodate the corrosive passage of time. But they have their breaking point as well.

The Bending Moment of Memory Words

Just how far can language be stretched to encompass the loss of the past? This question about the elasticity of memory words may be likened to the dynamic problems that preoccupied Galileo during his years at the University of Padua (1591–1600). Puzzled by the question of how much pressure a beam can take, Galileo came up with a new mathematical formula: the strength of a beam is proportional to its surface area and independent of its length.[13] This formula in turn revolutionized bridge building. The longer, lighter structures now possible were great improvements over the heavy stone constructions of Roman times. The problem of the "bending moment"—the tension and sagging that accompanies pressure on any longitudinal structure—was solved by a new vision of elasticity: a series of shorter beams could be used to make longer bridges.

Properly understood, force could be incorporated into and compensated for by the increased thickness of beams. A fragile structure, tested and sustained by pressure, could be made less vulnerable to collapse.

Chinese and Jewish tradition each faced its own bending moment in the twentieth century. The Cultural Revolution and the Holocaust, respectively, stretched the memorial resources of these two cultures to near collapse. In China, the stress became palpable as early as the 1920s, during which time the New Culture Movement, championed by radicals such as Zhang Shenfu and Zhang Ruoming, sought to replace the classical Chinese language with the spoken vernacular. Although the impact of this transformation took many years to be felt, its influence on memory was immediate. An entire world of traditional thought and feeling started to slip away along with the language of Han Yu and Su Shi. According to one contemporary scholar, Ci Jiwei, this memorial slide opened the way for the excesses of the Mao era: "Even though the forgetting of classical Chinese did not mean a total forgetting of a way of life, it did open up a linguistic-mnemonic space, and what has been put in that space is of utmost importance." [14] Ci, a victim of Maoist dogmatism, is especially mindful of memory's fragility. He predates the bending moment by focusing attention away from the murderous policies of the late 1960s and moving it to the remembrance lacunae left after the language revolution of the 1920s.

It is Ci Jiwei's aim to show how these mnemonic lacunae became filled with manufactured remembrances after the Communists' victory in 1949. Building upon earlier erasures, Mao Zedong demanded that his adherents purge themselves of the "bitterness" of the past and cling to the "sweetness" of the present. Once the nuanced vision of history nurtured by Confucianism gave way, a flatness of language and imagination took over. The old was bad and expendable, the new glorious and necessary. The Cultural Revolution of 1966–67 pushed this campaign for language and thought replacement to a breaking point, shifting the ground of revolution from politics and institutions to the depths of the soul. Each person had to go through repeated confessions known as *dousi*, which can be literally translated as "combating selfishness" but which more accurately connotes a war against the self. This assault was then combined with *pixiu* (criticizing revisionism), which seems to suggest an other-directed persecution. In fact, as Ci Jiwei points out, "both in formulation and in practice the institution of self-persecution turned people into wolves and sheep at the same time. And when Mao eventually wanted them to become sheep alone, they became sheep." [15]

But they also became something else—secret guardians of a vulnerable past.

Because memory can take refuge in silence, it is able to withstand huge pressures toward amnesia and self-incrimination. Mnemosyne, as the ancient Greeks knew, is a resilient mother of thought. The enforced forgetfulness of the Mao era, in the end, did not succeed in erasing China's cultural remembrance. During the most abusive moments of Mao's mnemonic tyranny, some refuge was still possible. Old words, like Galileo's beams, became tougher through the pressure of stress. In the 1960s, the way of the ancients was officially outlawed, though it continued to provide crevices of personal sanity for imprisoned, tortured intellectuals like Nien Cheng. A Western-educated woman, Nien was arrested and accused of various trumped-up charges throughout 1967–68. Sick with pneumonia and despair, she found solace in the words and memories of the past:

> I knew I was experiencing all the symptoms of mental and physical
> exhaustion that could lead to breakdown. For mental exercise I first tried
> to memorize some of Mao's essays. . . . But in the last analysis, to study
> Mao's books for many hours a day was a distressing occupation for
> me. . . . I turned instead to the Tang dynasty poetry I had learned as a
> school girl. It really amazed me that I was able to dig out from the deep
> recesses of my brain verses that had lain dormant for decades. Trying to
> remember a poem I thought I had forgotten was a joyful occupation.
> Whenever I managed to piece together a whole poem, I felt a sense of
> happy accomplishment.[16]

Nien Cheng was unwilling to be either sheep or wolf. Depressed and rendered almost powerless by her persecutors and Mao's works, she found solace in the works of Tang poets. Their condensed words helped her name the broken pieces of her life. Even after her daughter's death, during the first year of Red Guard Terror, the old masters remained more meaningful in her mind than the murderers of her child, enabling her to eventually talk back and to record what had been lost.

During the Holocaust in Europe, by contrast, amnesia nearly won. The language of tradition and personal experience was stretched so far that only deathly silence seemed to await those who managed to outwit the death camps. Hitler counted on the fact that no one would believe the ranting of escapees from hell. Furthermore, the persecuted would be struck silent by the nightmare they had seen. In such trauma, we now understand, time stands still, and the chronological sequence of events is arrested. Words and the mind are forced into something like a black box that assumes the form of a "time-eradicating chamber."[17] Nien Cheng, too, was shoved into such a black box in Shanghai. Cut off from the past and the present, she faced the risk of silence and a breakdown. When Mao's words failed her, she pieced her sanity together with the words of the Tang poets. She managed this spiritual feat because the trauma of history was never as suffocating in China as it became for Jews in the death camps.

Some might think that Jewish familiarity with the sufferings of exile was a solace in the black box. This was the assumption of Adolf Rudnicki, a non-Jewish Polish writer who wrote in one of his stories: "No other nation has so many synonyms for suffering as have the Jews. . . . Everybody knows that what the Germans did during the Second World War has no equivalent in history, yet it was all contained within the Jews' ancient vocabulary." [18] But Rudnicki was wrong. Not everybody knows the Jewish words for suffering, and even if people did, they would find them inadequate for what happened in the twentieth century.

Surely other nations also have a refined vocabulary for suffering. Classical Chinese, to mention one linguistic universe, was marvelously supple in describing the anguish of lonely guardians of historical memory such as Han Yu. Yet Han Yu never faced the threat of life-annihilating silence as did the Jews during the Holocaust. The connection between word and world held in the Tang dynasty and even in Maoist China. In the Jewish context, however, a terrible rupture took place. The violence of this bending moment is aptly captured by André Neher in an essay entitled "Shaddai: The God of the Broken Arch." [19] A survivor of the nightmare, Neher places the Holocaust in a context of tests. The Creator is always testing the Jewish people, testing Abraham, testing Isaac and, finally, testing Job. But in all other tests, the Creator himself waits on the other side of the bridge. He is the bridge of hope that encourages the person of faith to cross into the unknown. But in the death camps, the possibility of dialogue vanished. There can be no "test" of the Holocaust. What lingers after Auschwitz is simply the shock-effect of a brutal, experienced reality, the throbbing trace of an event. Neher's violent remnant is worlds away from Chinese traces of a spring dream. It leaves in its wake nothing but stammering speech and a wounded imagination. What bridge could possibly be built out of such stress-laden beams?

Any effort to speak about the God of the Broken Arch pushes language even further—beyond silence and beyond despair. Primo Levi was a survivor who ventured into this wilderness. A chemist from Turin, Levi was deported to Auschwitz, where the murderous reality of the death camp threatened to rob him of all sanity and words. Yet, after the terrible bending moment of the war, Levi reaffirmed the power of memory words. Returning to the language of

Genesis, he described the madness of the war years as *tohu-vavohu* (unformed and void). The tenth and eleventh words of the Hebrew Bible are used to evoke the chaotic, all-embracing loneliness that enveloped the world during the Holocaust. According to Levi, this was not so much a world without God as one from which the spirit of man had vanished. Shame and despair follow, along with a commitment to recollection. In his last book, *The Drowned and the Saved*, he clings to the life raft of memory, knowing how flimsy it is: "The memories which lie within us are not carved in stone; nor do they tend to become erased as years go by. But often they change, or even grow by incorporating extraneous features. . . . This scant reliability of our memories will be satisfactorily explained only when we know in what language, what alphabet they are written, on what surface, with what pen: to this day we are still far from this goal." [20]

Here, too, inscriptions on stone are challenged in the name of something more fragile: the alphabet of personal memory. Levi was fully aware that this is a loosely connected, ever-changing text. Yet in its very looseness and ephemerality lies its strength. As he writes about the scant reliability of memory, the chemist-survivor from Turin comes up with the same suggestion Galileo did in Padua. The elasticity of memory, like that of beams, has to be sought in the smallest surface unit. It is not the length of beams but their cross-section that helps them withstand the bending moment.

Galileo was concerned with the fragility of physical structures, Primo Levi with the flexibility of remembrance. How many extraneous features could it incorporate and still remain faithful to the events recalled? How much of the stress force that Galileo incorporated into the cross-section of his beams could be accommodated within the strained fabric of human emotions? Galileo had no doubt that short, stocky beams could withstand the bending moment. Witnesses to the historical horrors of the twentieth century had good reason to doubt whether their bending moment was even bearable. And still, their mouths were pried open by speech.

Primo Levi could have been silent, as Hitler had expected. The miracle is not that Hitler's plans failed but that they did not destroy the vocal cords of those who lived on after the Holocaust. This same miracle is repeated over and over again wherever brutal suppressors count on the verbal exhaustion of their victims. Stalin, too, expected silence in Russia, yet articulate witnesses somehow managed to stammer on about what they had been through. Silence might have been a graceful, perhaps even safe way out, but the will to stretch language to its limits prevailed. The work of Anna Akhmatova bears these stretch marks openly, even with pride. Akhmatova was a poet who took upon herself the guardianship of memory at a time when Stalinism choked nearly all possibility of truthful recollection. Her epic poem "Requiem 1935–1940" opens with an account of imprisonment in Yezhovshchina (the center for Stalin's secret-police activities in the late 1930s):

> One day someone recognized me. . . . Then a woman with lips blue with cold who was standing behind me, and of course had never heard of my name, came out of the numbness which affected us all and whispered in my ear—(we all spoke in whispers there):
> "Can you describe this?"
> I said, "I can!"
> Then something resembling a smile slipped over what had once been her face.[21]

The crooked smile of her camp mate increased Akhmatova's determination to speak. She went on using words in a world that would have liked nothing better than to silence her kind. She spoke and wrote not out of some noble urge to bear witness but simply because the enforced stillness was too deafening. And she did not speak about herself alone. If Akhmatova risked ungainly speech, it was for the sake of those around her.

This risk was increasingly rejected by the Belgian philosopher Jean Amery— Primo Levi's bunk mate at Auschwitz. According to Amery, the death camps had already stretched words to the breaking point. There was nothing left to say, or think. As a result, those most dependent on reason were condemned to the worst nightmare. After the war, those who once had believed in truth and beauty found themselves doubly bereft—dispossessed of life and of reason as well: "In the camp, the intellect in its totality declared itself to be incompetent. . . . The word always dies where the claim of some reality is total. It died for us a long time ago. And we were not even left with the feeling that we must regret its departure."[22] Whereas Akhmatova was sure she could convey what she had seen, Amery is certain that he cannot. It was not only speech that lost its meaning in the death camps but intellect as well. Under Stalin, the gulf between word and world was great but bridgeable. At Auschwitz it yawned so wide that it seemed pointless to even regret its existence.

Jean Amery's scathingly negative vision of language was shared by other Holocaust survivors. This outlook opened the gates of personal hell: Amery committed suicide in 1978, and Paul Celan in 1970; Primo Levi, though more patient with memory's twists and turns in both the public and private domain, also ended up choosing suicide, in 1984. These choices are something that those of us who were born after the Shoah can never understand. But we can, and must, see what is being rescued in the very process of radical doubt. Our words, our capacity to think and say something after Auschwitz, depend upon reckoning with the disillusionment of survivors such as Amery, Celan, and Levi.

The Recovery of Words

In China, the night of unreason during the Cultural Revolution was never quite as dark or as devoid of sense as were the death camps. Yet survivors of the Maoist era also faced the problem of language reclamation. The loveliest, most cherished words of Chinese culture had been repeatedly used and abused in the personality cult of Mao Zedong. The "Red Sun" that was supposed to burn in the heart of each and every one of Mao's followers demanded absolute loyalty and a willingness to betray family connections as well as personal memory. Older intellectuals and young Red Guards alike had rushed to incriminate themselves (and others) in order to prove their loyalty to the Great Helmsman.

After the death of Mao, in 1976, and after the first outpouring of the literature of the "wounded," a group of young poets turned their attention to the deeper problem of language erosion during the Mao era. Bei Dao, the writer who calls himself Northern Island, was one of the first to flee from the scorching certainties of the Cultural Revolution. In his poem "The Answer," he turned language on its head so as to extract from it the last bit of truth left after all the distortions of the political mobilization:

I don't believe the sky is blue;
I don't believe in the sound of thunder;
I don't believe that dreams are false;
I don't believe that death has no revenge.[23]

Here, a Chinese poet who is heir to the memory metaphors of Su Shi as well as to the slogans of Chairman Mao tries to reaffirm the possibility of genuine speech. To question the obvious beauty of the sky illumined by the Red Sun, to doubt the heroic clap of revolutionary thunder, to resist falsifying one's own dreams, is Bei Dao's way of circling back to cultural memory. If dreams (in the sense of fragile recollection) are not false, then death loses its senseless dominion over the present. The disbelieving poet thus reclaims the eroded terrain of his imagination. In another poem called simply "All," Bei Dao harks back to Su Shi as he writes:

All is cloud
All is a beginning without an end
All is a search that dies at birth
All joy lacks smiles
All sorrow lacks tears
All language is repetition
. . . .
All past is in a dream.[24]

No Chinese reader will miss the allusion to "dream traces" in this vernacular formulation of the classical insight. Clouds may be the only solace left in a world scorched by the Red Sun of Mao Zedong. The hopes of Bei Dao's generation had all been aborted by totalitarian rulers, their sorrows choked. Yet the very repetitive power of language, the idea of a dreamlike past manages, in the end, to talk back—and thereby defeat the Red Sun.

Chinese language, like the poet Bei Dao, has gone through a series of traumatic revolutions. The stammering quality of Bei Dao's vernacular is one of the consequences of this trauma. Classical Chinese was once marvelously well suited for Su Shi's images of spring dreams and wild-goose prints in the snow. But poets of the post-Mao era need a tougher language. They have, through terrible necessity, discovered Galileo's formula: shorter, thicker units make a stronger, more enduring bridge. If a poet and his words are to withstand history's relentless erosion, then memory and language have to grow more dense as well as more elusive. Little wonder that Bei Dao and his fellow poets were condemned as too murky, that their metaphors were censored as too obscure. Obsessed by dreams, these young poets threatened the politicians' dominion over what is real. Murky visions tend to complicate both speech and politics. Therein lies their danger.

Inside the suffocating boundaries of China's cultural Great Wall, these poets echo the elusive voice of Jewish survivors such as Dan Pagis and Paul Celan.[25] Celan, more than other poet-survivors, pushed language to its extreme. Having been orphaned during the war, he used words not as an alternative to loneliness but as the very embodiment of missed communication. To make matters worse, he went on writing in the language the Nazis had used to order the death of Jews. Each time he set pen to paper, Celan heard the echoes of death-creating speech. In January 1958, when he was invited back to Germany to accept a literary prize, Celan voiced in vague terms the hope that his Muttersprache may yet have some life in it:

Reachable, near and not lost, there remained amid the losses this one
thing: language.

It, the language remained, not lost, yes in spite of everything. But it
had to pass through its wound wordlessness, pass through frightful muting, pass through the thousand darknesses of deathbringing speech. It
passed through and gave back no words for that which happened.[26]

Nowhere in this speech does Celan mention German specifically; instead he limits himself to general terms such as "language" and "speech." Most striking by
its muteness is the reference to all that he lost as simply "that which happened."
To be sure, Celan is amply aware that he is speaking in the country that had
given birth to Nazism only two decades earlier. His audience would have to try
very hard to miss the meaning of this condemnation of their linguistic legacy. In
the end, however, he is concerned less with what they think than with what he
can tell them in his poems.

To resolve this bitter quandary, Paul Celan had to go beyond the dreadful
limits of German speech. In a poem titled "The Lock Gate" he circles back to
one key Jewish word—the word that connotes mourning and memory at once:

To
the worship of many gods
I lost a word that was looking for me:
Kaddish.

Through
the lock gate I had to go
to save the word back
to the salt waters and
out and across:
Yiskor.[27]

At the end of this poem Celan comes back to zakhor—the root of all memorial
expressions. He may have wished to worship many gods but two lost words
haunt him: kaddish, the service of the heart offered by the living in memory of
the dead, and yiskor, the prayer service in which individual and communal losses
are recalled. Celan has no choice but to join his voice in these prayers. He forces
his way through silence—the gate that blocks all words—in order to create
enduring verses about those who were to have no memories of their own.

Jewish tradition, like that of the Chinese, insisted upon the cultivation of
remembrance, but in the wake of historical trauma, memory had to assume new

guises. The specter of dark, misshapen experiences had to be accommodated alongside the loveliness of spring dreams and Lebanon wine. In the words of Chang Shiang-hua, a contemporary woman reflecting upon Chinese continuity from Taiwan, Chinese memory had to grow more coarse or else wither like a delicate hothouse flower left in blistering snow:

> The terrible fate of the Chinese people
> Is like an endless, unbroken vine of
> Strong rattan; a fierce will to survive
> Twisting under black soil
> The sprouts of faith encountering parasites
> That destroy them as soon as they emerge
>
> . . . .
>
> Every Chinese who has emerged from disaster alive
> Is a supreme philosopher of life
> Always springing back from deepest degradation.[28]

Clearly, this is not a poet taken in by foreigners' admiration for Chinese cultural inventions. Chang's subject is not the Great Wall but the broken vine of cultural continuity. She writes not about graceful silk threads but rather about coarse rattan covered by soil and parasites. The only philosophy celebrated here is the one that emerges from disaster. No lyrical wisdom of the East here, just the capacity to stay alive. With all this, Chang's poem lays claim to a lineage that goes back to Su Shi. It sings to us of the feel of the wind on the river and the light of the moon glimpsed behind the mountains. She digs beneath the soil of Chinese culture to excavate the fierce will to go on remembering, even if the subject of recollection is nothing but degradation, the terrible fate of her people.

Subterranean excavation is also the subject of Yehuda Amichai's poetry. He, too, probes the strata of his city for odd secrets, using geology as the metaphor—an intentionally odd twist on the "people of the Book":

> The Jews are not a historical people
> and not even an archaeological people, the Jews
> are a geological people with rifts
> and collapses and strata and fiery lava.
> Their history must be measured
> on a different scale.[29]

Amichai turns the tables on the vaunted textualism of the Jewish nation, evoking a fiery lava of historical explosions. Jews are privileged simply by their nearness to this furnace and by a determination not to run from its shattering heat. Outsiders might be dazzled by the well-preserved records of Chinese history and the uninterrupted tradition of Jewish biblical commentary and might marvel at the archaeological treasures of both cultures. But Jews and Chinese who dig beneath the soil of cultural memory come up with something quite different. It is not history that propels them forward but an attachment to recollection. Those who persist on clinging to memory, like rattan, are a tired lot. Not only do they have to dig up the past, but there is no assurance that their offerings will be welcomed in the present.

FOUR

Notes in the Wall

Personal Memory in the Crevices of Public Commemoration

Returning, he opened his eyes,
stood by the side of the road, uninvited,
wrinkled in his old jacket.
He remembered,
and recognized the night.
DAN PAGIS, "HONI"

Unwelcomed offerings are often memory's most precious gifts. An image long buried, a snippet of evidence suppressed, a nameless day that suddenly changes the whole calendar—these are fragments of remembrance recovered by individuals that sometimes alter the entire pattern of meaning established in the public domain. These disturbances may also enrich communal memory. By stretching the boundaries of acceptable commemoration, they create a more resilient historical narrative. This process of memorial augmentation has been going on in Chinese and Jewish tradition for centuries. Both these traditions nurture as well as guide the process of individual recollection.

In each of these cultures, the public past has been privileged, indeed monumentalized. At the same time, individual Chinese and Jews have developed over time many strategies for outwitting official history. Their need to transgress public remembrance was greatest when personal memory was least welcome. Dan Pagis captured this predicament in his poem "Honi," which describes the rememberer as a weary traveler. His wrinkled jacket is but one sign of his marginality with respect to the community. Troubled by his disturbing recollections, Honi nonetheless returns to face the night that better-dressed men might have good reason to avoid. Pagis was himself a traveler who accosted his contemporaries with dark tales collected on the side roads of public commemoration. A rumpled figure, he bore the burden of his own history quietly.

Pagis held his tongue as long as he could about the dark events that took the lives of his parents, trying to be a guardian of silence while crediting those who went before him with inventing grief.[1] Eventually, he wrote a few poems about the Holocaust, which were phrased in a fractured, reticent language. Pagis's poems simply (if such an adverb can apply to the skilled breaking apart of everyday cadence) squeezed a bit of truth out of words soiled by murderous events.

According to the literary critic Geoffrey Hartman, Pagis was in a state of "rebellion against memory" during most of his life in Israel.[2] He changed his first name to Dan—a common Hebrew name. And he did not dwell on the father who seemed to have abandoned him during the war nor on his hometown of Radautz, in Bukovina. His history, when finally spoken, had the gritty quality of sand in one's shoes: it made walking difficult and running toward some bright future quite impossible.

Pagis's voice marked a dark and troubling past that could not be readily incorporated into the optimistic history needed by a Jewish state bent upon building a new society after the Holocaust. The future of Israel demanded heroic predecessors, not broken men who spoke vague words snatched from a lifetime of silence. Yet the halting cadence of Dan Pagis became, over time, a unique gift to his community. His stammer perforated the narrative of collective memory. The latter, in Hartman's words, can be conceived as "a gradually formalizing agreement to transmit the meaning of intensely shared events in a way that does not have to be individually struggled for."[3] An agreement presupposes the absence, or at least the muting, of struggle. Individuals like Pagis, however, have no choice but to struggle, in that their work challenges the process that defines the boundaries of public remembrance. They want no part of the agreement to tame the past. Therefore, one must search for another metaphor to understand the thrust of their disturbance.

Another way of conceiving the relationship between public and personal memory may be to imagine individual messages tucked into the crevices of a stone wall—a sight that is readily available to those who visit the Old City in Jerusalem. There stands the Kotel, the Western Wall that is the only remnant from the Second Temple built during the reign of Herod. Huge boulders, pieces of a public past, are stacked one upon another, creating a solid mass that carries the eyes upward. But before one can follow this heavenly trajectory, one notices the myriad notes that are crammed into every opening between the stones and every crack in a single massive rock. Each fragment of paper tells of a grief, a hope, a sin, a blessing that is intensely personal. The notes in the wall blossom in interstices of the stones. They seem to give wings to a monument that is far more than a weathered shrine to the past.

The Kotel cannot speak by itself. Like public memory, it is an accumulation of massive facts. The First Temple was built by King Solomon and destroyed by the Babylonians; the Second Temple, one of Herod's grandiose schemes, lasted only ten years longer than the First. For those familiar with contemporary Israeli history, the Kotel also calls to mind the difficult war for the Old City fought

"Notes in the Wall," showing scraps of paper left in a crevice of Jerusalem's massive Western Wall, a fragment of the Second Temple built by Herod. (Photo: Zahava Strull)

in 1967, which returned the wall to Israel after prolonged Jordanian rule. In celebration, rabbis and soldiers blew the shofar to gather Jews for prayer at this once-forbidden site. The loud call of the ram's horn captured the initial excitement about the recovery of this symbol of Jewish continuity. As time passed, however, the Kotel settled into what it has always been: an embodiment of the living past. The crumpled pieces of paper that fill its crevices today continue to breathe new hope into the old stone edifice. Individual prayers, in turn, air the rocks, refresh them, as it were. Similarly, public memory, which defines the meaning of communally shared events that are to be transmitted to future generations, can be envisioned as a framework for personal recollection.

Public monuments and memorial ceremonies solidify the meaning of historical events until they become firm, like the stones of the Kotel. At the same time, canonized public history can become heavy, even burdensome for the individual. Its weight is constantly being assessed and renegotiated in both the official and the personal spheres—two realms that are not separated by a firm boundary. As the Spanish political philosopher Javier Roiz points out, "Inside the self are abundant public spaces."[4] Each attempt at recollection must reckon with the codes and contexts provided by public life. Memorials, like the Kotel, are not simply outer sites. They are also events that we internalize and that shape what we bring forth as individuals into the civic domain. According to Roiz, "Memory is an essential function of the growth of the citizen. Modern memory retains that matter which the citizen has obtained with much existential effort . . . and it is due to the contents of the memory that we, the citizens, can emerge afterwards as masters of ourselves amidst the city's chaos." [5]

Modern memory, as described here, promises us mastery of ourselves in exchange for the incorporation of the public past into our inner lives. Control over the impact of the past, however, can never be complete. Odd bits harbored by uninvited travelers like Dan Pagis keep on disturbing the official narrative. The process of internalization has not succeeded in taming history for either Jews or Chinese. The Kotel is anything but a controlling edifice. As a remnant itself, it cannot promise dominance over the vagaries of historical change.

The messages stuck into the crevices of the Kotel can also be used to conceptualize the power of personal remembrance: though bounded by the lexicon of public events (heavy as stone at times), individual memory goes beyond the linear attribution of cause and effect that is the hallmark of official historiography. The piling up of fact upon fact creates airtight stories told in granite monuments. The monumentalized, public past is a necessary container for individual recollection. Yet without the boulders of the wall, without the building blocks of communal remembrance, the individual would face personal history with no vocabulary at all. Without the bits and pieces of oddly stitched together personal remembrance, the public past would become a deadly weight on the present, and on the future. Dan Pagis broke through Israeli communal recollection with the force of his distinctive poems. The result was a richer sense of history and a more durable sense of community.

Such acts of perforation, always difficult for the individual, are even more troublesome in societies that actively enforce personal amnesia. Soviet Russia, like Communist China, depended on forgetting. The less people recalled from the past, the more likely they would be—or so the party propagandists hoped— to believe in the bright future the party had decreed. But what if the future did not look so bright or the past could not be swept under the rug? With the fall of Communism in Eastern Europe (and with its waning credibility in the Far East), we are able to see more clearly the power of personal memory under authoritarian regimes. Even in these societies, where official history was literally as massive as stone, individuals still managed to outwit the enemies of memory.

Rubie Watson, an American anthropologist, has described the personal strategies used to outwit public amnesia in totalitarian regimes:

> Remembrance was by no means confined to the choreographed event. There were also fragmented, and sometimes highly ritualized, personal acts of memory and homage: the flowers placed on an empty pedestal that was to have supported a monument commemorating the American liberation of Pilsen; the photos and personal documents of Stalin's "disappeared" posted on a Moskow street; candles lit at the mass graves of "secret" Yugoslav massacres; and the silent vigils commemorating violent confrontations with police in Czechoslovakia, Poland and Romania. . . . Often these acts of remembrances were both simple and direct.[6]

What Rubie Watson calls simple acts were, in fact, dangerous messages stuck into the edifice of official historiography. To place personal mementos of the disappeared in street shrines in Moskow was to threaten the entire superstructure that lent legitimacy to the Communist government. Secret graves in Yugoslavia could not be lit by private candles without dimming the bright light of socialist optimism. Because the edifice of official history was so rigid in Communist Europe, it could not withstand—much less incorporate—the challenge of personal recollection.

In China, by contrast, official historiography still manages to coexist with fragments of individual remembrance. Perhaps the wall of public forgetting was never as solid. Perhaps individual rememberers had more complex tactics for evading the official managers of the public past. Guardians of personal memory in China were, after all, heirs of Confucius, Han Yu, and Su Shi. They had inherited a long tradition of nuanced resistance to the demands of imperial historiography. These guardians were uniquely adept at recognizing interstices in the tightly constructed edifice of "facts" used to justify the emperor's rule. Long before Mao, they had learned to insert bits and pieces of personal recollection into the stony facade of the public past. A close look at one such crevice in the wall of official historiography may help illuminate this process of tacit resistance.

Beyond a Choreographed Event in China

In China, the Communist Party is still in power. The direct acts described by Rubie Watson in Russia and Czechoslovakia are more difficult to carry out. Nonetheless, the cultural landscape is dotted by bits of the personal past that do not fit the grand structure of official history. Individuals who insist on clinging to such fragments are, like Pagis's weary traveler, a lonely lot. I met one such guardian of the past—Yang Zaidao, the son of China's Gide expert, Zhang Ruoming. We met in the corridors of a former Buddhist monastery in Beijing, though Yang is not a monk. Yang Zaidao had never heard of Dan Pagis, but this scholar of literature wore the tired look of one who had faced the night. His tale was not filled with the terrors of the Holocaust, but it was dark enough that it could not be spoken in the halls of public remembrance. Our conversations took place in the first week of May 1989—the very week Chinese students had taken to the streets to commemorate the May Fourth Movement of 1919 and to demand more democracy from the current rulers of Beijing.

Yang Zaidao inhabited a world far removed from that of the idealistic youths. He wore a wrinkled blue Mao jacket, quite unlike the Western jeans favored by the demonstrators. Whereas the students radiated hope and energy, he had broken brown teeth and fugitive eyes. We began to talk at a conference in honor of the seventieth anniversary of 1919. Yang was not a distinguished guest and presented no paper. While other participants lectured in grandiose terms about the historical role of intellectuals in Chinese society, Yang had come to talk about his mother. The same woman who had graced the cultural life of Chinese intellectuals in France had, over the years, been forgotten in the annals of Maoist revolution.

Although Zhang Ruoming had been an active member of the May Fourth Movement and one of the earliest members of the Communist Party, there was no room for her history in this public symposium. Like Zhang Shenfu, Zhang Ruoming had withdrawn from the party early on. Her passionate and informed interest in André Gide was of no interest to the peasant leaders who consummated the Communist victory on the Chinese mainland.[7] Although Gide had felt well understood by this woman from the Far East, her compatriots at home saw Zhang as dangerously bourgeois. Like Zhang Shenfu and Zhang Dainian, Zhang Ruoming had been condemned as a rightist in 1957. The main difference in their fates is that the two men outlived Mao Zedong and managed to tell their tales in the era of reform that dawned after 1979. Zhang Ruoming, however, killed herself in 1960 and therefore did not witness the rehabilitation of former rightists that began after the death of Mao.

But her history-worn son did. Like other offspring of intellectuals educated abroad, Yang Zaidao had been marked by his parents' "bad" name in the new society. All he could do was wait for the day when his mother's early association with the Communist Party could be talked about in positive terms. Yang knew he had a revolutionary genealogy, but the revolution had been unwilling to recall its own cosmopolitan origins in France until the spring of 1989—when the wall of official historiography began to show cracks. By that time, the party was in the midst of changing the guidelines governing the discussion of historical characters. During the long era of Mao, only politically correct pingjia (criticism) was allowed, and only intellectuals directly linked to the peasant revolution were honored. But now pingjie (narration) was encouraged, and the sphere of commemoration was enlarged somewhat. Although Yang Zaidao was not invited to give a major address on May Fourth, he was provided an opportunity to recall, in open discussions, his mother's prominence during 1919 as well as in the Chinese Communist group that formed in Paris in 1921. His remarks constituted a message stuck in the crevices of the party wall.

In the new climate, Yang acknowledged that Zhang Ruoming had left the Communist Party, but he insisted that she had "remained loyal and sympathetic to the Chinese revolution."[8] With these words, the offspring tried to make his mother's sins less odious to the censors who were still in control of public memory in China. It was no easy task to make a case for the prominence of highly educated intellectuals in the Communist revolution while at the same time honoring the distinctiveness of the scholarly work that set them apart from the party's objectives. Zhang Ruoming had left her comrades in Paris not because she was against social revolution but because she wanted to pursue her interest in contemporary French literature by working toward a doctorate in Lyons. Yang Zaidao tried to explain this to a new generation of historians who understood the passion for scholarly work. They could not grasp all the details the son tried to bring up from his mother's life, but they were open to hearing an uplifting narrative about a female intellectual who had sympathized with the party and had wanted to serve the Chinese people throughout her life.

Away from the seminar tables, Yang Zaidao told a darker tale. Perhaps the mood of the former monastery had loosened a stream of more personal recollection, or perhaps he saw me as a safe interlocutor—an opening in the wall that would not be noticed in his own professional circles. Maybe he even sensed that I, too, was drawn to marginal figures—though I did not speak to him about my sister, whom I had sought outside the stone structure that encased the Children's Memorial in Jerusalem. Whatever the reasons, in the lunch hour after the open session on May Fourth intellectuals, Yang Zaidao drew me aside to reminisce about something that could not be said into a microphone:

Chinese intellectuals are naive, so hopelessly naive. Especially my mother. She turned me in to Party authorities in 1957, you see. In the middle of the Anti-Rightist campaign she tried to protect herself. Worried about being attacked for her own past, she turned over some of the letters I had written to her. In the end, she was not spared persecution. She committed suicide during a criticism campaign against her at her own university in Guizhou. She tried to protect herself and ended by blackening twenty years of my life. I was made a rightist in 1957. . . . Ah, how gullible she was! She trusted the authorities with everything. As if the Party were a benevolent, faultless father. She sacrificed her son for this heartless father. . . .

All to no avail. The authorities still blamed her for withdrawing from the Communist movement in Europe. Her academic studies in France were held against her. When she could no longer defend herself, she went mad. Then she took her own life.[9]

On the margins of public commemoration, a wounded son recalls his mother's betrayal thirty years after her suicide. Yang Zaidao might not have begun to talk about his mother's tragic faith in the party had the party itself not sanctioned a more open discussion of the role of intellectuals in history. A man in his sixties, a survivor of several campaigns against intellectuals, Yang could not go out on the limb of recollection alone. This dark kernel of personal memory was voiced only after some light has been shed on his mother's generation by public commemorations of May Fourth.

Only after the death of Mao and the reevaluation of the usefulness of intellectuals for "socialist modernization" could Zhang Ruoming be brought out of the night of public forgetting. Only after her contributions to Communist revolution had been acknowledged inside the seminar room could the more frightening subject of betrayal be broached in the hallway. In 1989, the corridor of a onetime monastery became the crack in the wall where a weary rememberer could insert a personal tale. Like Dan Pagis, Yang Zaidao had outlasted the long period of public amnesia and could now face it. On the margins of an official commemoration, he could begin to lay claim to a hurt that remained nameless within the conference hall. Yang took advantage of collective memory to probe a crevice in his own life.

The very concept of collective memory, as the French scholar Maurice Halbwachs understood so well fifty years earlier, depends on the conscious effort of groups to transmit and transform the remembrance of individuals.[10] Although the experience of memory is intensely personal, its expression is always social. In the words of Halbwachs's English interpreter: "Public memory is the storage for the social order. . . . For something to be remembered, it has to be compatible with political and philosophical assumptions."[11] Memory, in this argument, depends on language, on words that have already been used but that may yet carry new meaning. Yang Zaidao's recollection of his mother's "contributions" to the Chinese revolution was built upon such words and included her party activities in the early 1920s. What was new, what went beyond the officially approved version, was the story of how she offered up her son's letters in the 1950s. This, too, was part of the public past but had to be hidden. Ultimately, it became a note in the wall.

The wall of public memory endures in China even after Yang's confession. It is, however, a less rigid and airier structure. Insofar as there is room on the outskirts of Beijing to reminisce about what is still forbidden downtown, China as a whole becomes less suffocating. Its Great Wall, in turn, becomes a less powerful divider. Like the Kotel, China's wall was used to frame a people's identity. Within the framework of such monuments, individuals had to find (or rather create) their own space in which to think. Yang Zaidao's recollections augmented China's thinking space.

Monumental Memories

Chinese and Jewish traditions alike have venerated walls. The Great Wall and the Western Wall were built as outward manifestations of a collective attachment to memory—or, more precisely, to the transmission of remembrance from generation to generation. The will to remain connected to walls, and through walls to the communal past, was especially striking in the times of Ezra and Nehemiah, the leaders of the generation that returned from Babylonian exile in the fifth century B.C. Nehemiah arrived in Jerusalem in 445 B.C. and immediately requested permission from the ruling authorities to rebuild the ruined city walls. King Artaxerxes granted this and also made Nehemiah a provincial governor. When the walls were rebuilt, the people were ready for a renewal of their communal covenant. Ezra and Nehemiah conducted a public ceremony in which a written pledge was signed: "To walk in God's law, which was given to Moses . . . to observe and do all the commandments of the Lord our God and his judgments and his statutes."[12]

The walls around Jerusalem were thus concrete manifestations of the people's dedication to the covenant of their ancestors. The purpose of the pledge, both in stone and on parchment, was the same: to draw individuals back into the framework of communal memory. In China, too, the building and maintenance of walls were signs of a commitment to safeguard community. No city was considered safe or well ruled unless it could protect its inhabitants with stone barriers. The most outstanding reminder of this definition of security and good rule is the Great Wall, in northern China. Construction began during the reign of the first emperor, Qin Shi Huang Di, who ruled from 221 to 210 B.C. Although the emperor justified this effort as a defense against nomadic invaders, its true cost was political autocracy. Qin Shi Huang demanded such a huge expenditure of human resources for the sake of his grandiose project that the wall remained a sore point for centuries to come. Nonetheless, less autocratic rulers continued to rebuild the Great Wall and encouraged their officials to erect similar structures around all major towns. Over time, walls became symbols of communal security as well as imperial rule. They signaled the ability of the powerful to define, as well as to limit, the parameters of civilized life. The Dao (the Way) of Chinese culture was presumed to prevail within the boundaries of walled sites—in the form of settled, agricultural society. Beyond them lay so-called barbarism and the constant threat from nomadic tribes.

The omnipresence of walls in the Chinese landscape imprinted itself vividly upon the eyes of Western visitors. Lord Macartney, who went to China at the end of the eighteenth century, was only one of many who saw the Great Wall as a sign of power and virtue: "At the remote period of the Wall's building, China must have been not only a very powerful empire, but also a very wise and prosperous nation, or at least to have had such foresight and regard for posterity as to establish at once what was then thought a perpetual security for them against future invasion, choosing to load herself with an enormous expense of immediate labor and treasure rather than leave succeeding generations to precarious dependence on stringent resources." [13] Macartney rightfully recognized that the wall had become a symbol of cultural continuity in China. It marked the outer parameters of civilization that the individual was meant to incorporate within. The geopolitical fact that prosperity could not be maintained without stony protection added pressure on individuals to stay within the space marked by the Great Wall. China's rulers used geography to create a monument that safeguarded their power as well as the so-called Chinese way of life. By exacting a huge toll not only in terms of labor and money but also in terms of subservience to the imperial-bureaucratic system, they created a monument that over time became a symbol of political submission. In the twentieth century, the bondage embodied by the wall once again became a sensitive issue. In 1925 Lu Xun gave voice to this resentment in an essay entitled "The Great Wall." Written after the

May Fourth critique of Chinese tradition (and after Zhang Ruoming left the Communist Party to focus on Chinese cultural concerns), Lu Xun's work was a bitter indictment of public memory. It dissected the enduring self-enchainment of a people that, according to Lu Xun, feared its own autonomy more than the dreaded nomads of years gone by:

> Our wonderful Great Wall!
>
> This engineering feat has left its mark on the map, and is probably known to everyone with any education the whole world over.
>
> Actually, all it has ever done is work many conscripts to death—it never kept out the Huns. Now it is merely an ancient relic, but its final ruin will not take place for a while, and it may even be preserved.
>
> I am always conscious of being surrounded by a Great Wall. The stonework consists of old bricks reinforced at a later date by new bricks. These have combined to make a wall that hems us in.
>
> When shall we stop reinforcing the Great Wall with new bricks?
>
> A curse on this wonderful Great Wall! [14]

Lu Xun's curse resounds even today among Chinese intellectuals who debate the nature of political power. The authority to protect China from outside invaders has evolved into the right to control the thoughts of the population within the boundaries of the wall. The quarrel of those who rant against the Great Wall, however, is not with the stone structure running along the mountains of northern China but with the smaller, personal wall of subservience built up repeatedly by rulers who benefit from the unquestioning obedience of the Chinese population.

The wall cursed by Lu Xun commands the landscape of the mind. Such a structure binds the individual to community by reminding him or her of the dangers that lurk outside. In this sense, the Great Wall both depends on and nurtures cultural memory. Culture always defines the individual; it also can be used to create more freedom, as in the case of Yang Zaidao. Yang, like Lu Xun himself, understood the power of memorials to create a transmittable history. Like Chinese intellectuals who preceded him in the struggle with autocratic rulers, Yang appreciated the distinctive longevity of China's cultural traditions. The American philosopher Edward Casey, in his studies of Confucianism, has termed this quality "perdurance." Casey draws attention to a quality of lastingness that is found in Chinese tradition: "Remembering through and with others creates a presence, a sense of the past coming toward us." [15] Perdurance is the defining characteristic of a memory that can withstand wear and decay—like a wall.

There is no better way to promote perdurance (as opposed to the dead weight of the past cursed by Lu Xun) than through the active retelling of history. Friedrich Nietzsche praised this mechanism of memorial transmission, though he was neither Chinese or Jewish, nor particularly fond of historical remembrance. Yet he grasped the power of lively historiography when he wrote: "What good is it for one who lives in the present to observe the monumental past, to be concerned with what is classic and rare in the earlier ages? . . . He treads his path more confidently, because now the doubt that infected him in his hour of weakness—the doubt that he might be willing the impossible—has been soundly thwarted." [16] For Nietzsche, the monumental past mattered because it encouraged the quest for the impossible. Historical memory, in this sense, gave one courage to overcome individual limitations and to reach for greatness that existed in earlier times. If historic figures attempted the heroic, so could individuals in their own time. At war with his own doubts, the melancholic German philosopher looked to the past for models of the uncommon.

Chinese and Jewish rememberers, by contrast, sought to transmit more than the rare, the classic, and the edifying. In addition to ideal characters, the *Analects* and the Bible present saints and murderers, failed teachers and virtuous students. At the same time, both these classical sources have a didactic intent. Each uses the past to inspire subsequent generations to live more nobly, to face moral failure more directly.

In China, Confucian scholars believed that public morality was best maintained through a judicious apportionment of historical praise and blame. The "Spring and Autumn Annals," edited by Confucius, set a pattern of collective remembering that stretches forward in time to party historians who continue to apportion praise and blame when it comes to intellectuals such as Zhang Ruoming. These latter-day critics, however, have lost the broad-mindedness and abjured the moral responsibility that marked the work of the earliest Chinese historians.

One of the most perceptive of these ancients was Sima Qian (145–90 B.C.), Grand Historian of the Han dynasty. No other intellectual in Chinese history paid so great a price for his commitment to the transmission of collective memory. A high official in the court of Emperor Han Wu Di, Sima Qian spoke his mind in defense of a wrongly accused military officer. As punishment for this "crime," he was given a choice of suicide or castration. A person of noble standing was expected to choose suicide, yet Sima Qian chose castration in order to complete his great work *Shiji* (Records of the Grand Historian). For the sake of this opus,

Sima Qian decided to live with ignominy: "We reside in the world of the present but set our minds on the Ancient Way, that it may be a mirror for us." [17]

At first glance, this image of the mirror of history suggests complete faith in the transmission of the past—as if it were a monolithic entity. Indeed, Sima Qian's metaphor was used repeatedly by Chinese historians who sought to summarize the moral message of collective memory. The most famous among these was the Song dynasty scholar-official Sima Guang (1019–86), the author of *A Mirror for Government*. This text represented the culmination of didactic historiography by showing how public policy could be improved through scrupulous attention to the lives of the illustrious dead.[18] Yet even *A Mirror for Government* was not simply a morality tale. It was, like Sima Qian's earlier work, marked by a certain reticence about the power of history. Although the past was used as a repository of moral judgment, there was no guarantee that it would be used as such in the present. Sima Guang, like his Han predecessor, aimed for an encompassing and inspiring evocation of communal recollection. At the same time, he was also mindful that much of history could not be fitted into the boundaries of a monumentalized past. Sima Qian, at the end of a famous letter to his friend Ren An (in which he explains why he chose castration over suicide), succinctly captured the historian's reservations: "Shu bu neng jian yi" (words cannot embrace my meaning).[19] Although countless letter writers since the Han dynasty have used these five characters, none have captured the paradox of language and of public memory with more pathos than this impotent man who went on to become China's most renowned historian-rememberer.

Mirrors of History

After Sima Qian and Sima Guang, Chinese intellectuals inherited a double message: transmission of the past is a sacred obligation, yet no words can ever tell the full tale. This partiality opened up room for other kinds of memories. Along with the grand tradition of official historiography (the court-sponsored *chaoshi*), there proliferated in China "wild" histories (*ye shi*), written by individuals whose personal reminiscences could not be readily fitted into the public past. Interstices were either discovered or created in the monolithic facade of imperially sponsored dynastic annals. Bits and pieces of personal recollection found an outlet in marginalia.

The late Ming dynasty scholar Zhang Dai, for example, was one poet-scholar who resorted to the refuge of wild history. Zhang's recollections about life in the south before the Manchu conquest of 1644 were collected in *Dream Memoirs*—a moody, meandering text that stands in marked contrast to the Ming history officially sponsored by the victorious Qing dynasty. This work revives Su Shi's metaphor of meng hen while putting it into a context of political contestation. In a world in which daytime reality seemed to be the monopoly of foreign invaders, a Chinese patriot turns to the elusive language of night. Zhang's preface to this work emphasizes the memory spaces that are to be created at a time when public history becomes official propaganda. Speaking in the third person, the rebel-rememberer writes: "While living in constant hunger, he liked to amuse himself with brush and ink. And thus he would think on bygone days. . . . For this he must now suffer retribution." Then, as he calls up the heavy consequence of his fidelity to the past, Zhang Dai switches to the first person to justify this meticulous attention to "dreams": "How can I endure it? I think far back to events in the past and bring them before Buddha so that I can beg for pardon for everyone. . . . Isn't this a dream? . . . I will soon wake from the greatest dream of all, yet still I work on this insect-carving [writing]; this is mumbling in a dream." [20]

Personal memory here wears the familiar guise of dream work, fastening onto the deprivations of the present so as to bring to life the vanishing pleasures of the past. Buddhist metaphors abound in Zhang Dai's memoirs both because this unorthodox faith gave him courage in moments of despondency and because it allowed him to legitimate the conscious pursuit of vanishing recollections. The past itself seems nothing but a dream, a mumbling in the dark, yet the will to recollect remains undefeated. It goes on with the dogged job of "insect-carving,"—of recording personal memories—by focusing on all the details that had no room on the larger canvas of official history.

Times of political disintegration (such as the end of the Ming dynasty in the seventeenth century) were especially conducive to the transmission of personal recollection. The wall of official historiography was perforated again and again by the voice of some rememberer—be it Confucius, who described himself as qiu gu zhe (a seeker of the past); Sima Qian, who chose castration in order to finish his Shiji; or the dreamer Zhang Dai. As a result of their relentless insertions of the personal into communal memory, China's historical record remained vivid enough to become a true repository of moral values. Individuals shaped the contours of public history, thereby enriching its content immensely. The ancient goal of historically informed makers of history was realized in Confucian culture more than in the modern West, possibly because the past never became the monopoly of the powerful. [21]

In Jewish tradition, too, communal memory became the ultimate repository of moral values. In this context, however, religious texts and commentaries (rather than history as such) were consulted to sort out questions of right and wrong. This does not mean that there was no interest in historiography. Quite the contrary. The history of the Jewish people recorded in the Bible became a framework for interpreting and reinterpreting subsequent events in Jewish history. Geographically dispersed, Jews lacked the political means with which to codify historical events, and so they turned to the Pentateuch for lessons about key events.

Historical remembrance, as we have seen, was already a crucial element in the faith of the Jewish people who accepted the Torah at Sinai. The commandment of zakhor includes ongoing recollection of the Exodus, the Sabbath, Miriam, and even Amalek. What is carried forward in Jewish history from Sinai is not just two tablets of stone but a commitment to the transmission of memory, to doing something in time. Similarly, Jewish law, halakha, demands ongoing attention to the present in light of the past. The rabbis who decided which laws apply in a specific locality and time had to be mindful of local customs and to constantly adjust the lessons of history to the concrete circumstances of the Jewish people.[22] It was the oral Torah, as interpreted by the rabbis, that became, over time, the grid of meaning for Jewish memory. Religious leaders, more than historians, took upon themselves the tasks of explaining, amending, and elaborating the dense text of the written Torah. Rabbinical interpretations made this text into a living document.

Mindfulness of the past deepened the sacred and moral value of the present. The living Torah, Torat hayim—which included both written and oral traditions—allowed generations after Sinai to encode their history in the alphabet of religious recollection. This memory work was especially important to Jews who faced bewildering historical events. In the absence of China's court historiography, which could be amended by wild histories, Jews turned to the Bible for a way of structuring collective remembrance. The binding of Isaac on Mount Moriah (akedah in Hebrew), for example, became a paradigm for understanding the repeated martyrdom of Jewish communities in medieval Europe. This fragment of the monumental past inspired Shelomo bar Shimshon, the chronicler of mass suicide in Mainz, where fathers slaughtered their children, their wives, and themselves to avoid forced baptism at the hands of the Crusaders. At the beginning of the First Crusade, the leader of the Mainz Jewish community obtained protection from Emperor Henry IV. Nonetheless, despite spirited resistance, on May 27, 1096, the Mainz community fell, and over one thousand Jews died or committed suicide.[23] In his history of the Mainz martyrs, Shelomo bar Shimshon appeals to the lexicon of the Bible to make sense of the horror he has witnessed: "Who has heard or seen such a thing? Ask and see: Has there even been an *akedah* like this in all the generations since Adam? Did eleven hundred *akedot* take place on a single day, all of them comparable to the binding of Isaac, son of Abraham? Yet for the one bound on Mount Moriah the world shook. Wilt Thou remain silent for these, O Lord?"[24] Turning to the Bible allows this medieval historian to both interpret and interrogate the present. The binding of Isaac, in this case, became a mirror for the present. But just like Chinese rememberers, who use the mirror of history to question contemporary events, so, too, bar Shimshon's memoir wonders aloud about divine responsibility for the eleven hundred who died in a single day in Germany. Far more than a chronicle of events, history thus conceived becomes an interrogation and a prayer. The events in Mainz on the Rhine do not pale in comparison to Mount Moriah; they depend on it for meaning. This religious patterning of collective memory is distinctively Jewish. At the same time it echoes Sima Qian's faith that "we reside in the present but set our minds on the Ancient Way."

To be mindful of history in the Jewish way requires one to bear witness to the Torah in an active, often critical way. Historians, in fact, are not the primary custodians of this collective memory. Throughout much of Jewish history, rabbis and lay chroniclers took on the burden of holding up the mirror of the past to the present—not scholar-officials such as Sima Guang. In the Middle Ages, Jewish historical consciousness blossomed in *selikhot*, penitential prayers that commemorated various catastrophes in the life of the community. The related genre of *kinot* comprised lamentations originally recited when an important person died. Over time, these two types of lyrical expressions merged to foster a continual updating of religious memory in the light of unfolding events. They forged a link between the painful, often incomprehensible present and a past guaranteed by divine providence. One medieval lament is still recited annually for the commemoration of the destruction of the Temple on the ninth day of the Jewish month of Av. The words insist that no person be left out of communal grief and hope:

A fire kindles within me as I recall—*when I left Egypt*,
But I raise laments as I remember—*when I left Jerusalem*.

Moses sang a song that would never be forgotten—*when I left Egypt*,
Jeremiah mourned and cried out in grief—*when I left Jerusalem*.

The sea-waves pounded but stood up like a wall—*when I left Egypt*,
The waters overflowed and ran over my head—*when I left Jerusalem*.

Moses led me and Aaron guided me—*when I left Egypt*,
Nebuchadnezzar and Emperor Hadrian—*when I left Jerusalem*.[25]

The individual is hereby drawn into the circle of collective recollection. Egypt and Jerusalem stand for two poles of historical experience. The first marks slavery as well as the place where the various Jewish tribes became welded into a nation with a distinctive religious consciousness. Jerusalem, by contrast, recalls a site where holiness once prevailed. The terrible loss of the Holy Temple is meant to remind as well as to console. I, who left Jerusalem, will surely return. Enshrined by the cadence of the Bible, this "I" is audible throughout all the memoir literature that comes down to us from the Middle Ages.

The main reason why the connective fabric between Egypt and Jerusalem did not fray over time is that individuals and communities continued to record the events of the present in the light of the past. Although the pattern was ancient, the subject was constantly being renewed. This process of renewal is strikingly evident in the "memorial books" of various Jewish communities. These volumes were inscribed and read aloud during commemoration services for the dead as a way of keeping the details of communal experience in mind from generation to generation. Called *Memorbuch* in German, such texts would be kept on the reader's table in the middle of the synagogue. Each leather-bound volume contained special prayers to be recited after reading the Torah, as well as an ever-growing necrology of local and national leaders. Often a martyrology would be added to preserve the names of places and people struck down by persecution. The Memorial Book of Nuremberg, for example, records the life of the community from 1296 to 1392. It includes poems composed for the dedication of the synagogue, a list of benefactors, prayers in Hebrew and old French, and a martyrology of persecutions that took place in Germany and France from the First Crusade of 1096 to the Black Death of 1349.[26]

By contrast, the memorial book of the Jewish community in China was put together in the seventeenth century, at the same time as Zhang Dai's "Dream Memoirs." This text, recorded and preserved in the city of Kaifeng, details the ancestors of seven clans who claimed Jewish ancestry. Closed in 1670 (after the fall of the Ming dynasty but before the new Manchu rulers consolidated their control over southern China), the Kaifeng Memorial Book contains prayers for the dead in Hebrew as well as thirty-seven pages recording the names of community elders. Some names are in Hebrew, others in Chinese; some relationships are described in Hebrew, others in Chinese; and in some places Chinese family relationships among the clans are given in Hebrew transliteration.[27]

In 1851 the Kaifeng Memorial Book was sold to Christian missionaries, an act that eroded communal remembrance. Increasingly, the Jewish past receded from the daily concerns of this community of impoverished Jews in Kaifeng. Nonetheless, these Chinese heirs of the Jewish faith continued to seek contact with other Jews who came to live in China. Some even believed the Christian missionaries had been sent by overseas Jewish communities in order to revive the light of the Torah, given that descendants in Kaifeng could no longer read Hebrew and the ancient texts. A few of the Kaifeng Jews managed to maintain the tradition of circumcision—sending their boys to Shanghai, where experts in the ritual could be found in the aftermath of Jewish immigration from Iraq, India, Russia, and Germany.[28]

That the flame of historic memory was not totally extinguished among the Jews of Kaifeng testifies to the perdurance of both Chinese and Jewish tradition. The passing on of knowledge about the dead—their names, relationships, titles, and accomplishments—is, after all, a sacred duty according to both Confucian and biblical authorities. The Hebrew prayers and Hebrew names in the Kaifeng Memorial Book represent a Jewish framework for the recollections of a Chinese community. That framework underwent considerable change in China as the Kaifeng community became more assimilated in dress and manners. Eventually the rituals of filial piety and the veneration of male ancestors became prevalent. Yet, even as the meaning of being Jewish shifted radically in China, the veneration of the past endured. The Kaifeng Memorial Book, like Chinese ancestral temples (which are called Hao Gu Tang, or Loving the Ancients Hall), testify to the ongoing claim of history upon the lives of those in the present. "To love" one's ancestors is, in this context, to cherish their memory within a concrete framework of devotion to historical ideals. This understanding of loving the ancients is not what Nietzsche had in mind when he praised the utility of the monumental past. Rather, he envisaged a one-way street to the past by which moderns would be able to revisit paragons of radical will. Chinese and Jewish customs of memory transmission, however, show us a two-way road: they offer a pathway back to the ancients as well as a trail ahead into the unforeseen.

This dual engagement becomes all the more important in the second half of the twentieth century, when the need for historical markers gains urgency for Chinese and Jewish rememberers alike. Halls for loving the ancients no longer suffice, certainly not for Chinese who went through the Cultural Revolution (when many people were forced to denounce and distance themselves from their lineage). Classical poetry may offer moments of sanity to Nien Cheng during her ordeal in Shanghai, but it does not provide a framework of meaning for the atrocities endured. Nor does the monumental past suffice for Holocaust survivors. Records of bygone elders make sense in houses of worship that have a connection to graves in nearby soil, but what about martyrs who have no graves? What about those who went up in smoke? What pages could ever memorialize their names?

These questions haunt survivors and their children. In the end, the very paucity of the remains has required new kinds of memorials. In Israel and the United States, one now finds "remembrance rooms," in which bits of paper embody the dead for whom there are no markers. Memorial books for the decimated communities of Poland, Hungary, and Romania are like a garden in which no flowers grow.[29] In twentieth-century China, the old Confucian passion for hao gu has also undergone a profound transformation. The past is no longer securely monumental. For the victims of the Cultural Revolution, the absence of markers for the dead is a troublesome reality as well. Looking at the memorial dilemmas of the Jewish experience, the contemporary writer Ba Jin urged his contemporaries to build a Cultural Revolution Museum—a structure that would remind future generations of the atrocities of the past and thereby help them build a better future:

> The building of a Cultural Revolution Museum is not the responsibility of one particular person. It is our responsibility to do all we can so that our descendants, generation after generation, will guard the painful lessons of the past. "Don't allow history to repeat itself" should not remain an empty slogan. In order for all to see clearly, to remember truthfully, it would be best to build a Cultural Revolution Museum where . . . striking scenes would be reconstructed to bear witness to what truly took place in this country of China twenty years ago![30]

Here, a Chinese intellectual uses words almost identical to those of Jewish survivors, who also insist that we not let history repeat itself. Ba Jin wants a monument that will teach children the harrowing lessons of the past. His is a plea for communal action beyond the prerogative of the state or the individual. Ba Jin wants a collective reaffirmation of memory after the Maoist break with the past.

Yet China has no such museum today. Ba Jin's proposal touches too many sore spots on a collective body now consumed with the tasks of modernization. Jews, on the other hand, have erected many museums to commemorate the Holocaust. These structures command the landscape from Washington, D.C., to Los Angeles, from New York to Jerusalem. These museums and the commemorations they officially honor highlight the significance of Ba Jin's question: How do we prevent history from repeating itself? The continuing specter of atrocity in Cambodia, Bosnia, and other corners of the world only increases the relevance of this Chinese intellectual's query. Ba Jin wants clear lessons from history—a desire that places him in a lineage with Confucian scholars who believed that the past can and should be a mirror for government. But what if history is not a mirror? What if complex events cannot be used to provide a clear moral message? What if museums cannot illuminate the darker side of the events they are intended to commemorate?

The Cultural Revolution Was No Holocaust

Ba Jin's call for a Cultural Revolution Museum was based upon a belief in the moral authority of public monuments and on the parallel significance of Chinese and Jewish experiences with autocracy. Both these assumptions grew out of his experiences in the cosmopolitan period of the May Fourth Movement. After 1919, Ba Jin became a fellow traveler of the Communists, only to find himself revolted by the excesses of the Cultural Revolution. Ba's wish that his contemporaries learn from history was not a lonely cry, however. After the death of Mao Zedong in 1976, many other writers, poets, and memorialists were using Jewish history to reflect on what had gone wrong in their own country during the Red Terror of the 1960s.[31] Nien Cheng, for example, opens her memoir of life and death in Shanghai by recalling that she was reading the *Rise and Fall of the Third Reich* on the same night the Red Guards stormed her house to loot and search for "anti-revolutionary" materials.[32] The echoes with Kristallnacht (the night in 1938 that marks the beginning of Nazi terror for German Jews) are used to highlight Nien Cheng's predicament: her house is poised for destruction just like the world of European Jews—each painting, each vase, each curtain about to be torn or broken, bears witness to the parallel horrors.

The Chinese word for Holocaust—huojie, literally "plunder by fire"—has been gaining currency among victims of the Cultural Revolution. Used initially to describe Japanese atrocities in China during World War II, it has developed into a subtler, darker image relating to the fire of Maoist policies that devastated the lives of millions during the 1960s and early 1970s.[33] Yet the huojie of the Cultural Revolution was no Holocaust. Although the loss of life owing to prolonged beatings and hard labor was real enough (and the despoilment of the best years of several generations of young people is still felt in China today), those who endured the Maoist nightmare never experienced the depths of despair that engulfed Jews in Europe. This is partly because the struggle that took place in China from 1966 to 1976 was internal—a war of Chinese against Chinese. Some people armed with quotations from Chairman Mao took it upon themselves to persecute, beat, and even kill those deemed enemies of the Great Proletarian Cultural Revolution. Yet every Chinese was, in principle, capable of total obedience to the Red Sun. Mao Zedong had evolved from an earthly leader to a spiritual force that illuminated the life of each individual. Everyone was forced to memorize the chairman's quotations; everyone—even "class enemies"—was required to perform "loyalty dances."[34]

Mao's absolute authority in political and spiritual matters depended on very old, very traditional mechanisms. Unlike the breach between past and present experienced by European Jews, Chinese culture was stretched to accommodate yet another dictatorship. One Chinese critic has characterized this usage of traditional resources as sodality—or to put it more simply, a will to submit to the parental authority of the state: "Within Chinese sodality there is a guaranteed interdependence. . . . And, in typically infantile fashion, when a man's somatized needs are satisfied by another person, then he must surrender his Heart-and-Mind. Thus the individual comes to obey authority. In this way the Chinese adult never totally outgrows childhood. Throughout Chinese history, the Chinese common man has been the little child of a paternal, but dictatorial ruler."[35] The argument here is that the cult of Mao Zedong was abetted by China's long-standing proclivity toward interdependence. Putting aside the reductionist, quasi-Freudian vocabulary of this critique, the argument for an *internal* explanation of the Cultural Revolution is nonetheless compelling.

The Chinese who loved and venerated Mao, however, were quite different from the Germans who practiced the Nazi cult. Hitler was no Mao Zedong, nor could he ever be envisaged as a paternal figure to the Jews. Even Jews who found themselves working for the Nazis sooner or later came face-to-face with a Jewish identity that was thrust upon them.[36] Hitler was bent upon the total destruction of Jews, no matter if they spoke good German, had memorized his words, or were willing to betray their parents. The Holocaust was not an internal struggle but a strategy to dehumanize as well as exterminate the Jews. The concentration camps and gas chambers assaulted the human spirit, not just the body. In the words of Jean Amery, what died in Auschwitz was reason itself: "As a tool for solving the tasks put to us, [the intellect] admitted defeat. Beauty: that was an illusion. Knowledge: that turned out to be a game with ideas. . . . The reality of the camp triumphed effortlessly over the entire complex of difficult questions." [37] The essay from which this thought-defying conclusion is drawn goes on to detail the total devastation of the spirit in a world in which there were no books and no ideas, just hunger, humiliation, and death. Read by a Chinese survivor of the Cultural Revolution, Amery's work might recall the singling out of intellectuals for persecution in the 1960s. This was the era when old professors and learned persons from all walks of life were labeled qiu lao jiu (stinking ninth), the worst of the class enemies (after revisionists, capitalists, traitors, etc.) to be dealt with by the Red Guards.

But no matter how great the stench presumed to emanate from the educated in China, they were never degraded to the subhuman level described by Art Spiegelman in Maus, a book of terrifying cartoons that opens with Hitler's statement "Jews are undoubtedly a race, but they are not human." [38] There is no doubt that demonology thrived during the Cultural Revolution: common appellations for class enemies included "ox-devils," "snake-spirits," "rotten dog's head," "evil wind," and "pests and vermin." "Ox-pens" were set up in order to interrogate and beat prominent victims of the Red Terror—all in the name of "reeducation." [39] In the intense fervor of class struggle, the oldest, most violent folk beliefs surfaced, including the notion that it was beneficial to eat the heart and liver of one's enemies. We now know, from the scrupulous and unofficial researches of Zheng Yi (a writer who escaped from China after 1989), that cannibalism did take place in certain parts of China during the Cultural Revolution. In Red Memorial Zheng details fifty-six such cases in one county in Jiangxi province. Zheng Yi even goes so far as to trace down one poor peasant responsible for a public disembowelment. He finds the man accused of wielding the vegetable cleaver to be unrepentant and still quoting Chairman Mao: "Didn't Chairman Mao teach us: 'If we can't kill them, they'll kill us?' It's life and death. It's class struggle! . . . The government should have killed him, should not have left it to us. I just did the handiwork. The first knife didn't work, so I threw it away. I got him opened with the second knife. But I was not the one to pull out the heart and liver." [40]

Zheng Yi's book comes close to answering Ba Jin's plea for a memorial to the Cultural Revolution. Although Red Memorial is not a physical museum, it is a testament to the potential intelligibility of atrocity. By searching out the exact number of those disembodied in one county in southern China, Zheng Yi makes evil a documentable (and comprehensible) phenomenon. The interview with the knife-wielding peasant makes it clear that his hand did no more than what the government should have done. If the heart and the liver were fought for, it was because of beliefs that were part of Chinese folk medicine long before Mao's reign of terror.

Recollection of the disembowelment of Jews on their way to the gas chambers in Treblinka, by contrast, defies any reason. Some were disemboweled, many were kicked, most were gassed. No words such as class struggle apply here. No health benefits awaited those who took the lives of countless women and children—even if hair and skin had some practical use. This is what Jean Amery tried to suggest when he said that reason was murdered in Auschwitz. This is what sets him apart from a Chinese intellectual such as Zheng Yi, who presumes that it is possible to make sense of history—even though fact finding is still thwarted by the powers that be.

Despite the demonology, cannibalism, and violence that was China's daily fare for a decade, the Cultural Revolution never aimed to defeat sense-making the way that Hitler tried to in the death camps. Li Zehou, a Chinese philosopher who survived the dark decade of 1966–76, might well sympathize with Jean Amery's radical deprivations in Auschwitz, but he never experienced them. When Li was sent down to the countryside in 1972 (for what was then assumed would be a lifelong exile), he managed to hide Kant's *Critique of Pure Reason* among his belongings, which included the required Red Book of quotations from Chairman Mao. Less than a decade later, in 1979, Li was back in Beijing, publishing a critique of Kant's critique and calling for a revival of the philosophy of aesthetics.[41] Li Zehou, with one hidden book, managed to salvage what Jean Amery, with no books and a head full of useless quotations from German poetry, lost in Auschwitz: the hope of cultural regeneration through reason.

Because of this hope, China could return to a quest for normalcy after the death of Mao. The spiritual terrain, though greatly ravaged, could be reseeded. This is the traditional goal of harmony described by Ma Sheng-mei in an essay comparing the survival literatures of the Cultural Revolution and the Holocaust. Exploring the various strategies used by Chinese and Jewish poets to describe historical trauma, Ma points out the difference between the "obscurity" of poems that evoke the unspeakable facts of Holocaust and "murky" quality of works that recall the Cultural Revolution.[42] Jewish poets like Paul Celan war with language in the name of an ineffable history, whereas writers like Bei Dao preserve their faith in the healing power of literature. Beauty and harmony are words that retain some meaning for China's poets; they are empty of meaning in the world of Jean Amery.

Yet the corrosive power of history has its limits even in the darkest corner of Jewish nightmares. Poems continue to be written after the Holocaust by survivors as well as by their children. Theodor Adorno, in his famous statement about poetry after Auschwitz, affirms at once the reasonableness of despondency and the need to fight it off at the same time: "To write lyric poetry after Auschwitz is barbaric. . . . But (it) also remains true that literature must resist this verdict. . . . In art alone suffering can still find its voice." [43]

Numbness is therefore the first consequence of reckoning with Jewish history in the twentieth century. But to stop there would be to contribute to Hitler's grand plan. To go on writing after Auschwitz is to resist his verdict—not that the words we use can ever make old-fashioned sense. In challenging the universe of meanings before the war, post-Holocaust art comes a step closer to naming the nightmare.[44] This linguistic leap (actually a disintegration of previous verbal constructs) becomes the starting point for the recovery of memory. David Koening, a poet whose parents fled Vienna in 1939, puts this willful recovery in simple words:

> After the Holocaust,
> No poetry—
> That is what they say—
> But I write poems about it.
> . . . .
> Forgive me.
> I'm not unstrung.
> The poems keep me sane.[45]

Refusing to become unstrung is one way to talk back to reason-erasing events such as the Holocaust. Koening mockingly asks forgiveness for disobeying the first part of Adorno's warning, then proceeds to create a grammar that contains the ineffable. The sanity the poet seeks lies buried in metaphor—the same verbal construct that Cynthia Ozick praised in her talk to surgeons. Determined to find and guard the past the Nazis tore from his family, Koening, in this poem, becomes his own doctor. He ends by likening the effort to that of excavating "torn and injured pages from buried books of prayer."

The idea that books survived where people went up in smoke may seem bizarre. But such were the historical facts. Excavating material artifacts therefore becomes the first step in the commemoration of a world that no longer exists. How to excavate and how to commemorate, however, remain subjects of intense debate. Koening, as a poet, has a relatively easy task. He has to only imagine the dead in the buried prayer books, and it is as if they were back in the heart of

Jewish life. But in the public realm of museum building and communal commemoration, this becomes a much thornier issue.

Some Holocaust survivors have argued for the dignity of silence, whereas
others have focused their energies on public memorials. Elie Wiesel is one of
those who tried to do both. He has written volumes of stories, novels, poems,
and essays about the unspeakable events that took the life of his family and community in Transylvania. He also headed the presidential commission responsible
for planning the Holocaust Museum in Washington, D.C. If Ba Jin could have
consulted one expert in the art of memorializing shameful events, it would have
been Elie Wiesel. Yet, in the very midst of his tireless efforts to create linguistic
and cement structures aimed at preventing history from repeating itself, Wiesel
continually argued against the public tendency of squeezing moral lessons out
of history. Speaking about the risks embodied in a massive project such as the
Holocaust Museum, Wiesel warned: "Either this place will be a sanctuary or an
abomination." [46]

Stark as this contrast is, it does capture one prominent survivor's worry about
the monumentalized Holocaust. The metaphors of sanctuary and abomination
suggest that historical memory is a risky undertaking indeed. The idea that a
museum can be a place of authentic sanctity or a place of idolatry must ring odd
to Chinese ears, even to Ba Jin, who argued for the building of a museum.
Museums as public spaces for the codification of cultural remembrance did not
appear on the Chinese landscape until the late nineteenth century. Imperial and
private collections of artworks and books had sufficed for those with an antiquarian taste. When museum building began in earnest under the Communist
regime, it was both to tame and to reorder the past.

China's new rulers shared the assumption of their predecessors that history
must be made both intelligible and edifying. This assumption was the object of
scrutiny in the last volume of Joseph Levenson's trilogy, Confucian China and Its
Modern Fate. Levenson understood only too well that in creating museums to
house China's traditional legacy, Chinese Communists were in fact making history. By placing Confucius safely under glass and labeling his ideas as "feudal,"
they opened up new spaces for their own ideological project. This historicizing
impulse, according to Levenson, was simultaneously compensatory and cruel:
"Communists could try to have it both ways, killing the past for their own day,
yet relativistically fitting it into history. . . . One had to kill to be kind. The
kindness was a solace, a relief to the pain of killing." [47] Levenson is writing here
as a historian mindful of the dangers of relativism. He knew about the brutal
excesses of the Communist revolution during which killing had been anything

but metaphorical. He also wrote about museums as a Jew who appreciated the need to preserve the records of the past. When he wrote that one had to kill in order to be kind, Levenson was pointing to historical consciousness in general, to an outlook that sets the past apart and aside at the same time.

When the past becomes unsettling, however, all efforts to put it in its place are bound to fail. This is what happened to museums that attempted to represent Confucius during the Cultural Revolution. The past came terrifyingly alive, and Mao decided that no museum labels sufficed to mark off the parameters of safe meaning. Similarly, the Cultural Revolution is still too proximate a nightmare today to be securely included in a museum. In fact, this dark shadow is not ready to be housed anywhere on the Chinese landscape. The edification of the past symbolized by the museum leaves no room for the shame and rage that is the legacy of intellectuals like Zhang Ruoming's son—Yang Zaidao. Survivors of persecution continue to whisper on the outskirts of public ceremonies, their message being ill suited for public commemorations.

Beyond the Museum Lights

Nightmares, like Yang's betrayal by his mother, cannot be accommodated in structures dedicated to the lessons of history. Because they do not contain readily extractable morals, such personal memories get squeezed to the side. The quest for what cannot be memorialized in public goes on in other spaces. Like notes stuffed into the massive boulders of the Western Wall, personal memory demands its due. Crevices protect by their very size. Being small, they allow fractured visions to exist alongside eternalized rock. Absence, powerlessness, and despair have their place here.

The Holocaust Memorial Museum in Washington, D.C., has emerged as a site of public memory somewhat analogous to the Western Wall in Jerusalem. It is a place where individuals go to reconnect with a massive event. The immensity of the Holocaust is mirrored by the enormous amount of data compiled about this unfathomable atrocity. An individual can try to penetrate this edifice only by focusing on a particular image or exhibition. One writer described his way of sense making by focusing on two images: the pile of luggage assembled outside the boxcar that was used to carry Jewish victims to Auschwitz and a film about the mobile killing squads that he saw on television monitors. The mound of suitcases and the image of a little dog that kept wagging its tail during the silent executions helped this particular writer humanize an event that was utterly bewildering otherwise: "It made me think I could reach down and take up one of the bags and put my own toothbrush and pajamas and book to read inside and go somewhere. This was just luggage and it didn't know better . . . someone's shaving brush, a rain hat or a pair of stockings outside a boxcar at Auschwitz." [48] This act of imagination is like a personal message pressed inside the Kotel—a plea for understanding on intimate terms. The very absence and namelessness of the dead is encapsulated in the vision of one's own toothbrush and pajamas inside the suitcases that held the stockings of women who went up in flames. The barking dog, too, is a place to fasten the individual gaze when the enormity of the killing becomes too much to take.

For those who want to think about the full scope of degradation, such details are irreverent—and sometimes even obscene. The writer Philip Gourevitch was one visitor to the monument in the Washington Mall who came back disappointed by what he describes as "one more American theme park." [49] This scathing indictment comes from the son of survivors. Gourevitch begins his critique with an acknowledgment of his intimate connection to the Holocaust and by retelling a childhood nightmare. The core of Gourevitch's nightmare is made up of four words—"The Nazis are coming":

> I had a dream around the age of seven or eight, a dream I may have
> dreamed more than once, of a vast, darkened plain across which masses
> of people fled . . . Fire at the margins . . . the only possible outcome . . .
> isolation and annihilation. I survived, of course, because I woke up; the
> slaughter ended before I did. . . . I don't know if I thought the words in
> my sleep, or if I added them afterward. The experience seemed at once
> absolutely true and absolutely useless. Nothing could be learned from it,
> nothing taken away; there was nothing in it for life. [50]

This vision of fire threatens the entire edifice of public and personal memory. It is a fragment of history with no lessons at all. The nightmare is Gourevitch's chosen entrance ticket to the museum instead of the simulated "identity card" of a Holocaust victim of his own age and gender.

The Washington Museum is mandated to teach lessons, especially to Americans far removed from the center of the Jewish experience. The identity-creating entrance card is supposed to inspire empathy and to bridge the gap between individual questions and massive evidence. This is also the goal of the newly opened Museum of Tolerance in Los Angeles, which is intended to instruct Americans in the virtues of democracy and pluralism. The West Coast monument is called *Beit Ha Shoah* in Hebrew, or "House of the Catastrophe." In English, this monument translates the Holocaust into a well-lit message about the virtues of pluralism. Both the Washington and the Los Angeles museums stress objects, in that the Final Solution is incomprehensible to most Americans without them. A forty-foot re-creation of the Warsaw ghetto wall, an actual freight car brought over from Poland, a toy butterfly painted in Teresenstadt, a casting of the gate to Auschwitz, and heaps of hair are meant to saturate the eye, to stand for the missing past. A "Tower of Portraits"—the faces of fifteen hundred inhabitants of the shtetl of Ejszyski before the war—is yet another way to make history come alive.[51]

Yet the tower, like the heaps of hair, cannot tame the nameless terror of visitors like Philip Gourevitch. Such members of the second generation are dismayed by the very monumentality of these re-creations. In their eyes, these constructions are too perfectly planned, too solid to accommodate the nightmare of history. The Yad Vashem Museum in Jerusalem also struggles with the dilemma of representation. This site, after all, houses the official Memorial Authority of the state of Israel. Yet the main exhibit hall at Yad Vashem is free of the didacticism of objects. It focuses mainly on black-and-white photographs from the period of the extermination of the Jews. The grounds of the museum, by contrast, are filled with various objects and commemorative statues. Each tries to teach something, each wrings a tear through the use of stone and bronze. Two contrasting images linger for me following a recent visit: the massive Star of David recalling resistance fighters and the lean image of a man wrapped in talit and teffilin (prayer shawl and phylacteries), his face completely hidden in anguish.

The first monument stands at the edge of a stone plaza overlooking present-day Jerusalem. Dedicated on August 5, 1985, it commemorates the "one and a half million Jews who fought against Nazi Germany" in the Allied Armies, in the ranks of partisans, and in underground movements in occupied Europe. These were fighters who generated hope for their fellow Jews. This optimistic message is underscored by a steel obelisk rising to pierce the six massive rocks that create a sky-blue Jewish emblem between them. The weeping Jew, on the other hand, is hidden among bushes along a garden path. Leah Micholson, the sculptor who donated this work to Yad Vashem, calls it "The Silent Cry." No blue sky perforates the pain of this self-imploding figure. At the feet of the grieving man who makes no sound, the artist placed a mound of rough-hewn stones. These fragments of rock (unlike the massive boulders in praise of Jewish fighters) invite visitors to reenact a cemetery visit with the traditional gesture of placing pebbles on the grave.

Yet the sculpture of "The Silent Cry" marks no grave. It is merely a tradition-laden image of loss. To mark lives for whom there are no markers, we need another kind of vision that encompasses individualized records of degradation

Memorial to the more than one million Jews who fought against the Nazis, dedicated in 1985 at Yad Vashem, Jerusalem. The placement of the massive stones forms the Jewish star. (V. Schwarcz)

and grief, a vision that moves away from the symbolic to the historical. Here, Rabbi Shimon Huberband may be of help. Huberband, who recorded the daily nightmares of his people during the three years before his own annihilation in 1942, had no time for reflections on symbols. He put pen to paper out of a personal duty to chronicle the tragedies around him. In the village of Radzymin, for example, he witnessed the arrest of a fellow Jew by the Nazis, noting how the Germans forced the elderly man to put on his *shtreimel* (fur hat), prayer shawl, and phylacteries before leading him to the marketplace. There they tried to force him to kiss the cross. When he refused, they beat him until he lost consciousness.[52] Written in Yiddish, Huberband's notes were hidden in milk cans (together with the Ringelblum archives—which detail the life of the Warsaw ghetto). By this act of foresight, one fragment of humiliation and powerlessness has been reserved for posterity.

The preservation of such singular accounts required protective spaces. Huberband's milk cans were sheltered under a four-story building in Warsaw. But what about words, images, and stories that are exposed daily to the glare of official history? They need an even darker hue. Paul Celan became a master at creating poems that avoid brightness. His fractured lines written in the *Muttersprache* of the Nazis probed the depths of loss that are not apparent under the electrical fixtures gracing the museums in Washington, Los Angeles, or even Jerusalem. Out of the hard cadence of the German tongue, Celan created a "shawl" for the mother who perished in Nazi-occupied Ukraine. Then, having inherited her world of burning snow, he kept on trying to use words to name the cold that never left his bones. Chinese writers who went through the Cultural Revolution were spared Celan's ceaseless shivering. Nonetheless, they, too, inherited a linguistic universe in which every word that was once intimate, poetic, and cultured had been misshapen by the personality cult of Mao. The young men and women who were Red Guards in the 1960s and 1970s—who were faithful followers of the Chairman—experienced a scorching loss. They were robbed not only of schooling but also of affection for parents and teachers (who had to be castigated and at times even killed as enemies of the Cultural Revolution). Having once been fervently loyal to the Red Sun, they also seek refuge in the shadows of winter.

At the height of his cult, Mao Zedong called the Red Guards the "spring of China." After his death, however, they were determined to head toward colder climates. Slowly, with painful difficulty, this generation has been learning to give up a longing for the warmth of certainty. Younger than Ba Jin (who was initiated into student politics in 1919), Red Guards were born and raised in Mao's China. Mao's revolution was all the history they knew. Today, they do not call for the building of a Cultural Revolution Museum—museums are still too public for a generation once addicted to official ceremonies honoring Mao Zedong in Tiananmen Square. Instead of well-lit mausoleums, they seek refuge in the shadows of poetry. They map with worn words the space where loss and disillusionment have been most acute. This is a wintry landscape. The poet Bei Dao describes its chill in a work called "Zou xiang dongtian" (Head for Winter), addressed to his comrades who once believed in the sacred prophecy of Chairman Mao:

> Head for winter
> we weren't born for the sake of
> a sacred prophecy, let's go
> . . . .
> Head for winter,
> not sink into green
> dissipation, everywhere at ease

not repeat the incantation of thunder and lightning . . .
or hide behind a curtain
to recite with a stammer the words of the dead
performing the wild joy of the tyrannized
Head for winter [53]

In this poem, a generation that grew up parroting heroic words (referred to here as "incantations of thunder and lightning") is asked to purge its mind and its tongue. Bei Dao's comrades in the Red Guards had been accustomed to stammering slogans. Having once basked in the heat generated by the communal dance of the tyrannized, they are now asked to risk the cold comfort of truth.

The voice here is solitary, not projected by loudspeakers; the portrait is specific, not part of a tower of faces; and the message is bleak. Tolerance may be inscribed on a museum door in Los Angeles, but shame is what is whispered in this space. Away from mausoleums and museum lights, more complex regrets can be voiced. The Chinese writer Qian Zhongshu also pointed to shame in his preface to A Cadre School Life, the widely read Cultural Revolution memoir written by his wife, Yang Jiang (Yang uses the official label of "Cadre School" for the forced labor camps of the 1960s and early 1970s). A marvel of recollection in muted tones, the book is the account of an aged, cosmopolitan-minded woman who manages to bring to life the details of daily survival: a stray dog, a chance meeting with her elderly husband (who was also exiled to the countryside), the color of leaves after the rain washes off the dust.

Nothing in the book challenges public memory directly, however. Instead, the recalling eye fastens onto small, intelligible bits. Yang Jiang, a noted translator of Cervantes, is silent about the spiritual humiliations of the Mao era, but her husband is not. Qian Zhongshu's preface to her book challenges the narrative of public memory, drawing attention to a missing chapter of his wife's memoir: "Our only boldness was a lack of enthusiasm for the endless movements and struggles we participated in. . . . An acute sense of shame can result in selective amnesia. A guilty conscience can make you guarded." [54] By daring to mention "selective amnesia," Qian suggests that there was more than artfulness to this guarded memoir—more even than the party's official limits on what could be remembered about the Cultural Revolution after the death of Mao. Qian Zhongshu's preface hints at a difficult question: Might we have expressed more than mere lack of enthusiasm for Maoist movements? Beyond this question lies the shameful recollection of powerlessness.

This is also the terror that haunts the childhood nightmare of Philip Gourevitch. Powerlessness is what prevents him from appreciating the lessons of the Holocaust Museum. This same terror, magnified greatly, colors Primo Levi's reflections on memory after Auschwitz. In The Drowned and the Saved, Levi writes about the burdens of the Geheimisfrager—the "bearers of shameful secrets," a term used for Holocaust survivors who troubled the peace of mind of their contemporaries after the war. In this intentionally troubling and troubled work, Levi asks about the "gray zone" in which Jewish victims became instruments of violence against other Jews. He worries about the mythologizing that takes place as the Holocaust becomes ever more monumentalized in the public domain. And he always comes back to the question of memory itself: How can it offer any consolation where there is none?

In this book, Levi tells of his encounter after the war with the family of Alberto, an Italian inmate from Auschwitz. The forced death march of January 1945 swallowed Alberto's life, yet his family insists on better news. Could he have been rescued by Russians? Maybe he is recovering in a hospital. Primo Levi cannot give them such hope. What's more, he does not even share their longing for consolatory truths:

> The best way to defend oneself against the invasion of burdensome memories is to impede their entry, to extend a cordon sanitaire. It is easier to deny entry to a memory than to free oneself from it after it has been recorded. This, in substance, was the purpose of many artifices thought up by the Nazi commanders in order to protect the consciences of those assigned to do the dirty work. . . . Alberto never returned. More than forty years have passed. I did not have the courage to show up again and to counterpose my painful truth to the consolatory "truth" that, one helping the other, Alberto's relatives had fashioned for themselves.[55]

Unlike Alberto's relatives, Levi had a high tolerance for memories that do not set the mind at ease. He refused to set up a safe zone in which reassuring tales prevailed. Even after forty years, he insists on the naked fact: Alberto did not return. He reminded his contemporaries about the Nazis' efforts to cut off their own memory, to wall it off. Levi risked sinking into the painful morass of the past in order to prove the inefficiency of their cordon sanitaire.

This is a goal also shared by Ci Jiwei, the young survivor of Mao Zedong's mnemonic tyranny. Ci argues that the huge load of old memories carried by Chinese society had to be destroyed by Mao before his vision of a new society could take root. The past embedded in each individual had to be reshaped by what he calls "mnemonic engineering": "Bad things that could not be hidden were either given good names or else attributed to those who were dead. Bad things being done behind closed doors were conveniently kept there, safe from public scrutiny and public memory. Through a combination of ignorance of bad things and gratitude for good ones, the Chinese people showed a remarkable capacity for amnesia. And amnesia breeds obedience. . . . But political alchemy cannot long convert into the gold of amnesia a mountain of bad memories that is still growing." [56] The Great Famine of 1959–60 and the Cultural Revolution of 1966–76 kept the mountain of bad memories growing. Eventually, after the death of Mao, the cordon sanitaire became looser, and amnesia no longer had total dominion in public life. So Ba Jin could call for the creation of a Cultural Revolution Museum. Although it remains unbuilt, the compulsion to testify grows stronger over time. [57] Memorialists keep on accosting public amnesia by leaving bits of their wintry vision behind.

They keep putting notes in the wall. Jewish survivors, even more than Chinese, know how hard it is to say something distressing and concrete in a world looking for broadly inspiring messages. Yet they insist, since the alternative is the desiccation of all speech. Dan Pagis describes this effort in a work called "Sealed Transport"—a cycle of poems about the destruction of European Jewry. In these pages there is no replica of the cattle cars, no iron model of the Warsaw ghetto wall. With one foot already out of the nightmare and a new identity card in hand, the poet shows himself unable to give up the burden of discrete remembrance:

Imaginary man, go. Here is your passport.
You are not allowed to remember.
. . . .
You have a decent coat now,
A repaired body, a new name
ready in your throat.
Go. You are not allowed to forget. [58]

What better image for renouncing past recollection than a decent coat, a repaired body, and a new name! If we wanted to go beyond history's nightmare, this surely is the path. But Pagis did not take this road. All his life he remained the rumpled, uninvited guest at the feast of public commemoration. Yang Zaidao, too, could not avail himself of this alternative. Although his name did not link him to his mother, she remained the vortex that consumed his life after the betrayal of 1957. I, too, have a new name ready in my throat. This is the name my parents gave me after they survived the war. I also have a decent "coat"—

an intellectual covering for unnamed fears. My studies in Chinese history have provided many years of effective detour around Jewish memories. Yet this coat no longer fits. Chinese survivors of the Cultural Revolution remind me of Jewish questions that lie unanswered at home. So, I come back: back to the history of a Transylvania that I did not know but that is my inheritance nonetheless. I also trace my way back to another "Vera." For many years I did not know about this other offspring. I did not want to ask about her. Now, like Eudora Welty's somnambulist, this past will not stay asleep. It keeps calling my name.

FIVE

Light Passersby

Jewish Recollections of Shanghai . . . and Cluj

They have used the bodies
Of children as improvised bridges
. . . .
But they have lost the atmosphere
Which belongs to them

Light passers-by
DAVID SHAPIRO, "FOR VICTIMS"

C alling my name, I pick up a lost thread, though this is no golden guide through the labyrinth of family history. With my other sister, Agnes, I had at least a birth certificate, a date: January 10, 1944. The document records the ages of my mother and her first husband, and I am able to fill out some of the picture around the three letters—izr. But on my father's side, there are no such documents. Nothing points concretely to the existence, and the loss, of siblings before my time. Confusion and uncertainty dominate my mind. The other Vera, the one before me, keeps slipping through my fingers.

Once I thought my name was rather simple, that it belonged to me alone. I believed my mother liked the sound of Vera and the idea that it could mean both "truth," in Latin, and "faith," in Russian. Under the new Communist regime in Romania, she had tried to hedge her bets both ways. My name was to be a passport across the borders of time. It seemed a firm divider between the world before the war and the new society to be built after. But this divider was no solid barrier. It turned out that my name was part of what the poet David Shapiro calls "improvised bridges"—airy structures created by survivors to mark unspeakable loss.

Remembrance requires detours. Mnemosyne does not reveal her depths on demand. A meandering quest works better, because it mirrors memory's own circuitousness when nearing unknown terrain. My father's past cannot be mapped by facts alone, so my training as a historian is of little use here. Instead, I have to listen, simply listen to others who have lost the solid markers of their history. I did not ask about the other Vera until a few years ago. I never knew about her, though I had been told that my parents had been married to other people before the war. The only hint that my father had lost more than a wife in Auschwitz came from his sister, my aunt Magda, whom I visited in 1980, shortly before she died. Then living in a Jewish home for the elderly in the Transylvanian town of Timisoara, she gave me a bunch of old photographs she had stored in a shoe box. Among them was a bridal portrait of Rozsi Braun, the young woman my father had married in Cluj in 1940. "She had given birth to a girl named Vera, but the child died after a few days. She was also pregnant again when they deported her to Auschwitz." I write my aunt's words on the back of the photograph, to remind me to ask more later.

But I did not raise the subject with my aunt again, nor did I ask my father about his first daughter while he was alive. It was only after his death, in 1984, that I broach this with my mother. The scattered notes that my father called "Encounters Dictated by Fate" were all mixed up and lacked clear dates. In one place, Rozsi Braun had no children. In another, she had two. In yet another fragment, my mother's second daughter was called Vera. I knew this could not be so. I had documents to prove the name of Agnes Spitzer. Documentary facts are of no help in tracing the other Vera, though I continued to search for them. After my father died, I wrote to someone in Israel who knew someone who remembered Rozsi Braun in Cluj—and in Auschwitz. This lady could not recall any children but did not rule out the possibility that there might have been some.

Finally, in the summer of 1993, I wrote to Rabbi Joseph Schachter at the Hall of Names in Yad Vashem. Two years earlier he had helped me fill out pages of testimony about the specific persons who perished on my mother's side: my great-grandparents, my grandparents, and Agnes Spitzer. He also turned out to be a willing, helpful correspondent when I started to inquire about Rozsi Braun. Rabbi Schachter searched all the records for the city known as Cluj, Kolosvar, or Klausenburg. He looked at hundreds of pages bearing names similar to hers and found only one Rozsi. This woman had been married to a man named Sandor, who was deported with three children. Rabbi Schachter sent me a copy of the testimony page. After looking at it for a long time, I realized that I had been asking the wrong question.

In my mind and in Magda's stories, my father's first wife was always known as Rozsi Braun. But, of course, she was deported as Rozsi Schwarcz, since by 1944 she had been married to my father for four years. So I once again wrote to Rabbi Schachter, who this time sent me two more pages of testimony and a note: "Enclosed you'll find 2 Rosa/Rozsi from Cluj/Kolosvar—I doubt if they refer to your Rozsi. These two pages should have contained the 'infant' in the circled rubric. I feel for you in the difficulty of not being able to have gotten a straight answer. Most survivors react similarly as did your father." [1]

What is Rabbi Schachter trying to tell me? By now, I know that there are no straight answers to my questions about Rozsi Braun or her daughter Vera. Still, I want to understand why I was named after her—or rather, why I was led to believe that my name was new, mine alone. Then I reread the rabbi's note. It is not about names after all but about the problem of knowing. Survivors themselves were not sure of the abyss they were crossing when they built their improvised bridges. The second generation was left with a vague sense that we stand in another's place. Nadine Fresco, a daughter of survivors in France, explored this half-conscious realization in an essay called "La Diaspora des cendres." In this work, she points out that none of us ever strays far from the haze of ashes that emanates out of the death camp: we carry traces of fire in us through our very names. Many members of the second generation are named after someone who died. No wonder, in Fresco's words, that we often stand condemned as "usurpers" in our own minds.[2]

I, too, am one of the late usurpers. My parents lost their first spouses and first children in the Shoah. Much of what made them belong somewhere and to someone before the war was destroyed before my birth. They are truly "light passers-by," moving shakily on the postwar terrain. Many of my parents' friends had second families in 1947–48 and named their belated offspring after the dead. But there were so many names to chose from. Who was to blame them if they got confused? For those of us born after the Shoah, these names point toward an ever-present absence. How are we to map its parameters? My own cartography led back to the Cluj of Rozsi Braun rather indirectly. Like the meandering bridge in Mi Wanzhong's painting, mine is a path full of twists and turns. It slows me down. Like the two scholars who stop and admire a weeping willow, I linger along the way.

I stop in Shanghai on my way back to Transylvania. During the war, Shanghai was a place of refuge, of life, for Jews. Transylvania, by contrast, was turned into a large deportation camp. It is easier to start exploring Jewish recollections in a place that fostered survival than in a world that spelled almost certain death. Shanghai, whose streets I came to know only in 1977, is also a safe place for me. I know its alleys from twentieth-century maps, its classical gardens from Qing history. Cluj, the city of my birth, is considerably less tame. Before the war, each intersection had another name, another meaning, for my parents. Although I was born after the Holocaust, during the new age of Communist optimism, I sensed the hidden layers whenever people referred to Romanian streets by their older, Hungarian names.

My own Cluj was a cheerful if somewhat impoverished city. But my parents' Kolosvar and my grandparents' Klausenburg was an altogether different world.

During its more prosperous days, my grandfather ran a leather goods store in the main plaza downtown. Later, the city became a place of terror as inhabitants of the ghetto were gathered in the local brick factory before being sent to Auschwitz. My Cluj had the Szamos River running through it. Theirs did too. As a child growing up in Communist Romania, I often heard the Hungarian ballad "Szep varos Kolosvar." This folk song dwells on the beauty of the city and promises to lead back home anyone who drinks even a drop of the Szamos. To this day I feel the tug of this song, and of the river.

The dead who went up in smoke are not nostalgic about Kolosvar. This is also true for survivors like Willy Mund, a childhood friend of my mother's and my father's companion in the forced labor camps. When Mund recalls the city of his first marriage—from which his wife and infant son were deported to Auschwitz—he gets angry, not sad. One place to vent this feeling is poetry. In Miami Beach, in Hungarian (the language of his youth), Willy refuses to be charmed by a river that ran its normal course while his family was dragged toward death:

> He who drinks from Szamos water
> Has his heart pulled ever tauter.
> So the old saying goes.
> But not so my heart knows.
> Before I set foot again near the Szamos River,
> Time must flow and flow,
> And shiver.[3]

I never knew Willy Mund's Kolosvar, though I was born in Cluj. Before asking this family friend for his story, I sought out European Jews who survived the war in Shanghai. Their stories of miraculous rescue heartened me enough to start asking about Jews who stayed in Europe and never drank the waters of the Szamos River again. Shanghai is a daytime city for me, a city suffused with the light of my studies and with the life that Jews created there. Cluj is my late-night town, a city of the unconscious where, in the words of the literary critic Philip Kuberski, "quite unexpectedly, a sign, a sewer lid, or a broken clock will make one lose all sense of temporal and spatial identity."[4] The disorientation that Kuberski talks about is precisely what I had been fighting against through my studies of China. This country was far enough from my native ground that I did not have to worry about sewer lids or broken clocks. When I finally was ready to confront these gloomy signposts, I turned to the Fortunoff Video Archives for Holocaust Testimonies at Yale. In the cramped room where I began to listen to the voices of survivors, daylight streamed in reassuringly. I started by screening a testimony by Anschel W., a rabbi who had escaped with the Mirrer Yeshiva to Shanghai. Almost two years later, I watched the tape of Adrienne K., the surgeon who had been deported to Auschwitz from Cluj. Between the two testimonies lies a world of difference. In the first videotape, a religious Jew from Poland details his ongoing study of the Torah in a corner of war-torn China. In the second, a highly assimilated woman describes how her parents and younger sister were taken to the gas chambers and how she stayed alive by shoveling human excrement.

Yet there is a thread of continuity. Both witnesses face the same listener—Dr. Dori Laub, the psychoanalyst who founded the Yale Archives. He is able to draw out their disparate recollections of loss and survival in ways that may not be accessible to historians in search of hard facts about the Holocaust. Dr. Laub knows how to listen for what is not there, for what can never be put into words. In the essay "Bearing Witness," he writes about what it takes to accompany survivors on memory's circuitous road: "Each victim testifies to an absence, to an event that has not yet come into existence in spite of the overwhelming and compelling reality of its occurrence. . . . The listener, therefore, is party to the creation of knowledge de nuovo." [5] The idea that the listener adds to what he or she appears to be simply hearing is familiar to me. This is what my Chinese friends called zhi yin—the understanding that emerges between two sympathetic hearts. In Beijing, this expression based on a musical metaphor had a lyrical edge. In New Haven, it acquires a harsher tone as I follow Dr. Laub's voice in conversation with survivors.

I now know that I must also become a partner in the creation of knowledge de nuovo. Some of this knowledge I had sought to flee before, like the question of the other Vera; some had been closed to me because I was not well versed in the Torah, like Anschel W. So I use my knowledge of China to begin to inquire about Jewish memory.

With Shanghai in Mind

Shanghai, where some twenty-five thousand Jews survived the war, is a relatively young city. Until the opening of China to the West in the nineteenth century, it was a backwater town. By the early 1900s foreign and Chinese merchants, soldiers of fortune, coolie laborers, prostitutes, and artisans had made it the most cosmopolitan city in China. The place that ended up as home for Jews from Baghdad and Vienna, from the Polish village of Mir and the German port of Bratislava, was a hub of migration in the Chinese world as well. In the words of a local gazetteer, "Shanghai is a hybrid place that mixes up people from all over China. The number of outsiders outnumber the natives. Accordingly, the people from each locality establish associations of fellow provincials to maintain their connections with each other . . . and each established huiguan (native place associations). From this it is possible to know that Chinese people have the moral excellence of loving the group." [6]

The "moral excellence of loving the group" is also the main thread in Jewish recollections of the war years in Shanghai. Russian, German, and Central European refugees, carrying native worlds with them, created trade, cultural, and religious associations in that war-torn city.[7] What sustained them was a conscious attachment to the group and to Jewish tradition. This attachment comes through vividly in the Anschel W. testimony at the Yale archives. The tape opens with the conservatively dressed gentleman adjusting a black yarmulke on his head and a microphone on his chest. Dr. Laub then asks the rabbi if he would prefer to speak in Yiddish, the language of his youth and of the Mirrer Yeshiva— the only Jewish institution of higher learning to be saved from the Holocaust in its entirety by way of Japan and China. Rabbi Wainhaus, as he calls himself on the tape, chooses to speak in English. This is a clear sign that he intends to address his testimony to future generations who know little Yiddish and even less about the Torah learning embodied in the Mirrer Yeshiva. In English, Rabbi Wainhaus talks about the "miracle" of the rescue of his school from Poland and of his subsequent settlement in Shanghai.

The public history of the Mirrer Yeshiva begins in 1815, with the impact of enlightenment ideas upon Jewish institutions of higher learning. This highly intellectual movement, known as haskala (enlightenment), evoked a vigorous, rationalistic response within the observant community. The Mirrer Yeshiva represented this new approach and became one of the most prestigious institutions of Talmudic scholarship in prewar Poland.[8] Rabbi Wainhaus's testimony, however, offers more than institutional history. It is a memory-laced account pieced together in front of an empathetic listener. Along with the details of the rescue of the yeshiva comes the de nuovo knowledge of Rabbi Wainhaus's distinctive journey from his parents' home in a small Zionist town to the Beth Aharon Synagogue on Museum Road in Shanghai.

Rabbi Wainhaus's personal story is amplified further when we meet at his house in Brooklyn. In the safety of his home in Borough Park, the eighty-year-old survivor dwells on the vulnerability of Polish Jews caught in the struggle for power between Soviet Russia and Nazi Germany. As a young man, Anschel Wainhaus was drawn to Vilna, the capital of a briefly independent Lithuania. In Vilna, twenty-year-old Anschel had the good fortune of obtaining transit visas to Japan, provided by Senpo Sugihara, the Japanese consul in Kovno. Then comes a long tale about all the strategies the family used to outwit the NKVD, the dreaded secret police of the Soviet Union. Immaculately dressed and strong-voiced when talking about world events or Talmud scholarship, Rabbi Wainhaus speaks briefly, softly, about a younger brother: "I had already obtained the life saving visa for him. . . . Then I tried to meet him at a train station. . . . No luck. This brother, with my mother and three other children left behind in Poland, was betrayed by a shepherd. They were all taken to the gas chambers." [9]

Rabbi Solomon Schwartzman, born in Poland in 1914, uses a similarly sub-dued voice when talking about his family history before Shanghai. We are sitting in the conference room of a New Haven synagogue. The energetic septuage-narian with a European accent starts by recalling himself as a skinny young man who was a demobilized soldier in 1939. Later in our conversations, Rabbi Schwartzman shows me a photograph of himself as a yeshiva student in Warsaw: his face is beardless, his head covered by the square hat worn by Gerrer Hassidim. Aware of the dangers of Jewish life in German-occupied Poland because of the knowledge he gained through the army, he, too, decided to leave and seek safety through Lithuania. Like Rabbi Wainhaus, Rabbi Schwartzman did not find out about the fate of his family until after the war, when he stopped in Chicago on his way from Shanghai to New York: "My older brother Chaim, two sisters, and their spouses and children had been taken to the gas chambers . . . all except a younger brother who was killed jumping off the transport train." [10]

Rabbi Shimon Goldman comes from the same little Polish hamlet as Rabbi Schwartzman. In the dining room of his Crown Heights home in Brooklyn, this soft-spoken survivor frequently drifts into Yiddish as he recalls the color of the wallpaper at the Schwartzman home and a shared Sabbath meal. Born in 1925, and the youngest of these three men, Rabbi Goldman was only fourteen when he fled his native town. He started the long journey to China without the army experience of Rabbi Schwartzman and found his way to Shanghai without the communal contacts of the Mirrer Yeshiva that organized Rabbi Wainhaus's es-cape. Shimon Goldman left stealthily, with just one extra layer of clothing on his back. Having witnessed the bombing of his hometown and the local rabbi's en-treaties to be allowed to to bury Jews killed in 1939, this precocious young man understood that Jewish life in Poland at that time had reached a dead end. How deadly that end would be he found out only after the war, "when I learned that my parents died in the gas chambers." [11]

These three religiously observant young men came together in Shanghai. On the surface, they seemed to share little with the highly assimilated Jewish refugees from Germany and Austria, who far outnumbered the Polish group in war-time China. Yet, below the differences in religious observance lies a shared tale of fear and loss. This commonality is summarized in the words of the great medieval biblical commentator Rashi, who wrote: "Mourning is a sphere making a circuit in the world." [12] It brings together even those separated by geography and levels of ritual observance.

The year 1939, notable for the escape of the three yeshiva students from Poland, also spelled the end of the known world for Dr. Robert Sokal, a biologist born in Vienna. For the Polish Jews, the German bombing of Warsaw on the eve of the Jewish festival of Sukkot in 1939 marked the beginning of the end. For Dr. Sokal's father, the German occupation of the capital of Austria brought disaster earlier. In his daughter's home in New Haven, the eminent scientist who relies on reason for research as well as for recollection speaks of unreasonable events: "My father was taken to Dachau and Buchenwald from July 1938 to February 1939 . . . so we knew we had to get out. We left for Shanghai two months after my father was released from the labor camp, in April 1939. In China, we moved in with an aunt and uncle who had preceded us to Shanghai." [13]

That same year also figures prominently in the recollection of Kathe K., a journalist born in Breslau, Germany. In her testimony for the Fortunoff Archives, Kathe K. describes her arrival in Shanghai in 1939, what it felt like to be alone and disabled. Having suffered from cerebral palsy since childhood, this remarkably modern woman is nonetheless a kindred spirit to the young men who left family and the known world to seek refuge in the alien alleys of Shanghai. Kristallnacht, in 1938, had already demolished much of Kathe K.'s world in Breslau. By the following year her younger brother had left on a children's transport to England, and three sisters had also found refuge abroad: "Finally my parents started to look around for a way to leave. But it was too late. We were too late. We were too late for everything, so my father tried to get us to Shanghai. That was the only way out." [14] When family funds proved to be too scanty for collective salvation, the young woman left for Shanghai alone.

Forty-five years later, this vigorous woman in her late sixties faces the video camera with lively eyes behind dark glasses. Her cropped gray hair dances along with the animated tale while her body remains rigid in its metal brace. Good humor and articulate precision mark Kathe K.'s recollection: "On the day I left, France was invaded, the war spread. . . . When I arrived in Shanghai, I had no one. I stood alone on the pier not knowing what to do until a member of the greeting committee brought me to a 'Home,' a *heim* as we called them, a terrible place. I shared a room with six others, five of them deaf mutes. I decided I would not stay there. Not for me! I did not know where I would sleep but I would not go back there." [15]

Sheer willpower is a hallmark of survivors like Kathe K. But willpower is not all. Mindfulness of the collective fate of the Jewish people adds an edge of passion, and significance, to the years in wartime China. Along with a few belongings, each survivor brought his or her separate pain on this journey to a strange, often unheard-of country. Most Jews in China were largely unaware that the same city in which they endured great economic hardships was also a "lonely island" for Chinese laborers who dared to strike against Japanese business interests, for Nationalist politicians who plotted military resistance, and for writers like Zheng Zhenduo, who mourned the spiritual degradation of his fellow Chinese under Japanese occupation.[16] Few of the Jewish refugees knew about the loneliness and misery of patriotic Chinese. Instead, they crowded into small alleys surrounded by fellow Jews and impoverished, uneducated natives who lived day to day through bitter strength—through ku li.

These coolies, as well as the starving children and the dead bodies left out to rot in the night, dominate the Shanghai of the refugee's mind. One Jewish artist captured a corner of this utterly unglamorous world in a drawing entitled "Life in the Lanes of Hongkew." [17] At the bottom of the image, we see a little Chinese boy with split pants relieving himself in the open street. An angry local mother drags her daughter away from this all-too-familiar scene, while a German-Jewish family rushes out to receive an envelope from the postman. The European refugees grasp that piece of paper as if it were a lifeline to a world of cleanliness and material well-being left behind. Above the anticipation-filled Jews hang tattered Chinese robes—a concrete reminder of the strange new world in which these Europeans found themselves.

The crowded alleys that Jews were forced to inhabit during the days of the Hongkew ghetto led Polish refugees to look back with nostalgia to their brief stay in Japan—the transit station toward which the visas obtained in Kovno directed them. Rabbi Shimon Goldman, for example, recalls fondly the civility of Japanese women who started bowing to the yeshiva students, assuming that their frequent bending in prayer was a form of the greeting commonly used among polite Japanese. Rabbi Wainhaus also emphasized the cleanliness and politeness that the Mirrer Yeshiva encountered in Japan, as well as the welcome supply of food after the long train ride through Siberia. "I recall how impressed we were to be met by a Japanese professor, Kahzuka [Professor Setzuso Kotsuji] I think was his name, who spoke Hebrew and was a member of the Royal family.

"Life in the Hongkew Lanes," drawing by a German artist, ca. 1943. Hongkew, a poverty-stricken Chinese neighborhood in Shanghai, became the heart of the Jewish ghetto in 1942–44. (From David Kranzler, *Japanese, Nazis and Jews*)

He pressed our case with the Japanese officials and eventually converted to Judaism. He took on the name Avraham and asked to be buried in Israel." [18]

In Shanghai, no Chinese literate in Jewish ways waited to greet the refugees. There were no blue-and-white flags, as there had been in Kobe, nor was food plentiful. The spacious stone structures that housed the Mirrer Yeshiva in Japan were traded for unsanitary group "homes." After the clean streets of Japan, the littered alleys of wartime Shanghai provoked a rude awakening that grew more acute each day. "I will never forget the first morning I went out and saw the bodies of dead children left out because they had died of starvation or had frozen overnight," whispers Rabbi Wainhaus after he finishes talking about the exuberance of emigration out of Soviet Russia. "Then we had to get used to riding rickshaws. Imagine, using a human being as an animal. We were not trained for that, it is not the Torah way. . . . But you get used to it after a while. You realize that it helps a poor man make a living." [19] Dr. Sokal also recalls the human debris encountered on his way to the British public school that prepared young men for Oxford and Cambridge: "Each day one would pass three, four bodies on the way." [20]

In contrast to the Chinese poverty glimpsed through a hut window or inscribed on the stiff body of the abandoned dead, Jewish refugees lived relatively cultured lives. The Mirrer Yeshiva was most fortunate in this respect. Its students arrived in Shanghai from Japan before the High Holidays in 1941 to find an empty synagogue with exactly the right numbers of seats to accommodate them. The great Beth Aharon Synagogue, built by the Kadoorie family from Baghdad, turned out to meet the precise needs of the Polish yeshiva. It had two kosher kitchens, 250 seats for students, and was conveniently located on Museum Road. Because of this good fortune, the Mirrer group was able to resume immediately its prewar Jewish purpose. The large, imposing beit knesset (hall of worship) was now turned into a spacious beit midrash (study hall).

Through the eye of memory, the presence of two great religious leaders also accounts for the vitality of Jewish life in wartime China. Rabbi Meir Ashkenazi, the head of the Russian Jewish community in Shanghai from 1927 to 1947, imprinted himself deeply upon the life and imagination of refugees in Shanghai. Although Rabbi Ashkenazi was a Lubavitch Hassid, he was scrupulously fair to all the communities that congregated in Shanghai during the war. His white-bearded face was familiar not only to Anschel Wainhaus and Solomon Schwartzman but to the young Lubavitch follower Shimon Goldman. Each had occasion to be invited for a Sabbath meal at the home of this distinguished leader; each had occasion to hear him share his Torah learning.

An equally powerful reminder of the resilience of the Jewish spirit in times of adversity was the presence of Rabbi Shlomo Kalish, known as the Amshenover Rebbe. Not as publicly visible as Rabbi Ashkenazi, the Amshenover Rebbe was a different kind of "pillar of light." [21] In May 1942, when the first volume of the Talmudic tractate Gittin appeared in offprint in Shanghai, a public celebration was organized at the Russian-Jewish Club. Although bombs had already fallen on Pearl Harbor, although Shanghai itself had been damaged by Japanese war planes, the Jewish community celebrated the continuation of Torah study with fervor. Rabbi Kalish was at the heart of the celebration and bore witness to the joy of spiritual life in the midst of a world gone mad. In the words of a 1942 observer: "Those who did not witness the Amshenover Rebbe and Yeshiva students dance at receiving this marvelous gift, had never seen true Jewish joy and felt the secret of the Jew's eternity." [22]

Retrospectively, this briefly glimpsed "secret" of Jewish endurance grows more compelling, for it calls to mind the perdurance of Confucian civilization that was also based on a passionate attachment to texts. The ability to live in and through books was a quality cultivated by both Chinese and Jewish tradition. It was an aptitude that flourished even under the Japanese occupation of Shanghai. Rabbi Wainhaus, like Rabbi Goldman and Rabbi Schwartzman, recalled the extraordinary determination it took to maintain an unchanging study schedule in spite of all the dislocation. It was as if the fearful news of the war, the dead bodies on the streets of Shanghai, and the material deprivations of the German refugees paled before the urgency of Torah study. Isolation from news about the war in Europe certainly helped this feat of religious commitment. But the secret of Jewish endurance is not found in Japanese-imposed isolation from world events. Rather, it lies in willful concentration on the ultimate sources of Jewish life. Rabbi Wainhaus described his impression of how the Allies' war with Japan spread to China: "Sometime after Pearl Harbor, we heard bombing over the Shanghai harbor. I remember an Italian boat overturned in the river. That's all." [23]

Each day on his way to the study hall at the Beth Aharon synagogue, Anschel Wainhaus saw that overturned boat. Yet what mattered was not the battered present but the eternally compelling Talmud. The present, though manifest in the scuttled vessel, did not ignite the same curiosity as the texts to be studied, to be freshly appropriated in Shanghai. Dr. Robert Sokal also recalls the overturned boat (as well as its name, the *Conte Verde*) and the explosion of shrapnel that accompanied the Japanese bombings of Allied ships in Shanghai Harbor. Yet he, too, was focused on something else: a life of study, though mostly through secular subjects. An interest in biology, in Zionism, and in learning more about other Jews in Shanghai consumed Dr. Sokal as much as Talmud study riveted the Mirrer Yeshiva students. A capacity to turn inward to books, to the Jewish community, to newspaper publishing, to Yiddish musicals and theater productions—all this is part of the secret of Jewish endurance.

Circling Back to Cluj

Such structures of Jewish continuity had once been in place in my native Cluj as well. In Shanghai they continued to flourish, whereas in Transylvania they were erased by the war. Before 1944, Yiddish and Hebrew newspapers, Jewish high schools and rabbinical training institutes, the Goldmark Jewish orchestra, Zionist youth groups, Jewish banks to provide loans for the needy, and more than ten synagogues serving the Orthodox, Reform, and Hassidic communities had thrived in Cluj/Kolosvar/Klausenburg. Little remains today. How can one grasp the magnitude of this destruction? How to reckon with the vast difference between Jewish memories of Shanghai and Cluj? To my mind, this is somewhat like the gulf dividing the philosophers Li Zehou and Jean Amery. Li went into exile with Kant's *Critique of Pure Reason*, not just the required quotations of Chairman Mao. He drank of forbidden waters, sustained his mind, and rebounded with a new philosophy of aesthetics after the trauma of the Cultural Revolution. Jean Amery, by contrast, deprived of all books, wandered through Auschwitz in blind hunger, his mind filled with useless quotations from the German poet Hölderlin.

Such was the disparity between the Shanghai world of the Mirrer Yeshiva and the Cluj of my parents' youth. During one month, beginning on May 4, 1944, more than 150,000 Jews from Transylvania were deported to the gas chamber.[24] Ironically, the ghettoization of Jews lasted longer in China than in Transylvania. The Hongkew ghetto, established by order of the Japanese authorities in Shanghai, began to forcibly aggregate Jewish refugees in February 1943. All through the summer of 1944, its alleys continued to swell with Jews pulled in from other parts of China. When the bombs fell over Hongkew, the Mirrer Yeshiva went right on with its schedule of religious studies. Even the Chinese writer Zheng Zhenduo, who took refuge in Shanghai's lonely island, managed to console himself with books. In the very hour when Japanese aggression threatened to destroy his country, Zheng used what little money he had to buy and preserve Yuan dynasty drama scripts, his people's "national treasures." [25]

Life in the Cluj ghetto, by contrast, was a short, devastating nightmare. "Operation Margarette," the pretty-sounding name for Hitler's plan for the occupation of Hungary and Transylvania, was carried out with efficiency. The order for the establishment of the Cluj ghetto was given on May 3, 1944. By June 1, Endre Laszlo, dubbed "the Hungarian Eichmann," wrote a report to Berlin announcing that 275,415 Jews had been deported from the Cluj and Kassar districts.[26]

Among those taken to Auschwitz from Cluj were my great-grandparents, Judah and Sarah David; my grandparents, Herman and Cecilia David; my father's first wife, Rozsi Braun; and Adrienne K., who gave her testimony to the Yale archives. In these tapes, the Cluj-born surgeon talks about the end of her childhood. Born in 1923, Adrienne K. is four years younger than my mother. Both women were born in Cluj and both belonged to well-to-do families, but there the similarity ends. Adrienne K. comes from nonreligious parents. Her mother and father were both doctors, "the well-known Matyas doctors . . . connected to the Matyas hospital owned and managed by my uncle, who had married a Christian woman." [27] The large family house comes vividly alive as Adrienne K. recalls having three separate governesses to teach her and her younger sister

French, English, and German. Lack of parental attention was compensated by frequent, lavish gifts. Yet the older daughter, the only one in the family to survive the war, seems different from the beginning. She recalls the Christmas tree in her house as well as the effort to seek some Jewish education on her own: "We knew when the Jewish holidays were, but did not celebrate them. . . . Other children had Hannuka and Pesach. I was jealous of them, so when I was a ten-year-old girl, it was my own decision to go to Dr. Hirsch, an orthodox Rabbi, and ask him for lessons. These continued from age ten until age seventeen."[28]

My mother, Katherine, grew up in a religious home. Her father was a member of the orthodox *hevra kaddisha*, a select group of observant Jews who take upon themselves the commandment of honoring the dead by caring for the body before burial. My grandfather also belonged to the synagogue of the Kallemaier Rebbe, a Hassidic leader who prayed with his followers in a small courtyard on David Frencz Street. My grandmother wore a wig, as was the custom among religious women. They spoke only Yiddish during Sabbath and required their children to do the same. Wealthy enough to afford maids and a German governess, the David family lived in a different world from the socially prominent Matyas doctors, who had begun to intermarry with Christians.

When the catastrophe came, however, it hit both families with equal force. Adrienne K., like my mother, dates the beginning of the end to 1940, the year when Hungarians occupied Cluj. Although Polish Jews, like Rabbis Wainhaus and Schwartzman, had already glimpsed Nazi terror by 1939, Cluj got its share indirectly, and rather mildly at first. Under the Vienna accord of August 30, 1940, Transylvania was to be partitioned, with Cluj and a few smaller cities in the north going to Hungary (which had controlled this region before World War I). My mother recalls sitting on a park bench and being sick with anger as she witnessed the Hungarian armies march into her native town. My father, in his memoirs, also wrote about the flood of new announcements put up on shop windows forbidding the use of any language but Hungarian.

In 1940 Adrienne K. had just begun her medical studies. Her testimony dwells on the *numerus klausus*, the racist laws limiting the number of Jews allowed into a university. Dr. K.'s wealthy father used his connections to secure her a place at the medical school in Budapest. A year later, he was able to use his connections once again to send a Gentile detective to bring his daughter home to Cluj, where anti-Jewish policies had not yet become as life threatening as they were in the Hungarian capital. Three years later, in 1944, Dr. Matyas was no longer able to protect himself. On March 19, 1944, Nazi troops entered Hungary. By March 28, the Gestapo had installed itself in Cluj and began arresting the heads of wealthy Jewish families. All the softness of tone, all the pleasure in rambling recollections of her childhood, vanish from Adrienne K.'s voice when she comes to the story of her father's imprisonment: "They picked up sixty families who were known to be rich. . . . My father and I, in the middle of the night before, buried foreign currency, gold coins, sterling, dollars. . . . During the interrogation he revealed nothing. I went to see him once and he told me to unbury the stuff and throw it in the river. . . . His hair had turned white over one night." [29]

Adrienne K. was not imprisoned in the Cluj ghetto. Along with her mother and sister, she was sheltered in the hospital of the uncle who had married a non-Jewish woman and converted to Christianity. Yet Adrienne K.'s mother chose to join the father in the cattle cars on the day of his deportation: "My father was in the last transport from the ghetto on June 7th. . . . My mother got hysterical. After a phone call from him, she panicked. She packed in haste, taking an umbrella but not a toothbrush. She got into the cattle train voluntarily, she was not picked up." [30]

At the train station in Cluj, the family was reunited. On June 11, they arrived in Auschwitz, not knowing where it was. They were greeted by a cacophony of voices and the sound of German: "Loss! Loss! Schnel! Schnel!" (Move! Move! Fast! Fast!). There was no way that a young woman raised by a German governess could miss the meaning of these harsh words. But a note of uncertainty lingers in Adrienne K.'s voice from the nightmare: "They put us in two columns. My memory tells me we went to the left, my sister and mother to the right. . . . Is my memory failing with me?" [31]

The scrupulous surgeon who faces the camera turns inward. She knows all about the historical documents that single out Mengele—the "doctor" who decided the fate of Jews on the Auschwitz train platform. She knows that left led toward death and that right meant life. Yet she is confused. On the night of her selection, the doctor on the Auschwitz platform was not Mengele, but Dr. Kapezius, a face she recognized immediately: "He had been the representative of the Bayer German medical firm before the war. He had visited my parents often, had tea at our house, brought gifts for my parents, a cigarette case, a desk set." [32] Adrienne K.'s father had also recognized the SS officer at the Auschwitz train station. He pleaded to be allowed to go with his wife and younger daughter. "Good, that is very good for you," was Kapezius's response.

These words, this last vision of her parents and her little sister, linger in the survivor's mind. In 1967, Adrienne K. went to Frankfurt to testify against Dr. Kapezius. Although her memory was uncertain about right and left, she had no trouble picking out the photograph of the man who sent her parents and sister to death. "Dr. Kapezius got nine years of which he was already in for four. So he got another five years and was out. He is still alive in Germany. He has a chain of pharmacies and is a millionaire." [33]

I have no such details about the day my mother's parents and grandparents were deported from the Cluj ghetto. By 1944, my mother was married and living in Budapest, using Christian papers provided by her former maid. My older sister, Marian, was two years old when Eichmann marched into Hungary that April; Agnes was four months old.

In a recent letter, my mother alluded to those days. Not to the death of her second child but to the failed effort to save her parents: "When my sister came to me in a German car, I begged my parents to come, but they wanted to be together with the rest of the family!" [34] In the spring of 1944 my mother had been wealthy enough to hire a car and send it from Budapest to Cluj to fetch her parents. Leopold Spitzer, like Dr. Matyas, had business contacts with Germany. The car came back only with my mother's younger sister, Edith. My grandparents, like Adrienne K.'s mother, chose to join their relatives in the cattle cars.

On my father's side, the sense of time is more slippery still. I do not know the date that my father's first wife was taken to Auschwitz or the name of the German doctor who decided her fate. It might have been Dr. Mengele or Dr. Kapezius or someone else altogether. To clarify these details, I seek out Willy Mund, whose wife had worked with Rozsi Braun in a Jewish bank in Cluj before the war. But Willy remembers nothing of Rozsi Braun's fate. His memory is weighed down by his own nightmare: "I was privileged to work outside the ghetto. I even had the use of a car. I would sneak into the ghetto each day to bring milk for my infant son since his mother was too ill to feed him. Then one day, I made up my mind to take him out. Everything was arranged. The car, the papers. I even had a coat made with extra large pockets to hide the child in. . . . Then my wife's mother pleaded with me to leave the child. She said the baby would help the mother recover from her illness. Later, I heard they both died in the transport car to Auschwitz." [35]

Dark shadows cover the face of my parents' friend as he recalls this. We are talking in his daughter's spacious house in New Jersey. She was born in 1947, the child of a second marriage, a post-nightmare offspring like myself. All seems ample and secure in this country home. Yet the shadows linger. They are present in Willy's determination to observe a yizkhor—a memorial day marked by a special candle and prayers—for his first wife and child. He has chosen June 6, the day in 1944 that the Cluj ghetto was emptied. He has tried to write his memoirs several times but can't get past that night in the ghetto when he had his son in his hands, when he might have given his child life in the big pockets of his army coat.

The Cluj ghetto also towers in the recollection of Rosita K., another survivor whose video testimony I watched at the Yale library. A tense woman wearing dark glasses faces the camera. She never takes off the glasses and avoids the question about her full name. Her thick Hungarian accent is identical to that of my parents and of Willy. She is a Cluj native who was in the ghetto for the full four weeks of its existence. She describes in detail the meadow near the brick factory in which the makeshift tents were erected: "About eighty thousand people were crowded there, no bed linen, just straw. We were sleeping on the floor. . . . The Gestapo started to interrogate people they thought had money. . . . We were supposed to go to the promised land of Rhodesia to work. . . . We were told we were going to do agricultural labor there." [36]

The woman in the dark glasses seems to be frightening herself all over again with the terrors she recalls: the burning of her fiancé's nipples during the interrogation, the hell that broke loose in the train during the transport from Cluj. "In one freight wagon were ninety-two people," she says. "Five days to get to an unknown destination. As a young girl I saw giving birth, death. . . . We were thirsty and hungry." [37] The slow-paced retelling goes on even as the glasses tremble. Rosita K. recalls her arrival in Auschwitz, the humiliation of having her genitals shaved, her rectum examined for diamonds. She continues memory's trail all the way to the night of January 1, 1945, when she was reduced to sleeping with dead bodies, seeking warmth in the bitter winter of Bergen Belsen. The protective eyewear almost comes off, but, in the end, she keeps her glasses on: the injury is too severe to be seen. Rosita K. states simply that she was not able to have children after the war, that many of the *lager schwesters* (concentration camp "sisters") are in mental hospitals in Israel.

The contrast between the fragile sanity of this survivor from Cluj and the rugged voice of Kathe K., the disabled woman who survived the war in Shanghai, comes to me sharply. It explains (somewhat) why this study of memory began with China rather than Europe. Vigor had to be located first before terror could be allowed into the framework. Otherwise, dread would have overwhelmed my capacity to proceed.

Still paralyzed today, Kathe K. seems to almost leap off her chair as she recalls editing a German newspaper in Shanghai and the lovely old gardens before the establishment of the Hongkew ghetto in 1943. I have walked through these gardens often. They silence none of the danger that radiates from behind the sunglasses of Rosita K. Childless after the war, she does not even have the solace of "improvised bridges," the postwar offspring that console my parents and their friends. For Rosita K., emptiness lingers unassuaged. She is left on the precipice of memory without any consolation, an inheritor of what one poet calls "white pain":

> I unfold their absence, the white pain.
> Like this we go on so many nights,
> surviving ourselves, in memory together,
> perched here, bartering ecstasies
> song to wing, pinions to the cracked melodies,
> under heaven, fathomless,
> the night sky at the back of our breath.[38]

Peter Cooley, the author of this poem, is not a survivor of the Holocaust, nor even a Jew. Yet his words mirror the magnitude of the absence that weighs down the testimony of Rosita K. The metaphor of cracked melodies captures the broken cadence of her words. The fluttering lips are like the wings of a motion-less bird—although nothing in the video testimony can be construed as an ec-stasy. What cannot be said on camera is like the night that colors each breath. Rosita K.'s dark glasses separate her from the camera and from me. Yet her accent brings her terribly close. It takes me back to the city I was born in but know less well than the Shanghai conjured up by Kathe K. I am familiar with the alleys of China.

In April 1993 I returned to Cluj. I found the house I grew up in, and I looked into the courtyard where my grandfather Herman David used to pray. I took a photograph of the store where his leather goods used to be—it was a privatized shop once again. Old markers were in place, but this was no homecoming. All around me absence prevailed. When I went to visit the courtyard where my father's sister used to live, all that greeted me was new paint on her old door. The woman who had talked about the other Vera and Rozsi Braun was nowhere to be found. I spoke to old Jews in Cluj. I visited three cemeteries. Nothing satiated the need to know. Back in the town that was no longer my home, I finally understood my father's rage after the war. He, too, had returned looking for family. They were nowhere to be found. In his memoirs he describes the fruitless search:

> Soon after getting to Cluj, I went to my former apartment. I knocked on
> the door. A woman opens it. Instinctively, the first thing I did was to grab

her neck and bang her head against the wall: "You beast! You fascist! What are you doing in my apartment?" I never gave her a chance to explain herself. I never let her say that she was some kind of concubine or wife to my brother-in-law. Or that she, too, had barely survived the camps and took over the apartment only recently. Banging at her was more convenient. It was a way of dealing with the horror I felt at the empty place. Everything was gone. All my clothes, all my furniture, everything was gone.[39]

The Question of Meaning

What sense, if any, is to be made of such emptiness? The dread of emptiness leads here to the banging of a woman's head. My father, late in life, could look back and see that he had attacked the occupant of his old apartment simply because she was there and Rozsi Braun wasn't. In memory's eyes, it is easier to note the absence of clothes than the vanishing of his wife. My father resisted the temptation to moralize. He even resisted the appeals of a rabbi who came to visit him in the hospital. Many years after the incident in the apartment, this pious man tried to persuade my father to see higher meaning in his ordeal. My father spoke of his desire to leave a factual record about "my own particle of experience during the Dark Age of our people."[40] The rabbi suggested that the true significance of these experiences lay in encounters dictated by faith. My father was touched by the man's interest in his memoir—and was also not so rash as to argue with a religious leader from his sick bed. To his dying day, however, he insisted that the title of his manuscript was to be "Encounters Dictated by Fate."

The rabbi had spoken from his special position as a guardian of inspirational stories. He sensed in my father's recollections the possibility of turning Jewish suffering into an occasion for the sanctification of God's name. He knew that my father was not conventionally observant, but he also knew him to be full of religious feeling. "Faith" was a word the rabbi used to appeal to those emotions. But my father was full of other feelings, too, which he left out of the hospital conversation. Those passions, in the end, guided the selection and coloring of most of his Holocaust stories. Faith, in the rabbi's sense, could not serve my father's storytelling purpose. It could not explain how my father's life was spared by the SS trooper who had been an apprentice in Timisoara before the war. Unexpected moments of goodwill rounded out my father's notion of fate. He clung to this theme because it wove some coherence into a bewildering world.

A similar quest for coherence animates Rabbi Wainhaus's testimony for the Fortunoff Archives. This observant survivor is close in spirit to the rabbi who wanted to put faith at the heart of my father's recollection. Rabbi Wainhaus, however, did not go back to an empty apartment in Poland. He heard about the death of his mother and brother later, after the war. He did not have to bang on doors or on heads. In Shanghai, the Mirrer Yeshiva continued its prewar routine of Torah study. Memory's eye, heartened by this outcome, could fit history into the traditional framework of a "miracle." This is the word that Rabbi Wainhaus and other memoir writers from the Mirrer Yeshiva use most often to describe their escape from Poland. It is the word that comes up over and over again when he is asked about his final thoughts for the Holocaust testimony. The last minutes of the tape are taken up with a history lesson: "They ask, why is? In old times happened miracles. We don't see miracles now. People ask. I tell you: old times also did not see it. For instance the story of Haman and Ahashverosh. It happened in twenty years. One year a fraction. Five years a fraction. Here Vashti killed. Here Esther taken away. Ten years later Mordechai nominated. It is only a fraction. But when you are back of it already, look with an eye on all twenty years, you see a miracle. The same thing with us. When we went through it, who can see a miracle?"[41] These words capture the power of precedent. Miracles, Rabbi Wainhaus suggests, happen to those prepared to see them. The Purim story is retold in this testimony as a framework for the epic of the Mirrer Yeshiva. Faith in miracles gives meaning to this tale beyond the fraction of one man's life.

In Shanghai, the thread of history was weakened but did not unravel. Fragments of good fortune could be connected to form a coherent vision that sustained religious faith. This vision depended on the absence of sense-denying nightmares. Jewish refugees heard little about the gas chambers during the anti-Japanese war. Most got news of their murdered kin only after they left China. In Shanghai, they evaded the dead bodies of native coolies and the foreign bombs and managed to continue to study Talmud, to edit newspapers, to perform plays in Yiddish.

Such daily miracles were not part of the life of Adrienne K. She had seen her parents and sister taken in front of her eyes; she knew the face and the name of the murderer. The time lag in her realization about the fate of her family was much shorter than that of Polish refugees like Rabbis Wainhaus and Schwartzman. As Adrienne K. recalls, hardened Kapos, Jewish women themselves, pointed to the smoke stacks and told her: "You see that smoke there? That is your families! There is your father."[42] The mind's effort to comprehend was frustrated in the concentration camps. Even after the war, even four decades after the nightmare, Auschwitz defeats all questions of meaning. When Dr. Laub asks Adrienne K. for an epilogue—some summing up thoughts, as he did with

Rabbi Wainhaus—the response is very different. The last few minutes on this tape are more somber, the voice of the witness softer as she circles a past emptied of all lessons: "I am ashamed that we were stupid . . . [that] we went like cattle to the slaughterhouse. I am ashamed that we were so naive."[43]

The interviewer tries to press beyond the worn metaphor of "cattle to the slaughterhouse." He confronts this fellow doctor directly: "You are a surgeon. . . . As you operate, does the past come back in your work?" The articulate witness stiffens, then a new flood of words comes forth:

> In my work, no. Not in my work. My work is completely different. The past is a nightmare. . . . Nothing hurts like it hurt forty years ago. . . . In one particular nightmare I am separated from my parents and my sister. My sister is crying for me and I cannot go to her. In my nightmare I always see her crying. . . . I still see her face as vividly as I have seen her. The other recurrent nightmare is related to hunger. I want to eat and I cannot find any food. . . . I am ashamed and sorry to tell you that I lead a normal, everyday life. I do two, three operations a day. In the evening I am glad to get my bones rested, and I am glad to be able to read medical journals.[44]

Recurrent nightmares and a willful separation between past and present is the epilogue provided by this survivor from Cluj. The sister cries on at night while the doctor continues to do surgery during the day. Medical journals are part of a boundary maintained with difficulty. There is no thread of continuity between day and night, no talk of miracles, though Adrienne K. also recalls odd instances of kindness from Germans, just like my father did. There is no effort to create some enduring framework of meaning.

Adrienne K. speaks about the hope that this testimony might forestall public forgetting. This is why she went to the first Gathering of Holocaust Survivors in Washington, D.C., in 1983—and took her daughter with her. She also took time for the video testimony (these early videos were the beginning of the Fortunoff Video Archive). Adrienne K. also testified against Dr. Kapezius in Frankfurt. Yet despite all these activities, the question of meaning remains. It cannot be forced into any resolution—not in public, not in words. Dr. Laub, who has also been through the nightmare, tries to press beyond the veil of facts. Earlier in the taped testimony, he asks Adrienne K. to describe her feelings on the cattle train that took her and her family out of Cluj: "You are so matter-of-fact. You are going to Auschwitz, and you are so matter-of-fact."[45] Here, the barrier holding back the past is challenged directly.

The witness freezes for a moment, then turns her head from the camera. The effort to regain perspective about a past that can never be shaped into meaning is written all over the stiff shoulders, the drawn mouth. Yet she goes on, answers the challenge: "I know these things. I never let myself forget it. And I am so matter of fact, I got used to it through the years, it's part of my life. I still have my nightmare. Every night, I see my parents. I still see my sister. . . . But I live with reality." [46] Nighttime questions and daytime reality are both given their due.

This tension between day and night is the inheritance of survivors deprived of miracles. Patterns of meaning embroidered with daytime reason do not hold up in the loss-ridden night. These are the "light passers-by." Sometimes they talk to their postwar children about relatives gone; sometimes they give testimony. Some may even have the opportunity to be witnesses in a German court. But the nine-year sentence given to Dr. Kapezius, the "meaning" accorded the victim's history after the war, can never answer the gaping questions of the recurring nightmare.

Back in Cluj in 1993, I also went looking for signs that mark the empty circle left by the deported Jews. I returned to the city of my birth asking questions about a history that had nothing to do with the bright memories of my childhood under the Communist regime. In the cemetery for Orthodox Jews, I found a monument: a large marble stone topped by a brass menorah. Under the menorah were two words in Yiddish and twelve lines in Romanian. The Yiddish reads Rif Zeyfa—an allusion to "Pure Soap." My guide, a man who lost his mother and sister in Auschwitz, tells me: "You know, people came back from the lager (concentration camps) carrying nothing but pieces of soap. That is all that was left of their relatives. Some of those pieces were collected and put underneath this stone." Certain historians, I know, argue that Jews were never made into soap by the Nazis. Maybe not, but Rif Zeyfa sticks on the tongue and in my mind. It points to the will to bring back something. A fragment of soap need not be one's mother or father or child, but it can be placed under stone markers and made somehow pure, even if never whole, again.

I am troubled by the discordance between the two Yiddish words and the longer commentary in Romanian that follows. The former refers to a deadly degradation that is now honored as martyrdom. The loquacious Romanian inscription, by contrast, rolls off the tongue smoothly: "This stone was erected on the symbolic grave of the Jewish martyrs from the city of Cluj who entered the ghetto in the year 1944 and were deported and exterminated by Fascist elements in the death camps. We will guard their memory forever." The wording here is not so different from other plaques one might find on monuments for national heroes. The menorah in the Cluj cemetery, at least, commemorates Jewish victims explicitly, unlike some other Holocaust monuments in formerly Communist countries like Poland, which point in vague terms to the victims of fascism.[47] This stone monument was designed by the Transylvanian artist Egon Lowith and reflects the complex compromise between public and private memory played out in Communist Romania after the war. The Yiddish words preserve a distinctively Jewish mourning. The Romanian explanation pulls the history of the ghetto into a larger national framework. A quotation by the French Communist poet Aragon at the entrance to the memorial plaza underscores the extent of the state's penetration into memorial practices. In the words of Mr. Weintraub, the head of the small community of Jews remaining in Cluj today: "In those days, we were more Communist than Jewish."[48]

The stone memorial in the Cluj cemetery has a life of its own, occupying a central place in all public ceremonies relating to the Holocaust. Originally, Mr. Lowith had conceived a more grand monument than the simple tablet with the menorah on top. But Dr. Moses Rosen, the chief rabbi of Romania, found it difficult to raise funds to commemorate a community that perished, officially, under the rule of a Hungarian government. So a tug and pull about Jewish history goes on after the war and in the post-Communist regime. Jewish memory, it seems, is still a contested piece of political currency. In a recent article about Jewish artists from northern Transylvania who died during the Holocaust, a Romanian scholar blames their fate on "the revanchist and revisionist interest and intentions of Hungary."[49] The author, Raul Sorban, seeks to charge current neighbors with crimes committed fifty years ago. In the political struggle between Romania and Hungary over Transylvania, Jewish victims are dragged in once again to buttress the claims of one side against the other.

No talk of "revanchist interests," however, will ever assuage the unremitting absence of the Jews in Cluj. Such political discourse does not soothe Adrienne K.'s nightly encounters with her missing sister and parents, nor does it answer my questions about Rozsi Braun or the other Vera. The enduring absence of my grandparents remains with me, and with my children.

Willy Mund is similarly marked by loss. He goes over the same fragment of remembrance and cannot complete his memoirs. In one poem called "Toprenges" (which in Hungarian means "soul turmoil"), he recalls the rooster feathers that adorned the cap of the policeman who came to round up Jews from the ghetto on March 3, 1944. Then, he describes the day his son turned six months old. Finally, Willy writes about June 6, the day he returned to the emptied ghetto to get the falsified news that all was well with those sent off in "hospital cars." In another poem, called simply "Marcika" (the Hungarian diminutive for his son's name), a father who cannot stop mourning his infant writes:

> My little son, I held you in my arms,
> Your small body racked by rough winds.
> I wanted to snatch you out of the throat of death,
> To save your young life . . .
> That day still grinds away at my soul
> Like a mill stone making flour.
> The ache of the past cuts through my body,
> The bitter memory still scorches my heart.[50]

For Willy Mund, to remain alive is to be subject to the grinding force of memory. Day and night the millstone turns, shaping the soul and softening the heart. To some, this going around and around the same subject may seem like emotional paralysis. But there is also something freeing about this attachment to remembrance. One day, one hour, one child, keeps cutting through to the present. All other days take shape around this circle of emptiness. Willy Mund had another family after the war. Now, having retired, he lives a full life of community service. All that is new and good in his postwar years shines with the added light of a past that will not fade.

This connection between grief and a vibrantly ailing heart comes through also in the poetry of Li Yu (937–978), the last ruler of the southern Tang dynasty. Born to great power, Li Yu might seem an unlikely link to Jews from Transylvania. Yet this Chinese ruler, too, became one of the "light passers-by." In 975, the capital city of Li's empire was sacked by the invading Song armies, and the self-indulgent, artistically accomplished ruler was taken captive. Away from the landscape of his youth and glory, the deposed ruler wrote some of the finest poems about memory in Chinese literature. As his natal world faded from view, he found ways to reevoke it lightly, as only one who is familiar with irreparable losses can:

> The past is fit only for grieving,
> Its traces rise up before me, hard to brush aside
> Autumn winds empty the courtyard, moss invades steps . . .
> No one comes all day.
> My golden sword lies buried deep in loss,
> My youth turned to weeds.[51]

An overgrown courtyard is all that endures in the mindscape of the former emperor. The poet approaches the moss-covered steps of the palace he once ruled with gnawing regret. It is remembrance that allows the autumn winds to sweep in a dark mood. The golden sword of power lies broken, left behind in the lost homeland. Li Yu did not defeat the invading armies (he died a captive after drinking the poisoned wine sent him by the new rulers on his fortieth birthday). Yet his poems preserve a kingdom that is no more. Recollection adds luster to the buried past and diminishes, somewhat, the victory of invading mosses. In the end, this may be memory's main achievement: to loosen the flow of grief.

SIX

The Master's Tears

Memory and the Healing of Historical Wounds

If you lose the past, the zither too laments.
And the Master's tears for the loss of the past
In those days fell streaming in torrents.
MENG JIAO, "AUTUMN MEDITATIONS"

The flow of grief does not return one to the past, because time has been broken. It is impossible to recover the fullness of life before our time. Li Yu understood this when he resorted to words instead of the golden sword of youth that lay buried in his lost kingdom. For my family, there was no such image to mark the site of loss. The mind goes over and over loose threads that are insufficient to weave a complete story. It is a great temptation to imagine that there is some restitution for what is irrevocably gone. But that comfort is not real—though survivors of the Holocaust like my parents have received German reparations for their suffering.

To remember is to come face-to-face with the gulf that divides us from the dead. That abyss may not be papered over either with money or with narratives about the meaning of history. All we can do is glance into the depths. Can this be called healing? Chinese and Jews who cling to recollection do not speak about remembrance in such medically uplifting terms. Instead, they accept the pain that memory brings and persist in its circuitous paths. Their aim is not to bring back the past but to mark its traces upon those living in the present.

One of those who registered these traces with great skill was Meng Jiao. Born in 751, he became one of the young men who joined the running-back-to-the-ancients faction. Meng Jiao, like the cantankerous poet-essayist Han Yu, rejected not only the style of his contemporaries but their faith in Buddhism as well. Drawn to Confucius, Meng used him as an exemplar of how to cherish a fragile connection to the ever-vanishing past. Unlike Han Yu, however, Meng Jiao never achieved a high official position.[1] He spent most of his life in poverty, living off friends and powerful patrons. His personal life was marked by the tragedy of his sons' death in infancy. Loss and bitterness added passion to Meng Jiao's "Autumn Meditations." These poems, composed in the early ninth century, reflected a literary tradition that sanctioned the use of one's later years for cultural introspection. But they went one step further: they became a dirge against the dangers of forgetting. Without the will to arch backward in time, Meng Jiao insists, "the sword snaps" and there is nothing left to defend in the present. Without an attachment to history, "the zither too laments," and sorrow becomes the sole inheritance of future generations.

Yet this promise of cultural renewal through remembrance is marred by tears. Neither the sword nor the zither soothes Meng Jiao for long. Instead, he dwells on China's loss of memory. Confucius (referred to in the poem simply as Master) was the first of many to weep over a weakening attachment to the ancients. Had Confucius been able to overcome the urge to look back, he might have become a tough-minded statesman dealing with dilemmas of his time. But he chose to grieve over amnesia. Over time, he became an emblem for those who refused the consolations of Old Lady Meng. After Confucius, the problem of Chinese memory grew more acute. How was traditional culture to strengthen a bond with the ancients if the Master himself had shed such copious tears? How were the fragile truths of personal recollection to imprint themselves upon the hard surface of public history? And, finally, how does the historian heal the wounds that memory leaves in its wake? Meng Jiao did not have the answers, but he dared to ask such questions.

The Burden of Memory

Remembrance enriches and revives us, but it also troubles us, by bringing us close to the contemplation of loss without consolation. For this very reason, China has a long tradition of ambivalence about the dark powers of memory. In particular, the Daoists, who valued a reflective state of mind, viewed memory as the root of all disquieting emotions. To be human was to be a sentient being who remembers. Yet to engage in recollection was to be in a state of inner flux. The third-century classic *Jinshu* summarized the paradox of memory: "Qing you yi sheng, bu yi ze wu qing."[2] No words in English can capture the condensed reservations expressed in nine simple characters. The first four summarize ancient psychology: emotion is born out of remembrance. The next five advise the wise to stem this process of arousal altogether: where there is no remembrance, emotion will dissolve as well. The point, simply put, is that distress causes memory. To be sure, it is human to have feelings, but this can be curbed by a willful quieting of the emotional upheaval caused by remembrance.

This reluctance to give in to the turmoil that memory stirs up is further amplified in the writings of Han Yu. He, too, shared the traditional assumption that human nature is best nourished through calming influences, even though he was on intimate terms with distressing emotions such as grief and sorrow. When a person loses calm and balance, Han Yu observes, the "tidal flow of the heart's blood" (xin xue lai chao) is unleashed—not infrequently in powerful and moving poems: "Whatsoever thing loses its calm and balance, is bound to make a noise. . . . The human voice, condensed and purified, becomes language, and literature is language further condensed and purified."³ Han Yu himself was a master noisemaker. A disgruntled conservative in matters of aesthetic taste, he poured his suffering into memorable poems and essays. Yet even this creative outlet did not prevent him from longing for a state of undisturbed harmony, before the billows of sorrow overcame the memoryless self. Through this longing, Han Yu partakes of the fatalism embedded in traditional Chinese psychology. He, too, assumes that strong emotions, especially pain and suffering, do little more than increase bitterness and rancor.⁴

Jewish tradition is similarly mindful of the burdensome feelings that come along with memory. Simcha, the Hebrew word for "joy," has as its root macha, meaning "to remove" or "wipe away."⁵ To be joyful, in this sense, is to be free of the tearful weight of the past. The Bible elaborates this vision, along with the numerous commandments to remember the Sabbath, the Exodus, the giving of Torah, and the attack of Amalek. In Isaiah 25:8, for example, the prophet promises the abolition of grief: "And the Lord will wipe tears from all faces." This image of faces unmarked by grief is not unlike the Chinese metaphor of a lake unrippled by the turmoil of painful memories.

In the end, however, neither Chinese nor Jewish rememberers settled for the peace of a memoryless world. The opposite of quietude can be found in the story of Lot's wife, in Genesis. Here, a woman who refuses to walk away from history is turned into salt—a concrete symbol of endless weeping. Lot's wife captures the need to remain connected to the past and dares to stand still when the known world is about to crumble. Although some might argue that Lot's wife looked back with nostalgic regret for past pleasures, Anna Akhmatova, in the poem "Lot's Wife," suggests she did so out of her refusal to become deaf to the grief embedded in the past:

> The just man followed then his angel guide
> Where he strode on the black highway, hulking and bright;
> But a wild grief in his wife's bosom cried,
> Look back, it is not too late for a last sight

. . . .

Who would waste tears upon her? Is she not
The least of our losses, this unhappy wife?
Yet my heart will not be forgot
Who, for a single glance, gave up her life.[6]

Here, Akhmatova laments Lot's wife in a way that echoes Meng Jiao's dirge for Confucius. She does not let the unhappy wife sink back into forgetting. The "just man" is Lot, who willingly walks away from disaster. Such righteousness does not appeal to a poet who witnessed so much grief and silence. She refuses to save herself through lack of weeping. Like Lot's wife, Akhmatova gave up her life under Stalin for the right to glance backward.

Elie Wiesel, like Akhmatova, is an inconsolable rememberer. In his early memoir of the Holocaust, Les Chants des morts, he makes his painful allegiance to Lot's wife amply apparent. Neither the biblical character nor Wiesel can turn away from the past. Like Lot's wife, he embraces the risk of endless grief. Furthermore, Wiesel argues, Jewish tradition demands that we turn back, to follow the model of the accursed wife: "Know where you come from, said the sages of Israel. It all depends on the inner attitude of the one who turns toward the point of origin. If it is out of intellectual curiosity, the quest turns you into an ornamental statue."[7] In this passage, Wiesel takes us back to the sages of Israel as well as to Han Yu. He lets us know that there is nothing inherently virtuous about turning to the past. If one cries to make a scene, to hear the sound of one's voice ripple across time, it is just emotional indulgence. Elaborate displays of feeling, like ornamental statues, are often ridiculous.

What matters, above all, is one's attitude in inaugurating the quest for historical memory. If it is done simply out of curiosity, the heart's blood is spilled in vain. If, on the other hand, the rememberer knows the responsibility that recollection brings—if the noisemaker does not disturb only to be noticed—then descent into grief is not in vain. Elie Wiesel has risked this descent over and over again. In his speech accepting the Nobel Prize, he summarized the emotional difficulties and moral urgency of remembrance: "It is memory that will save man from despair. Let's put it simply: hope without memory is like memory without hope. The opposite of the future is not the past but the forgetting of the past."[8]

Here we have a Jewish rebuttal to the Daoists' caution against remembrance. According to Wiesel, there is no way to be fully human except through the risk of remembrance. He does not deny the pain that memory brings in its wake, but he insists that without memory we drown in despair. The future cannot come toward us except through our openness to the past. Elie Wiesel insisted on this insight from Jewish tradition while speaking to a cosmopolitan audience in Oslo. The Nobel Prize speech is filled with concrete references to the Hebrew Bible and to remembrance. To be Jewish is to refuse the consolations of amnesia, no matter how restful it may be to adopt forgetfulness. Wiesel's appeal to the religious sanction for remembrance is not found in the works of Meng Jiao or Han Yu. Ardent Confucians, they sought to counter their contemporaries' religious interest in Buddhism with the ethical teachings of the ancient Chinese sages. Unable to draw upon a theology that transcends the natural universe, they could only weep for the loss of the past and (artfully) plea for a return to memory.

Jewish writers, by contrast, had the mandate of the commandments behind them. Primo Levi, for example, was not a religious Jew, yet he used the power of the Bible to demand attention to the memories of Holocaust survivors. His poem "Shema" starts out with the most fundamental religious practice: the affirmation of divine unity that Jews undertake each day and that Levi must have heard on the lips of the dying at Auschwitz. This central prayer insists that we be mindful of the role of providence in Jewish history while walking, lying down, waking up, or talking with our children, while at home or on the road. Levi uses this practice to bridge the gap between two widely disparate historical experiences:

> You who live secure
> In your warm houses,
>
> . . . .
> Consider that this has been:
> I commend these words to you.
> Engrave them on your hearts
>
> . . . .
> When you go to bed, when you rise:
> Repeat them to your children
>   Or may your house crumble,
>   Disease render you powerless,
>   Your offspring avert their faces from you.[9]

This poem was written in January 1946, barely one year after the end of the war. Levi's tone is as frantic as anything we read in Meng Jiao, but there is a religious urgency as well. The writer assumes a prophetic voice as opposed to the mournful cadence of the Confucian scholar ignored by Buddhist contemporaries. He calls up the specter of wholesale destruction—of toppled dwellings, diseased bodies, hateful children—unless his message is heard. Meng Jiao wept over broken swords and silent zithers. Primo Levi uses much harsher metaphors to call up the faces of those who labored in mud, who fought for a crust of bread, who were so disfigured as to seem neither man nor woman:

> With no more strength to remember.
> Eyes empty and womb cold.
> As a frog in winter.[10]

Since they had no strength to remember, we must. Since they could no longer cry, we must. Since they had no warmth, we must not take our homes for granted.

In this poem, Levi goes back to the language of Deuteronomy. When Moses reminds the Jewish people of what they heard at Sinai, he is not simply teaching a history lesson. He hopes that his words will scorch the memory of those about to enter the Land in the same way that the fiery voice from Mount Sinai engraved itself upon the hearts of their ancestors. In the Promised Land, as in our lives after the Holocaust, comfortable houses and friendly faces seem to prevail, yet we are called upon to look back and to become mindful of another sight: the survivor in the wintry landscape who cannot bring forth children from her womb—a woman like Rosita K. Primo Levi's "Shema" draws upon more theological sanctions than were available to Chinese rememberers like Meng Jiao. Instead of the zither's lamenting, the house crumbles. Nonetheless, the Jewish chemist and the Chinese scholar-official point in the same direction: to the powerlessness that comes as the aftermath of forgetting. Although yi (memory) brings up unsettling emotions, and simcha (joy) depends on wiping away old aches, remembrance remains the only way not to betray the past.

"We Must Drop the Methods of the Past"

This Chinese and Jewish commitment to remembrance runs against the grain of the modern Western notion that we move forward in time through the powers of reason alone. The Cartesian idea that the philosopher discovers all-important truths through solitary cogitation is the antithesis of the past embodied in the Master's tears. No wonder that the study of history (especially its darker side, where loss and trauma predominate) suffered neglect during the Enlightenment. This turning away from the past is at the heart of the work of Eugene Rosenstock-Husey, a modern historian who wrote an audacious work called *An Autobiography of Western Man*. Wrestling with the two World Wars, Rosenstock-Husey reconceived the historian's task. More specifically, he reinstated memory in a cultural climate that had little use for testimony by survivors: "We must drop the methods of the past. They were based on either physics or metaphysics. As a survivor, man smiles when realizing how narrowly he has escaped. This smile, unknown to the dogmatic idealist or the dogmatic materialist, twists the face because a human being has survived danger and therefore knows what matters. Humor illuminates the essentials. Our modern sciences, on the other hand, die from carloads of inessentials that are dumped daily on the student's brain. . . . The man who survives is starting, starting, starting."[11]

At first glance, Rosenstock-Husey seems to have little in common with Elie Wiesel and Meng Jiao. He appears to call for an emancipation from the "methods of the past," whereas they insist on the need to hold on to the past. He appears to treasure humor, whereas they are on intimate terms with tears. Beneath these differences, however, lies a shared distaste for "inessentials." As a professional historian, Rosenstock-Husey wants to shake up fellow practitioners of the science of history. He demands attention to memory in terms that neither physics nor metaphysics can grasp.

To listen to the voice of memory, as I discovered in my oral history project with Zhang Shenfu, does indeed require "starting, starting, starting." Little of what I knew about Chinese history prepared me for the chuckle of the octogenarian or the succinct expressions from classical Chinese with which he summarized his life in our conversations. In these talks, sometimes heavily veiled, sometimes less so, lay one survivor's effort to make sense of his life apart from the dictates of the Maoist revolution. Zhang Shenfu's rebellion against official historiography was never overt; he enjoyed his status as a marginal intellectual and proceeded to document that marginality in our conversations. The historiographical rebellion championed by Rosenstock-Husey in 1964, by contrast, was explicit. Yet both Zhang and Rosenstock-Husey confront historians with the problem of narrative: how to tell the story in a way that does justice to the fractured visions of our subjects? We can no longer assume that Clio will reveal her truths on the basis of so-called facts alone. History, after all, is the daughter of Mnemosyne—the mother muse who knows only too well the twists and detours of memory. The demand for rational explanations in history runs counter to the content of historical evidence. According to one feminist critic, Carolyn Steedman, Clio is nothing but a "blank-faced girl" who cannot tell us anything that we have not already told her in the first place. Steedman's point is that we must come to terms with our historicity before we can produce an explanatory narrative: "To imagine Clio in this way, as the blank-faced girl with nothing to say, is to recognize history as a form of cognition and a form of writing. . . . History cannot work as either cognition or written narrative without the assumption on the part of the writer and the reader that there is somewhere the great story that contains everything there is and ever has been—the jump of an electron from one orbital position to another, as well as the desolate battlefield, the ruined village." [12] Although the "great story" waits to be told, it exists nowhere in our evidence, be that electrons or the battlefield. To recognize history as an act of cognition is to come up against our ignorance as well as our embeddedness in the facts we seek. We are part of the story we chase. Ancient Greeks, having confronted the empty stare of Clio, understood that without the aid of memory history cannot but flee from ruined landscapes. Without Mnemosyne, Clio asserts a rather desolate dominion over the accumulating debris of past experience. The quest for systematic explanations is the modern approach to clearing up debris. We keep looking for the great story, because this scattering of bits troubles us. The prospect of having to remap our paradigms of narrative is distressing. Yet a historian who would venture into the realms of remembrance has no choice but to abandon the methods of the past.

This abandonment is the subject of *Waterland*, a novel by Graham Swift. In it he describes the dilemma of a historian who faces the difficulty of pressing beyond the accepted parameters of historical understanding: "So I began to look into history—not only the well-thumbed history of the wide world but also, indeed with particular zeal, into the history of my Fenland forebears. So I began to demand of history an Explanation. Only to uncover in this dedicated search more mysteries, more fantasticalities, more wonders and grounds for astonishment than I started with—not withstanding a devotion to the usefulness, to the educative power of my chosen discipline—that history is a yarn." [13] Swift is moving here from History as Subject to his own histories as an ever-puzzling mystery. He finds himself in this bewildering terrain by following the yarn of forebears. He lets old stories from long ago take hold of him. This is not easy at first, since he had hoped to find a more watertight explanation. But no string of historical words sufficed in this wilderness. Then, he looked for some edifying lessons. No golden nuggets were found in history, either. He is brought back, again and again, to Waterland—the slippery ground where memory dissolves all attempts at comprehensive reasoning.

In German I Do Not Exist

I, too, have begun to look into the history of my forebears. In this demand for an explanation, I have been sorely frustrated. Like Graham Swift, I am left to reckon with lacunae or, rather, to fill them with snippets that history discarded.

Even before I received Rabbi Schachter's letter from Yad Vashem, I knew there were no straight answers to my questions. The depth of the "fantasticalities," however, struck home much later. I had hoped that the study of Chinese history would set aside confusing mysteries and reveal some intelligible core of facts. Instead, my China studies only amplified the problem of narrative. The more I listened to the voices of intellectuals like Zhang Shenfu, the more difficult it became to weave a seamless web around their lives. To have attempted this would have been to mirror the Communist Party's strategy of assigning singular meaning (or, more often, de-meaning) to lives broken up by the Maoist revolution. The alternative to the seamless web is more difficult to fathom. My parents' memories provide some clues, but before I can pick up these threads, I have to confront the problem of reparations—a concrete way to seemingly give meaning to the past.

Both my parents participated in a process the German government called *Wiedergutmachung*—"making good again." The decision to grant reparations depends on the survivors' ability to produce a coherent, convincing narrative of their sufferings during the war. The "reward" for a well-told tale is monthly payments from Germany. The idea of making good again is troublesome to me. It connotes a recovery that I do not find in my parents' lives, in their memories, or in my own effort to come to terms with our family's losses. In a letter to Nadine Fresco some years ago, I even misspelled the German word to read *Widergutmachung*. It took the trained eye and historical sensitivity of this other daughter of survivors to point out my war *against* reparations—*wieder* meaning "again" or "in return," *wider* meaning "against" or "in opposition to." One missing vowel turned the word around from a seemingly healing award to a reminder of what cannot, will not, be made whole again. The gaps in our lives remain in spite of German payments. They are marked with bitter precision in Dan Pagis's poem "Draft of Reparations Agreement":

> Everything will be returned to its place,
> paragraph after paragraph.
> The scream back into the throat.
> The gold teeth back to the gums.
> Look, you will have your lives back,
> sit in the living room, read the evening paper.
> Here you are. Nothing is too late.[14]

Reparations, like the quest for an Explanation, repair nothing, least of all our injured understanding. True, Jews like my parents do sit in the living room and read the paper. And they do not scream any more. The terror that Dan Pagis evokes in his poem does not rule, especially in daylight. Their bodies are as if covered by new skin and bones. Life after the war has gone on. My own birth is proof of that normalcy. Yet something dark is also palpable at the edge of the circle of light. That darkness waits to be looked at—though it cannot be fully known. For many years I sought refuge from such shadows. But Meng Jiao, Han Yu, and Zhang Shenfu all pointed back to familiar dilemmas. Pagis's words— "Here you are. Nothing is too late"—are an apt description of this inevitable return.

My pathway back was suddenly quickened in the spring of 1993. I happened to take a few days to watch Adrienne K.'s testimony at the Yale Video Archives while my mother was visiting Connecticut. I asked her if she knew this surgeon's prominent family back in Cluj. My mother answered: "Of course. She even wrote a letter for me for my wiedergutmachung case." In the split second after this response, I realized that my parents' legal documents for the German government may contain the only "facts" I will ever have about our family history. Here may be found whatever bit of fractured truth I hope to gather. So I asked my mother to send me from Florida the complete reparations files, both hers and my father's.

To my surprise, she agreed. After a war that took the life of her parents, grandparents, first husband, and second child, my mother had preserved every piece of paper relating to reparations. Unlike my father, she had been rather taciturn about voicing memories, but she was scrupulous in collecting evidence relating to the legal case. After I received the large box, it took but a few minutes to locate the letter from Dr. Adrienne Matyas Krausz, dated January 11, 1972. In this letter my histories converge. The public tale of the Holocaust in Cluj and the silences surrounding my parents' experiences are all there. I am no longer watching a video at the Yale Library. In my own house, I read, in German:

> Mrs. Katherine Savin, a resident of 87–86 165th St. apt 508, Jamaica, New York, has been my patient since 1967.
>
> Mrs. Savin was 48 years old when she first consulted me for excruciating abdominal pain of crampy character, diarrhea alternating with constipation, malaise and low-grade temperature.
>
> Since no organic cause could be demonstrated, my firm opinion is that we are dealing with a psychosomatic type of spastic colitis that is strictly dependent on the patient's anxiety syndrome. . . . Surgery is not indicated since no organic changes can be demonstrated.[15]

No longer a voice on the screen, Adrienne K. is the internist who gives medical explanations for my mother's long-hidden "condition": the terms psychosomatic colitis and anxiety syndrome name something I had sensed earlier. I have, of course, known about my mother's spastic bowels, though the surgeon's terminology takes me aback. I also know that my parents had to collect a large medical dossier to justify their demand for reparations.

But I am not prepared for the waves of terror the dossier unleashes in me. What could possibly be made good again through these documents that catalogue loss? I recall the dread that the German word for reparations evoked in me the first time I heard it whispered between my parents. At the time I was a high school student preparing to go to an American college; I did not want to hear talk of the world we left behind in Europe. Yet this strange German word worked itself into my nightmares like the powerlessness that haunts Philip Gourevitch at the Holocaust Museum in Washington, D.C. Much later, it surfaced in a poem that raged against the injustice of being left out of the process of compensation. Not that I ever wanted the money from Germany. What I hated was being left out of the claim to loss, out of firsthand knowledge of our family's grief:

Their nightmares poison my day.
If I could wash the venom off
I would. But it has ground
Too deep into my bones.
If I could shout:
"I'm whole" I would.
But their broken lives
Make me ashamed of mine.
Last night, a dream outwit the shame;
A covered basket houses a snake,
An injured bird, no room for me . . .
I wake up whole, and rage
Against the crippled bird
Against memories not my-own.
This is an injury
For which there is no *Wiedergutmachung*
As yet.[16]

The nightmare of the snake and the bird draws me closer to Dan Pagis, into a strange territory of monstrous pain. Like Pagis, I am both angered by and at a loss in this terrain. Hence the bitterness of Pagis when he wrote his "Draft of a

Reparations Agreement." Although I still hate the word, I search my parents' wiedergutmachung documents for a way out of the embrace of the injured bird. I am no longer the child who asks to look into the covered basket. The bloody wings recede somewhat as my daytime eyes read Dr. Adrienne Matyas Krausz's letter about my mother's illnesses once again. I use these documents to make my own case against History.

History, in this case, is that version of my parents' lives that satisfies the German government's definition of "suffering," which has to be prepared in German for presentation to a German court of law. Some survivors refused to be part of this system after the war. Some do not qualify because they lack sufficient connections to German culture—a requirement both my parents meet amply because they were educated in German-language schools. There are official go-betweens for survivors who qualify and who want to pursue the reparations process. My parents' agent, a Hungarian-Jewish lawyer who lives in Berlin, orchestrated the collection of documents. He suggested where more suffering was needed and knew which doctors provided such documentation in New York. This lawyer then presented the materials to the German government and received a hefty percentage of the final settlement.

I know the parameters of this odd dance between survivors and the German government. Yet I scour the legal documents for missing facts. I inspect Dr. Krausz's letter for what it adds or changes about my mother's history. The medical terminology underscores the absence of organic causes for the pain in whose shadow I was born. The surgeon's letter points away from the knife to an anxiety syndrome. Thus labeled, my mother's grief almost dissolves in front of my eyes, swallowed by the medicalized vocabulary that transforms a sufferer into a victim. This is a metamorphosis that Arthur Kleinman, a fellow China scholar and psychiatrist, has been arguing against. His criticism of posttraumatic stress disorder (known as PTSD) helps me rethink the meaning of reparations: "We need to ask, . . . what kind of cultural process underpins the professional transformation of a normal sufferer to victim to someone with pathology? What does it mean to clothe those traumatized by political violence with the moral status of victim or patient?" [17] Kleinman's questions are a call to conscience. They are prompted by his work with survivors of the Cultural Revolution and by his concerns with the uses to which "disability" is being put in America.

I read this critique and readily see that my parents' documents are the creations of a "cultural process." It is obvious that part of the German government's goal is to clothe victims in the language of pathology. Still, some naked data come through the technical vocabulary. It is these discrete details that I now fasten upon as I go on to probe the extensive documentation provided by Dr. Conrad Mehler, director of the Lincoln Hospital Unit of the Bronx Psychiatric Center. The five documents that bear his title in my parents' folders are the longest, the most detailed, and the most unsettling parts of my family history.

I read and reread a document dated March 25, 1974, six single-spaced pages in German that attempt to summarize and analyze my father's trauma. The "facts" start straightforwardly enough with my father's birth in 1911, his German *Gymnasium* graduation in 1930, and his marriage to Rozsi Braun in 1940. Personal and world history begin to crosscut each other in 1942 when "the patient was, as a Jew, sent away to do forced labor." The details about my father's labor-camp experiences are crisper, more dramatic in this psychiatric document than in all the stories I had heard before: Gherla, Gomel, Nowioskol, Staryskol, Budyeni, Brianck, Winica, Lawoczne, Hutor Bondorowka, and Dorositz are all listed as camps to which my father was taken for forced labor. I had only heard about the first and the last. I had not matched my father's sicknesses to a chronology of the retreating Germans: "typhus in Staryskol, hospitalization in the military hospital at Dorositz" (where my father is described as suffering with high fever, unconscious and receiving insufficient care). "After several weeks, the hospital caught fire and many of the fleeing prisoners were shot to death by the SS to prevent the spreading of the epidemic." [18]

I read on, hungry for facts that seem to be present in abundance. On the second page, the psychiatrist describes my father's return to Klausenburg to search for his wife, his child, and other family members. "He learned, then, that his wife had been deported to the concentration camp in Auschwitz, with his little daughter Vera, and that they were killed there." [19]

My stomach twists, like a rag wrung dry. Is this the answer I have been looking for? So Vera did exist? This, then, was the name of my father's first child? I'm almost ready to stop reading because I have found what I sought for so long at Yad Vashem. But I read down the crowded German page, to the section that chronicles my parents' life after the war: "On the 23rd of November, 1946, he married his current wife and adopted her daughter, Marian, from her first marriage. This marriage remained otherwise childless." [20]

Something snaps inside me like a rubber band stretched too tautly. Only louder, more like Meng Jiao's sword that might wound your hand when it breaks in two. I am back in the night of dark fears described by Graham Swift. I came looking for an Explanation but am left with confusion and rage. Rozsi Braun had a "Vera," whereas I, the postwar "substitute," can't even be mentioned? I reread the German words and want to shout German accusations against my parents. How dare you describe the marriage as childless? What is the meaning of *kinderlos*? What do you mean I do not exist? I am here. You lived and loved after the war: I am the proof. Why must this be erased for the convenience of the German authorities? Have they not erased enough of our lives already?

Later, when the child's rage subsides somewhat, the historian in me takes another look at the German documents. My mother's native tongue is not the German she uses to address the court. My father's Gymnasium training did not prepare him to deliver his life up to the scrutiny of wiedergutmachung officials. He probably never heard of such business as a boy. Yet as a man, he had to translate what he went through and what he lost in terms They could understand, to deliver an explanation in terms They would pay for. The Jewish lawyers, surgeons, and psychiatrists who wrote this new History had to put it in words the German courts would find acceptable in keeping with their criteria of suffering. Kinderlos was one such word. In my hunger for explanation, I had mistaken it for a fact.

Dr. Conrad Mehler's letter of November 11, 1974, helps me understand my error. It summarizes my mother's syndrome in terms required by the German courts. For these authorities, it was not enough that my mother lost an infant daughter during the war. More vivid wounds than Agnes's birth certificate had to be produced. So the infant is made to die of starvation in my mother's arms rather than in a bombed-out Budapest ghetto. I read on, no longer arrested by this disparity in facts. I no longer read with Their eyes. Dr. Mehler's letter of November 1974 was written as a rebuttal to questions raised by a German doctor who evaluated my mother's case for wiedergutmachung. The German doctor asked, as I had earlier, how she could have married and worked as a bookkeeper after the war when she was supposed to have been sickened by it. Dr. Mehler takes on these questions directly: "Dr. Bucken reasons further in his assessment that the patient followed a completely normal life path after the end of the persecution. Missing here is the *break in the lifeline*, which is characteristic for intense persecution-contingent psycho-reactive disorder conditions. Now Dr. Bucken seems to forget that Mrs. Savin did, after all, lose her husband, both her parents, and her child during the period of persecution and that she never recovered from the loss of these next of kin." [21] Here are the bare bones of whatever truth memory has to offer. I have added emphasis to "break in the lifeline" because that is the only kernel I truly understand from all the complex medical and legal analysis. This is the simple fact that I know to be true in my bones. Dr. Mehler, the Jewish doctor, reminds the German court what the German doctor seems to forget: that my mother lost four of the people that mattered most to her. Yes, she was able to love and live and work after the war, but the break in the lifeline endured. It is the break, not the line, that has to be understood. This is memory's job. There is no reparation possible for this break. The idea of wiedergutmachung is obscene if taken literally. Memory can repair, however, by mapping the divided self and healing the wounds that come from denying the breach.

Vehicles of Grief

Mother tongues that have grown sour with the passage of time are one vehicle of memory repair. This means of bridging broken time is not available to those who cling to the sweet cadence of early youth. The Yiddish term for mother tongue, mama loschen, suggests warmth and continuity—words used to hush a whimpering child on the verge of crying. But once the night has been pierced by the cry of an infant who has not been cradled or cannot be protected from the ravage of history—like my sister Agnes—the mother tongue is no longer sweet. It becomes, in the words of Nadine Fresco, a "guttural tongue." [22] Fresco's parents, like mine, used to speak German to each other whenever they wanted to protect their children's ears. But children's ears are finely tuned to secrets, especially those that cannot be spoken. So Fresco grew up both drawn to and suspicious of her German Muttersprache.

This strange predicament is familiar to those who were forced to leave their native lands. All exiles carry within them a seed of home that will not flower because the ground is forever missing. Exiles from history suffer no less than those exiled from land. In both cases, homecoming is a longing that can never be fully assuaged. The pain caused by this distance from home led Johannes Hofer, a Swiss doctor, to coin the word "nostalgia." In his 1688 work Medical Dissertation on Nostalgia, Hofer combined the words algos (pain) and nostos (return home) to describe a malady that admits no remedy other than a return to a fatherland that remains forever inaccessible. [23] This longing for a lost home is, according to Fresco, the common affliction of those of us who were born after the war. The term "second generation" does not explain what causes us to mourn (sometimes knowingly, more often unknowingly) for siblings, parents, and grandparents lost in the Shoah. Second suggests a generation of augmented possibilities. I am second after my parents, second after Agnes, yet no more complete for having been born after the war. We are, in Fresco's words, "like amputees who lost a hand they never had. A ghostly sorrow takes the place of memory." [24]

This ghostly sorrow, I believe, is our only gateway to memory. Yet it is not ours alone. Such sorrow also permeates the work of Yu Guangzhong, who now lives in Taiwan. Yu writes a great deal about the pain that comes from losing a part of his natal ground, the Chinese mainland whose reality can be mapped only in the longing to return. Even when physical access to home is once again made possible (as it was for many Chinese after the death of Mao Zedong in 1976), homecoming is still denied. An awareness of broken time is at the heart of Yu Guangzhong's poem "Nostalgia":

> When I was small,
> Nostalgia was a tiny postage stamp,
> I, on this side,
> My mother, on the other.
>
> . . . .
>
> Later on,
> Nostalgia was a low tomb,
> I, outside.
> My mother, inside.
> And now,
> Nostalgia is the coastline, a shallow strait.
> I, on this side,
> Of the mainland.[25]

The Chinese expression for "nostalgia" is *xiangchou*, literally "village sadness." More concretely than Johannes Hofer's phrase for the "pain of return," xiangchou describes the grief that accompanies the traveler who cannot find a way back to the home village. Nostalgia, for Yu Guangzhong, is not a geographical predicament but a spiritual state of being. First he finds himself outside the mother as a tiny emblem of apartness, then he is the man who contemplates her tomb. The shallow waters of the Taiwan straits are, similarly, not only a spatial divide between the island and the mainland but a reminder of the longing for, and the impossibility of going back to, ancestral roots.

This state of suspended animation is also familiar to Qian Zhongshu, a well-known literary scholar from the Chinese mainland. Qian, a student of Zhang Shenfu on the eve of the Sino-Japanese war, became a prominent victim of the Cultural Revolution and, along with his wife, Yang Jiang, was sent down to forced labor in the countryside. A broken but unrepentant old man, he dared to write about the shame of tacit collaboration when others sought to recall only the victimization of the 1960s. Qian Zhongshu's willingness to explore the unsettling past also comes through in an essay titled "Poetry As a Vehicle of Grief." Delivered as a lecture in Japan, this work suggests that *yuan*, or grief, is the source of China's most powerful aesthetic expressions. Qian himself is on intimate terms with this troubling emotion. Yet, in the opening words of the talk he describes his predicament as a survivor-rememberer in muted terms. He likens himself to a man who cannot find a house with sheltering eaves, so he must content himself with "spreading a cloth on the tip of a stick." [26] Homelessness and an umbrella made of scraps is all that accompany this seasoned critic as he reflects on the poetry of sorrow. An improvised shelter of words is all that is left for those betrayed by the mother tongue.

Qian Zhongshu did not go to Japan to catalogue his own losses but rather to speak about the depths of literary expression achieved by other Chinese who have suffered from history. The title of Qian's address in Kyoto is drawn from the Confucian *Analects*. In this work, the ancient Sage suggests that poetry has several functions, one of them being to convey sorrow: "Shi ke yuan" (Poetry may be used to grieve). The word *yuan*, however, does not connote merely "grief" and "sorrow" but has the added edge of "rancor" and "grudge." Qian Zhongshu, the man who has refused to be rancorous in public about his suffering during the Cultural Revolution (even in the preface to his wife's memoir about their years of persecution in the countryside), managed nonetheless to convey the complex mind-set of those racked by pain.

Away from his native land, through the roundabout route of literary criticism, he crafted insight out of pain. Qian makes use of his personal experience with the disturbances of history to clarify the sorrow of others. Foremost among the predecessors thus illuminated are Sima Qian, the historian-eunuch of the Han dynasty, and Han Yu, the Tang dynasty poet-official-essayist who wrote about the noise of disturbing emotions. By situating himself in a lineage of men literally and figuratively deformed by history, Qian Zhongshu shows how grief need not lead to rancor. Instead, through the alchemy of poetry, it can become something meaningful as well as beautiful: "a pearl bred by the sickness of the oyster." [27] This metaphor is intended to draw attention to the disquiet bred by the memory process. Like Cynthia Ozick, who sickened the doctors when asked to speak about memory and metaphor, Qian Zhongshu went to Japan to talk about a Chinese illness. The ability to craft beauty out of grief, however, is not reserved for Chinese writers alone. They, like Jewish rememberers, have only had a longer time span to get used to the predicament of history. [28]

Lot's wife, too, suffered from and increased the disquiet of those around her. Like Han Yu, she stirred up trouble by refusing to look away from the past. She became a rememberer and paid the price by turning into salt—the stuff of tears. In this sense, Lot's wife is a kindred spirit of Chinese poets who cherished the tears of the ancient masters. They share a common belief: to refuse memory's claim is to court disaster in the future. This intuition about recollection and sorrow is borne out by the burden that weighs on China after the shootings of 1989. Bodies of the victims could not be claimed, counted, or mourned. Unappeased at home, grief found its outlet elsewhere. For Fu Hao, some solace came from the burning words of Yehuda Amichai. For a group of Chinese artists who managed to go abroad, mourning could be enacted on the stage of the La MaMa theater in New York. One year after the tanks ran over students' tents in Tiananmen Square, a Chinese dancer battles a rope on the stage of La MaMa. This small, congested sanctuary for experimental art becomes a sheltering place for Chinese memory—a place where its "pearls" can be harvested more readily. Artists who, literally, cannot go home again put on a performance entitled: "Threshold: A Dance Theater of Remembering and Forgetting."

From the balcony of the darkened room, the husky voice of a Chinese woman reads in halting English: "We are born into history. This is an attempt to escape it. . . . What I forget comes back to me in dreams. Cuts me open like a knife. . . . Mother? Motherland? Comrade." [29] While the staccato voice both draws near and flees from the memory of the Chinese mainland, the young man wars with a crimson rope on center stage. He is trying to make his way to a distant door, to cross its freedom-promising threshold. He tries to cut memory's umbilical cord, to be born anew, but he collapses on the way to emancipation. The young man is left embracing an unbreakable tie—the history that cannot be forgotten and the dreams that cut like knives.

Away from China, where comrades murdered students trying to show love for the motherland, these Chinese artists probe the meanings of cultural identity. Exiled from their country, they pass beyond the fixed borders of inherited knowledge in search of new (and dangerous) insights about the maternal world left behind. [30] At "home" in China, remembrance is controlled by political authorities. Abroad, it is free to acknowledge those killed in Tiananmen Square. It may cry out with the wounded voice of nostalgia, of the xiangchou so familiar to Yu Guangzhong. Away from Beijing, memory becomes an opportunity for self-becoming. In New York, the revolt against the masters of forgetting can be enacted more openly.

Homecoming is possible only after recollection makes room for irreparable loss. The Chinese artists in New York show this solace by pointing to the one place of solitude still sanctioned on the mainland: the privy. On the stage of La MaMa, the Chinese dancer struggles to get into and stay in a cramped bathroom. The voice on the loudspeaker cries out: "I love the toilet! . . . It is the only place to be private. I love the toilet, especially when there is no toilet paper. Then, you can use anything at hand. Old history books are best!"[31] Like the rope of cultural connectedness that cannot be uncoiled, the toilet of privacy cannot contain the wish to be rid of history. There is trouble here: the Chinese artists' toilet backs up with debris from the past. Far from the heart of the Chinese political world in Beijing, young artists are calling the mother country to task. Their "Threshold" transgresses the bounds of permissible memory at home. By performing a "Dance Theater of Remembering and Forgetting" about the events of 1989, they expand the meanings of history. They change, in effect, the lessons that history would teach them at home.

The Historian as Physician

The lessons of history are more mutable at the periphery of the Chinese cultural world than at its center. A dance performance about remembering in New York can challenge, though not quite dislodge, the forgetting being institutionalized in Beijing. The Chinese government's strategy of political reeducation following the shootings of June 4 was meant to enforce forgetting about the true purpose of the student movement for reform. "Memory is a fragile thing," reported Elizabeth F. Loftus, a professor of psychology who researched Chinese methods of promoting amnesia after 1989. According to this American scholar, the Chinese people who were forced to repeat lies about the events of 1989 became more and more vulnerable following June 4: "All the right psychological ingredients are in place for the lie to become truth . . . reason for us to view the future of memories of Tiananmen Square with pessimism."[32]

Yet this psychologist's pessimism turned out to be premature. Loftus, reporting to the American Psychological Association two months after the crackdown in Beijing, focused on the harsh measures that were being imposed on the population in the capital. But a historian can see that strategies for enforcing amnesia have been far from effective. Each year when June 4 nears, "protective measures" are enacted to make sure no commemorations of the student movement take place in Tiananmen Square. Beyond the large chunk of pavement the government controls, the policy of repression is even less effective. Since 1989, poems, memoirs, and collections of documents about the events of that year have been pouring out of China. Published abroad for the most part, these materials invariably find their way back home, where they continue to disturb the "peace" of forgetting that Loftus worried about in August 1989.

The future of memory is, I believe, far from bleak on the Chinese mainland. But questions about its authorship remain: Who will design the parameters of public remembrance? How will personal meaning be extracted from officially mandated histories? Might China become so flooded by memoirs of 1989 that it will become more difficult to reflect on other, less dramatic events? Charles S. Maier, a historian of German and Jewish culture, has recently drawn attention to what he calls the problem of "surfeit memory." [33] Maier believes that modern society is in danger of an addiction to memory at the cost of political action: "Let me summarize the political argument: the surfeit of memory is a sign not of political confidence but of retreat from transformative politics. It testifies to a loss of a future orientation, of progress toward civic enfranchisement and growing equality. It reflects a new focus on narrow ethnicity. . . . I believe that when we turn to memory it should be to retrieve the object of memory, not just to enjoy the sweetness of melancholy." [34] Maier's point here is that remembrance has a tense relationship to action. He argues that the more we recall our special moments—be they tragic or triumphant—the less likely we will be to assume an active role in civic affairs.

This argument, however, rests on a problematic assumption: that memory is a retrievable object. It is as if the rememberer (either an individual or a community) sent a pack of hunting hounds back to the past. Driven by the scent of melancholy, they carry back to us something concrete and tasty. But is this really the case? Does not memory disintegrate in our hands whenever we want to hold on tight, whenever authorities try to squeeze it for political messages about "civic enfranchisement"? To be sure, some of the ways in which Chinese and Jewish memory is being regathered in our time does reinforce ethnicity, but this quest is not motivated by the "sweetness of melancholia." When Yu Guangzhong writes about his mother or graves or barbed wire, he is not enacting a retreat from transformative politics. Rather, he is dissecting the bitterness of loss and of the knowledge that homecoming is forever denied. Yu's metaphors do not allow for a purposive vision of memory—there is no object to retrieve, nothing to rescue or bring back whole from the past. Instead, we read about a dissecting loss. The young artists at La MaMa, inspired by Yu Guangzhong, talk about knives that cut one open.

If remembrance cannot be charged with the mission of retrieval, then it must have another potential—perhaps one that can be couched in medical metaphors. Rosenstock-Husey's work probes the mission of the historian in precisely these terms. Although he does not deal with recent happenings in China or the proliferation of Holocaust memoirs in the Jewish world, he points out what can be done to counteract amnesia in the modern West. His recommendation is nothing short of a total redefinition of the historian's task. Far from being a collector of facts, he or she (though Rosenstock-Husey always refers to the historian as "him") must now become a "physician of memory": "It is his honor to heal the wounds, genuine wounds. As a physician must act, regardless of medical theories, because his patient is ill. So a historian must act under a moral pressure to restore a nation's memory, and that of mankind. Buried instincts, repressed fears, painful scars come for treatment to the historian."[35]

Rosenstock-Husey's call to conscience places great responsibility on the historian. To be sure, "the patient is ill" not only in China, where strategies for forgetting are applied rather nakedly, but also in most of the Western world. Yet this diagnosis does not explain the further assumption: that the historian is capable of healing the wounds of forgetting. Nothing in the *Autobiography of Western Man* justifies this faith in recuperative powers of historical analysis. Nor does the history of historians' own entanglement in public forgetting warrant the claim that they can be safely trusted to deal with the treatment of "buried instincts" or "repressed fears." Arthur Schlesinger deflated this hope when he wrote: "Too often it is those who can remember the past who are condemned to repeat it."[36]

In other words, the historian is as sick as the society whose memory he or she seeks to cure. Whatever the mission, the historian is ill served by outworn notions of medical healing. Even Freud, the first doctor to try to actually become a physician of memory, was more modest than Rosenstock-Husey about his ability to restore the memory of humanity. Precisely because he spent most of his life researching buried instincts, repressed fears, and painful scars—both in the individual patients he analyzed and in the social crises that dominated his later years (spent in the shadow of rising Nazism)—Freud was cautious about the nature of healing through memory.

In his essay "Remembering, Repeating, and Working Through," Freud directly addresses the problem of recovering forgotten events. The goal of psychoanalysis, according to Freud, is to fill in gaps of memory. The transformation thus effected will, in Freud's view, enable the patient to move beyond forgetful repetition: "The patient does not remember anything of what he has forgotten and repressed, but acts it out. He reproduces it not as a memory but as an action; he repeats it, without, of course, knowing that he repeats it."[37] Freud the doctor, like Rosenstock-Husey the historian, is concerned with freedom from repetition. For both theoreticians, remembering is key to the emancipation from an endless acting out of the nightmares of history. Psychoanalysis tries to effect such liberation on the individual level, and sometimes succeeds. Historians' works, by contrast, rarely penetrate the layers of the collective unconscious to the point of arresting the process of repetition.[38] If the cycle of memory and repetition goes on, as Arthur Schlesinger warned, what may be an even more modest metaphor for the historian's task?

If the historian is neither hound nor physician, perhaps she is simply a cartographer. If healing the wounds of forgetting is an impossible task, the historian may map the traces that amnesia leaves on the bodies and spirits of those whose words cannot be heard, or spoken. Doctors and poets working with patients traumatized by history offer some guidance to the historian here. They know, as Dori Laub puts it, "the feelings of absence, of rupture, and of loss of representation that is the daily diet of survivors."[39]

Similarly, Arthur Kleinman and Joan Kleinman (working with Chinese survivors of the Cultural Revolution) have described the process through which social narratives penetrate and break down the individual. In an essay entitled "How Bodies Remember," they point out how enforced forgetting translates into personal dizziness, exhaustion, and pain: "To be dizzy (or vertiginous, Chinese patients do not make a distinction between the two) is to be unbalanced, to experience malaise, to be diseased. . . . To experience dizziness is to live and relive the memory of trauma."[40] The Kleinmans' work takes seriously both the testimony of Chinese victims and the cultural traditions that frame their experience. They draw upon classical Chinese medicine and philosophy to understand the process through which Chinese patients somatize their memories of historical trauma: "Fatigue and weakness in traditional Chinese medical theory express loss or blockage in the flow of qi (vital energy). Devitalization is understood to affect the body-self and the network of connections (guanxi wang), the microscopic local world and the macroscopic society."[41] The body, in this context, does not represent suffering but conveys it in living form.

This connection between the body and the remembered past is also manifested in the life of Sima Qian, the historian of the Han dynasty. By choosing the shame of castration, he gained time to finish his comprehensive work on history. This exorbitant sacrifice made cultural memory all the more problematic for Sima Qian's successors. The Grand Historian himself found courage for his choice in the belief that the well-being of future generations depends on the density of their connection to the past. The historian, according to Sima Qian, should aim "to console the dead for their sorrows" and "to instruct the living and the unborn."[42] Even with these lofty goals in mind, Sima Qian limited himself to recording carefully the variety of human characters and actions embodied in actual events. To "console the dead" was, after all, the starting point of moral responsibility. By taking on this duty, Sima Qian acted wholly in keeping with the Chinese practice of ancestor worship.

In a very different religious context, lingering alongside the dead is also the goal of Jewish memory. Rabbi Carmilly-Weinberger, editor of the Memorial Book about the Holocaust in Cluj, describes this as his main purpose. This work is similar in tone and style to the yizkhor books published after the war. Each seeks to memorialize a specific community, to bring back some specificity, if not consolation, to the dead who have no graves.[43] Written by survivors, the Cluj/ Kolosvar/Klausenburg memorial book shares this mission. Yet it also speaks in a distinctive voice, most apparent in Carmilly-Weinberger's introduction, entitled "God Also Cried." This essay seeks to reach out to all generations of Jews: "to those of you who are here today . . . and to those who are yet to come."[44]

Sima Qian's commitment to the dead takes on an added religious dimension here not only because the author is an observant Jew but also because the lessons of this history are so full of dread. To approach his terrible subject, Carmilly-Weinberger uses both Transylvanian geography and ancient Greek mythology. In a cartography of grief devoid of the healing promises made by other historians, he retells the story of "Killer Lake," the body of water near Cluj created long ago by volcanic forces. In 1944, this name took a literal significance as Cluj became the site of mass extermination. Carmilly-Weinberger conjures up the image of the murderous lake along with that of Medea, who tried to collect the pieces of her butchered children. He uses these mythic props to frame his own effort to piece together the history of Transylvanian Jews. With the aid of these metaphors, the editor of the Cluj Yizkhor book finally enters the city of his nightmares:

> May 1944, when everything was falling apart in Hungary, when you could hear Russian guns in the Carpathian Mountains, our enemies had the heart to drag away 600,000 Jews from Transylvania and make ashes out of them. Then, the tears in God's eyes became a flood because the fumes from the ovens of Auschwitz had blackened the skies. . . . In Pata Street there were fewer and fewer children who learned the Bible. Instead of Jewish songs, the flies were buzzing around empty bottles of beer. In our destroyed temples, drunken soldiers were singing and dancing. The Tablets of the Covenant were destroyed. The words "Do Not Kill" and "Do Not Rob" no longer troubled the soul. Yet, later, when they saw Jews coming back like skeletons they were frightened and wondered:

"Are there Jews still left in the world?" Yes, there are and will continue to be Jews—my brethren who remember.[45]

Here, the remembered past claws its way back across time. The author's aim is to make sure that we are not immune to the memory of those taken from us. Care is taken to name an exact place, Pata Street, to point to the absence of children. Although God's tears may seem abstract, the degradation of 600,000 is not. To further this concretization, the Cluj Memorial Book was printed in three languages—Hungarian, English, and Hebrew: "In Hungarian, because we are bidding farewell to our Hungarian past, whose sorrows and oppression outweighed joy for us. In English, because the world should know about the massive anti-semitism that prevailed and took the lives of Jews in Transylvania. In Hebrew, because we want to weave together the past of the Jews from Transylvania with future generations in Israel."[46]

I am addressed in all three tongues. I no longer avoid looking into the black hole of my birth town. I listen more alertly to the voice of Sima Qian, the emasculated historian who also wanted to console the dead and guide the unborn. The broken and frenzied voices of Chinese and Jewish survivors remind me that the historian is no omnipotent healer of wounds. The recovery of memory is a modest undertaking. We can only turn on a bit of light in dark corners where fears have plenty of reason to grow. To remember is not to become well or whole again. It is, as Maya Angelou put it so well in her 1993 inaugural poem, simply the hope that we may not have to shed the same tears over and over again:

History, despite its wrenching pain,
Cannot be unlived, but if faced
With courage, need not be lived again.[47]

Not to repeat the past is the only hope memory imparts to those who heed her voice. The wrenching ache that Maya Angelou speaks about is intimately familiar to both Jewish and Chinese rememberers. They keep on taking the risk of historical knowledge—not because it is a glorious or healing undertaking but because it is their only way of being fully human. Old Lady Meng may be handing out the broth of oblivion, but they keep on crossing the Bridge of Pain unaided by her potion. Their fears have little to do with the two demons of Buddhist folklore: Life-Is-Not-Long and Death-Is-Near. Instead, Chinese and Jewish guardians of memory worry about finding words for the darkness they've seen.

Conclusion

And If There Was No Bridge?

Now we see more symbols, more
words. Some of us stand
in the middle of the traffic
screaming: THERE IS NO BRIDGE!
ANDREI CODRESCU, "FRANCHISING THE FIGHT"

ndrei Codrescu, my compatriot from Transylvania, does not lack the courage to cross the bridge of pain. A poet who has traveled across several language worlds, he is troubled by mere symbols. His need to shout "There is no bridge" comes from a quarrel with empty words. Codrescu and I share a heritage of being uprooted from both language and native land. Back in Romania, we both had to set aside our particular histories. Codrescu was born Perlmutter, a Jew like me. He changed his name in order to be able to publish poems in Communist Romania. My father also changed his name from Schwarcz to Savin under pressure from the party. To survive in Transylvania in the 1950s, one had no choice but to acquiesce to the dominion of symbols over reality. As a result, the urge to reconnect world and word surfaces more strongly abroad.

But the connection is never perfect. Codrescu's work outlines the gap that continues even when the poet is far from the mother tongue. In an essay entitled "Notes of an Alien Son," he describes the predicament of being a stranger to both words and worlds. Alienness, here, is a state of mind quite distinct from that of the refugee. Codrescu attributes the latter status to his Jewish mother, while choosing the outlook of an exile for himself: "If someone had asked my mother in the mid-sixties if she was a political refugee, she would have said 'Of course.' But privately she would have scoffed at the idea. She was an economic refugee, a warrior in quest of Wal-Mart. In Romania she had been trained at battling lines for every necessity. In America, at last, her skills would become handy. Alas. But if somebody had asked me, I would have said: 'I am a planetary refugee, a professional refugee, a permanent exile.'" [1] The son who decodes his mother's memories is familiar to me. It is so easy for those of us born after the war to see our parents as economic warriors. It is even fun, at times, to focus on their skills at shoving to the front of the bread line or the meat line or the line for tickets to a vacation—pushy Jews held back by silly Communist egalitarianism. If we can paint them as warriors in the economics of survival, we are free to be broad-minded cosmopolitans. The burden of a specific history falls from our shoulders, and we can then play the role of planetary refugees, a role that once tempted me as well. Chinese history, too, seemed to offer some relief from Wal-Mart warriors.

When I went to live in China, however, the lessons learned in Romania took on new significance. True, many people in Beijing, Shanghai, and Canton would barter their cultural inheritance to get a bit more of our Wal-Mart benefits. But it was in China, as well, that I learned to see beyond the scramble for survival. Chinese friends who have endured, and outlasted, a system bent upon reducing them to "class enemies" allowed me to reclaim my parents' history. It was in China, too, that I came to appreciate ren, the ideogram for "endurance" represented by a heart beneath the cutting edge of the knife.[2] Ren is key both to remembrance and to survival in Chinese culture. This source of personal and cultural continuity is less visible than the economic gains of the past decade. Nonetheless, it can be discovered provided one is willing to follow a circuitous path.

This path through mere words troubles Andrei Codrescu. Remembrance is not an alternative to simple speech but a constant wrestling with its limitations. The Transylvanian poet who left behind his mother's world, including the enforced Jewishness that was part of anti-Semitism back home, issues warnings about the bridge ahead. I am a historian who cannot but build bridges.

The Chinese and Jewish rememberers brought together in this book are separated by language as well as religious and historical differences. The disparity between world and word perceived so acutely by Codrescu exists in both Chinese and Jewish culture. Poet-survivors like Paul Celan (the Czernowitz-born Jew who wrote poems in German after the war) and Bei Dao (the former Red Guard who calls himself "Northern Island") inhabit worlds in which words have lost the power to heal. Can such disparate voices ever be woven together? Perhaps Codrescu is right. Perhaps there is no bridge.

Yet I believe that the French essayist André Neher is closer to the truth when he dwells on Shaddai, the God of the broken arch.[3] Neher witnessed the Nazi atrocities in France and cannot claim the luxury of distance from native worlds. Before the Shoah, according to Neher, everyday speech, like that of Abraham and Ruth and Job, was put to the test, placed at dangerous crossings. Yet words, like the biblical heroes, overcame the risks: "The man left out on these bridges risks dizziness, certainly in sizing up the silent and obscure depths over which he makes his way. But he risks neither life nor destiny, for Another keeps watch over the two ends of the bridge, firmly anchored in solid ground. And the man sent out will reach his destination and will hear the Other say to him, 'Here I am!' " [4] The reassurance that another will hear and meet us along the way withered during the Holocaust. Too many interlocutors turned a deaf ear. Adrienne Krausz, talking to her father's business partner, Dr. Kapezius, on the platform at Auschwitz, heard this deafening silence. When the possibility of human dialogue is cut off, one is left lonelier than ever before. Remembrance brings no relief from the predicament of words severed. It points to, but cannot repair, the broken arch.

Memory Matters

In trying to bridge disparate Chinese and Jewish memorial experiences, I am especially mindful of broken arches. Yet I persist in this project because memory matters; it is the cord that attaches hope to despair. To continue to explore various layers of remembrance, we must gain access to what historian Jacques Le Goff describes as "connectors" to worlds gone by. Le Goff has embraced the study of memory because it promises not only to repair our relationship to the past but also to "democratize" it: "It is incumbent upon professional specialists in memory . . . to make of the struggle for the democratization of social memory one of the primary imperatives of their scientific objectivity. . . . Memory, on which history draws and which nourishes in turn, seeks to save the past in order to serve the present and the future. Let us act in such a way that collective memory may serve the liberation and not the enslavement of human beings." [5] Le Goff's work summarizes several decades of research on the various manifestations of social memory. Titled *History and Memory*, this book is not addressed to historians alone but is meant to inspire the work of anthropologists, sociologists, and journalists as well. Although I am sympathetic to Le Goff's appeal, I do not see myself as a memory specialist. I am not sure that collective memory (even if enlivened by non-elite voices) can live up to the grand project of "scientific objectivity" or the "liberation of human beings." My materials are too fragmentary to allow for such an encompassing goal. Most of the time, they defy purposive inquiry altogether. To hear the voice of Adrienne K. or of Zhang Xianliang (the author of *Getting Used to Dying*) requires a redefinition of the historian's task. To be sure, I have no quarrel with Le Goff's assertion that memory is the primary source for our sense of history. But I find that I must keep on redefining what history means if I am to do justice to the actual voices of rememberers I meet.

Far from being liberating, memory seeks to arrest us in our flight toward the present moment. It would be such a relief to be done with the past, or better yet, be headed for the future with a confidence unburdened by the details of sorrows gone by. But memory won't leave us alone. It catches up to us, often in some grief we cannot shake or in a flurry of images that come to us whenever memory breaks through the curtain of necessary amnesia. These ruptures in the dominion of the present are the subject of Jean-Philippe Antoine's psychological study of the art of memory. Unlike Le Goff, Antoine is not taken by the democratizing potential of his subject. Instead of broad calls for the liberation of all human beings, he focuses on discrete strategies that remembrance uses to make us hear her voice, which is anything but grandiose. Precisely because forgetting is so pervasive, and so seemingly salutary, memory comes to us as an afterthought. Yet as Antoine makes clear, this is an afterthought that helps us map our place in the world: "The art of memory accepts as valid elements for the building of images, materials that would be rejected from other types of language. . . . If the art of memory is not a mere antiquarian's curio and deserves to be studied on its own ground, the balance between what it has to say about the economics of the soul and what belongs to a particular episode in cultural history is a delicate one." [6] Antoine, unlike professional specialists in memory, is willing to explore the inchoate spaces of cultural life. He is not afraid of absurdity, low taste, or lack of relevance in his search for the process of figuration that is the art of memory. He is not embarrassed to talk about the "economics of the soul," which is also what concerns me in this book about Chinese and Jewish memory. The balance between individual and cultural history is always difficult to maintain, especially when the voices of cultural recollection are varied. This balancing act depends on odd materials, like poetry, that are frequently rejected when historians are tempted to elaborate encompassing explanations of past events.

Odd materials are strewn all over China and Israel alike. Cultural debris abounds, waiting to be noticed by the historian of memory. Working on this book on Kibbutz Maaleh Gilboa, I was in daily contact with scraps of time that were far from metaphorical. They were pieces of barbed wires left over from the Jordanian occupation and broken turrets used by Israelis in various wars. One day I tripped on a barrel from the 1960s, which brought to mind these images:

Someone dumps an old barrel of cement
into my dream.
Scratched on its grass-streaked side: Memory—

a garbage treasure found on kibbutz,
rusty, worn, bulging with grief.

Nothing wasted, nothing erased.

Another night, I am rebuilding
an old house on the hill: History—
a tall cupboard exposed on all sides
in danger of toppling.

Nothing wasted, nothing erased.
I am learning to prop up the scaffolding . . .

Worlds I feared lost
are stripped to rusty wiring.
No memoryless flight to wind-kissed jasmine,
no path but this.
I am learning to prop up the scaffolding,
to refuse the dread of a pulverized past,
to use refuse.[7]

Several months after writing this poem, I find myself at Yad Vashem looking for documents about Rozsi Braun. Nothing tangibly useful has turned up, but on the way out from the archive, I pass a painting titled simply *Memories*. Away from the glaring sun that bathes the monument to the heroes of resistance, I stop in front of this work by Chava Pressburger. A strange edifice of muted colors, it starts with a vague animal pedestal below and ends in a large, blank clock face above. In between, layers of stone lie at various angles, their once-rough edges now smoothed by the passage of time. The pyramid looks as if it might topple were it not for the fine network of raised lines running across the massive blocks. This network does not tie anything together, yet it weaves coherence into a barbed-wire embrace.

Chava Pressburger is no stranger to barbed wires. Born Eva Ginz in Prague in 1930, she was interned in Theresienstat during 1944–45. Memories of a girlhood in the Nazi inferno mark much of Pressburger's work, especially since she was very close to her brother, Peter Ginz, a poet, editor, and painter who later perished in Auschwitz at the age of sixteen.[8] In Theresienstat both brother and sister produced realistic watercolors of stone buildings and oddly resplendent flowers. Only later, after death had taken its huge bite out of life, after possibilities of representation were exhausted by the nightmare of history, did Chava

Memories, painting by Chava Pressburger.
(Courtesy of Yad Vashem Museum, Jerusalem)

Pressburger develop her abstract style. In the Memories canvas, pieces of the past are preserved, but only as odd building blocks of an ill-balanced edifice. The tenacity of this edifice shows through in the web of scattered lines cast across the broken-up units of time.

A very different structure is manifest in Chen Yifei's painting Looking at History from My Space.[9] The title of the Chinese work is longer, more didactic than Pressburger's. And also more distant—since Chen Yifei is part of the "generation after." Born after the founding of Communist China, even after the worst excesses of the Cultural Revolution, Chen can almost afford the leisure of an armchair contemplation of history. But the chair stands empty in the foreground, because the young man refuses to sit and contemplate. Instead he turns to face the past, allowing memory's disconnected and often violent images to flood him. The sight that arrests him (and us) is primarily that of the Nanjing Massacre of 1937–1938. The vulnerable body of a naked boy and a young girl with her bared back symbolize the suffering of a whole nation during the brutal war with Japan. The memory of this event had been long dormant in China and actively

Looking at History from My Space, painting by Chen Yifei. (From Joan Lebold Cohen, The New Chinese Painting, 1949–1986)

suppressed by text books in Japan. Now, in this large canvas, Chen Yifei takes a direct look at history. He allows himself to be disturbed by his countrymen's helplessness. The young man has his sleeves rolled up. He is willing to try to do something, even if it is simply evoking memories once shut out of both Chinese and Japanese history. By painting this work, Chen Yifei takes upon himself the burden of questioning the past. By the 1990s, this conversation had developed into a social movement with the appearance of such groups as the "Global Alliance for Preserving the History of World War II in Asia" and "Action to Revisit Chinese History." The Nanjing Massacre, far from being a forgotten event, is now widely talked about as "The Chinese Holocaust." He begins a dialogue with forebears muted by death.

Broken Layers and Winding Rivers

Chinese and Jewish guardians of memory use disparate metaphors in their dialogue with the past. At first glance, what is most striking is their shared insistence on reanimating the old. By breathing new life into the remains of history, they are revived in turn. Confucianism and Judaism provide concrete guidance as to how to pursue the dialogue with the past. In seemingly similar terms, the Book of Lamentations urges Jews to "come back and renew our days as of old," while the Analects speak about reciprocity as "the one word that may guide one's conduct through life." [10] Yet beneath this shared emphasis on a life-sustaining relationship with the past lies a whole world of cultural and theological differ-ence. The Confucian connectedness to history was based on naturalistic com-munication with heaven and with the sages of long ago. Jewish faith in the renewal of history, by contrast, is grounded in the relationship to a divine force that transcends nature and time.

To understand these disparate ways of reanimating the old, one has to reckon with the geographies of Chinese and Jewish imagination, which are as different from one another as the Jordan River is from the Yangtze. The first is a narrow, winding divider between the Jewish homeland and the red mountains of Moab. The second is the unifier of central China. Physically, the Jordan River of today does not resemble the mighty waters of the spiritual: "The river Jordan is deep and wide." It is, in fact, a narrow stream that often runs dry in the summer. Far broader and more majestic, the Yangtze cuts a swath through China's landmass as well as her art. Known in Chinese simply as the "Long River," it starts from the Tibetan plateau and meanders through the great gorges of Sichuan all the way to the expansive greenery of Henan and Hebei—provinces named after their respective locations, "South of the River" and "North of the River." The narrow Jordan River separates Jews from other nations, whereas the Yangtze is a grand symbol of unity in central China.[11]

How, then, can such different worlds be bridged? By scrupulous attention to the voices of those who cross dangerous waters. Andrei Codrescu discovered these dangers when he changed his Jewish-sounding name. He had intended simply to outwit the censors, to pick a word that seemed to be paying homage to local geography. Codrescu, in Romanian, calls up a homonym for the dense forests of Transylvania. Later, he tells me: "I discovered it echoes also Codreanu, a fascist of the Iron Guard."[12] Codrescu shares this insight during a meeting in the Berkshire Mountains, when we are both safely distant from our native land, as well as from the nightmares that marked our parents' lives. Away from the terrain of the mother tongue, discomfiting nuances can finally surface. It is often abroad that historical memory accosts us most acutely.

This, too, is the experience of Yu Guangzhong, the Chinese poet who also became a planetary exile. His poetry is full of longing for and rage about the world left behind. The farther he strays from his native landscape, the more tenacious its hold on his mind. In a poem written on Memorial Day in America, Yu chronicles the history written in his veins. Cruising the highways of a foreign and brashly young nation, he writes about a distant world that will not leave him alone:

China, O China,
When shall we stop our quarrels?
China, O China, you're big in my throat so hard to swallow!
The Yellow River flows torrential in my veins.
China is me. I am China.
Her every disgrace leaves a box print on my face. I am defaced.
China, O China, you're a shameful disease that plagues my thirty-eight
    years.
Are you my shame or my pride, I cannot tell.[13]

Far from his country, the Chinese poet can express his ambivalence about the beloved who pulls him back into history and shames his face all at once. Codrescu has Jewish history embedded unwittingly in his very pen name. Yu Guangzhong lays claim to the pain of history more directly. In China, his sentiments might be considered disgraceful, unpatriotic, unfilial; abroad, memory appears both as pride and as shame. In exile, Yu can acknowledge his quarrel with China as well as the wish that their lovers' quarrel might cease—all the while knowing it cannot.

For Jews, exile has been a long familiar predicament. Codrescu does not invent it afresh. Although the memory of Jerusalem was never eradicated, the Jewish people were forced to recall it from the rivers of Babylon, from the cities of medieval Spain, from the shtetls of Eastern Europe. Yu Guangzhong locates his quarrel firmly in the ancient soil of the Chinese people. He carries the Yellow River in his veins. Dislocation from his natal world is temporary, self-created. Not so for Jews who had to nurture memory through prolonged exile from the land of Israel. Over time remembrance became its own homeland. No matter how slippery its ground, how tenuous the hold on the past embedded in texts, memory has kept Jews Jewish. Even after the establishment of the state of Israel, historical remembrance has remained the primary framework for both self-understanding and sympathy for others. This ongoing rootedness in recollection comes through in a full-page advertisement in the New York Times. Printed in September 1988, on the eve of Rosh Hashanah, it quotes a key passage from the High Holidays prayer book: "The memories of all creatures are known to You." The Jewish Theological Seminary sponsored the advertisement in the hope that it would reach Jews, but not only Jews. A dramatic central message—"My Memory fails me"—was intended to remind the world that Jews owe an allegiance to the past as well as to the world around them. The concluding words of the 1988 New Year's greeting were: "We wish for all humanity a year of broadened vision and shared perspectives." [14]

This message from the Jewish Theological Seminary called up an image of a world that would become more compassionate as a result of the memory covenant embedded in the religion of the Jews. Three years later, from across the Atlantic, came a resounding rebuttal of this wish for empathy through memory. In 1991, Mahmoud Darwish, a well-known Palestinian poet (who has been given honorary citizenship by several Arab countries and was chosen to be a member of the PLO Executive Committee in 1967), cursed the Jewish attachment to remembrance. In a work called "Song of Stones" he asked Jews to get out of his history, his land, and his memory altogether:

> Live where you wish but do not live among us.
> It is time for you to get out
> and die where you wish but do not die among us. . . .
> Get out of our land,
> our continent, our sea
> and our wheat, our salt, our sore,
> our everything, and get out
> of the memory of memories. [15]

Jews, the Palestinian poet cries out, must leave. They are asked to evacuate the present, and the past. All evil is attributed to a people who have inserted themselves too deeply into the "memory of memories." Jews stand accused of monopolizing not only material but spiritual resources as well.

After the publication of this poem, and the outbreak of controversy in Israel, Darwish tried to explain that he only meant that Jews should get out of the lands occupied after the Six Day War. But the poem's call goes beyond the political debates surrounding Gaza and the West Bank. Precisely because he is a poet, and because he does not gloss his meaning with humanistic prose, Mahmoud Darwish's bitter "Song of Stones" cuts to the heart of the Jewish remembrance.

Those Who Won't Let Go of the Past

Darwish understood that Jews can't leave the past alone. They might hope that a sharing of memories will result in broadened sympathies. But this often fails (though Israeli politicians continue to demand that foreign dignitaries visit Yad Vashem, as if paying a visit to Israel's official Hall of Remembrance is synonymous with an empathetic embrace of Jewish history). In Darwish's eyes, Jews have appropriated not only land and water, wheat and salt, but remembrance as well. They have become contemptible because of their rootedness in the past.

This obsessive concern with ancestral roots has also been attributed to Chinese immigrants in Southeast Asia. Called the "Jews of Asia," they too have been stigmatized because of remembrance. The negative link between Chinese and Jews dates back to the seventeenth century, when European travelers saw Chinese as somehow too clever, too successful in areas beyond their border. Edmund Scott, an English trader in Java, was the first to contrast the "proud" Javanese with the "crafty" Chinese merchants, who, "like Jews, rob them of their wealth of the land and send it back to China." [16] Chinese are likened to Jews because they have a center of loyalty far from the geography they inhabit. Scott had observed a new fact and put it in the context of old prejudice. To be sure, the Jews of Asia were indeed omnipresent in that landscape. They were "good at marrying surplus to scarcity, and vast numbers were involved in distribution. Retailing was everywhere seen as a Chinese monopoly." [17] The commercial services of Chinese immigrants, however, did not win them appreciation in their host countries.

Two centuries after Edmund Scott, the king of Thailand published an anti-Chinese pamphlet entitled The Jews of the East, in which he claimed that both Chinese and Jews "worshipped one God, the God of Money." [18] He accused the Chinese of being too clever at the accumulation of material wealth. Underneath all this talk about the "God of Money" lay rage against Chinese cultural apartness. The king was maddened by the determination of Chinese immigrants to maintain distinctive cultural traditions even after having resided in Thailand (Siam) for over a century.

It is not the fact that Chinese and Jews are ancient peoples that irks their neighbors. It is their ongoing efforts to maintain a connection to history. Those who resent Chinese and Jewish commercial successes have no trouble bridging their disparate traditions. This negative link between Chinese and Jews must be undone before we can build new bridges of genuine understanding. Whenever I hear praise of the common "cleverness" of Chinese and Jews I, too, want to scream, like Andrei Codrescu: "There is no bridge!" Quick-wittedness, like moneymaking, is a mischievous commonality glimpsed through the eyes of prejudice.

But what if there was no bridge at all? Without an appreciation of their distinctive cultures, Chinese and Jews remain endangered guardians of historical memory. Brought into the same semantic universe, these two traditions may yet enrich each other. This possibility was given visual form on the cover of a 1991 booklet commemorating the wartime rescue of the Mirrer Yeshiva. On the

兼善天下

‏וכשאני לעצמי מה אני"‏
"If I am for myself alone, what am I?"
—HILLEL

"Talmud Scholar and Asian Sage," illustration for the
Mirrer Yeshiva tribute held in 1991 in New York.
(Courtesy of the Mirrer Yeshiva Institute)

winding path of an ink-brushed mountain stand two figures. The bridge, a common element in Chinese landscape painting, is not shown here—as if it were no longer needed, as if a crossing between different worlds had been successfully consummated. Two figures stand alongside each other, close yet at a respectful distance. Their faces are indistinct but their garb embodies a whole world. The Asian scholar wears long robes and a straw hat, the student of the Talmud dark pants and a dark hat. The two men stand together on the lonely mountain capped by one ragged pine—a symbol of moral rectitude in Chinese art. Above them shines the moon and two messages in finely crafted calligraphy. The thicker Chinese brush expresses a core belief of Mencius, Confucius's most famous disciple: "Jianshan tianxia" (Seek to unify and benefit all under Heaven). In thinner Hebrew script, we read Rabbi Hillel's well-known dictum: "V'chesheani l'atzmi ma ani?" (If I am for myself alone, what am I?).[19]

The four Chinese ideographs remind us that we are put on earth for something more than our personal benefit. According to Mencius, it is not only the

Ruler who has the power and responsibility to improve the world. Each person must also strive for the perfectibility of the universe, because each partakes of the unity of heaven. Rabbi Hillel insists on the same broad-mindedness in the words of his own tradition. He knows that a person, like a nation, must look out for his or her own survival. This is why his first question—memorialized in the *Pirkei Avot* (Ethics of the Fathers)—states: "If I am not for myself, who will be for me?" But concern with survival is not enough. Jewish tradition, like Confucianism, demands a universal morality. I am forbidden to be for myself alone. So Rabbi Hillel adds, "If I am for myself alone, what am I?" and "If not now, when?"[20]

It is this active engagement with the world that matters to Chinese and Jewish guardians of memory. They seek to infuse the present with the light of the past. Rabbi Hillel, like Mencius, draws on the vocabulary of his tradition. Although these two sages never met, we can imagine their talking together under the ragged pine, each experiencing his world more deeply as he listened to the other.

Notes

PREFACE

1. Hart Crane, *The Complete Poems and Selected Letters and Prose of Hart Crane*, ed. B. Weber (New York: Liveright, 1966), 163.
2. Ilona Farkas, "Interview with Vera Schwarcz," Radio Kolosvar, Romania, April 23, 1993.

INTRODUCTION

1. Joseph Brodsky, *Less Than One: Selected Essays* (New York: Farrar, Straus and Giroux, 1986), 3.
2. For further discussion of the etymology of the Chinese word for "endurance" and "tradition," see Zhong Zhiyun, ed., *Zhongwen da cidian* (An encyclopedic dictionary of the Chinese language) (Taibei: Zhong gongchuban bu, 1973), 3:314.
3. For further information about the etymology of the Hebrew word for "tradition," see Ibn Shushan, *Ha Milon Hahadash* (Jerusalem: Kiviyut Safter, 1980), 56; and Edward Horowitz, *How the Hebrew Language Grew* (Jerusalem: Kitav, 1960), 51.
4. The plethora of recent writing about memory defies review here. The following are some of the more encompassing studies dealing with the role of memory in the maintenance of cultural continuity: Edward Casey, *Remembering: A Phenomenological Study* (Bloomington: Indiana University Press, 1987); Thomas Butler, "Memory: A Mixed Blessing," in *Memory: History, Culture and The Mind*, ed. Thomas Butler (New York: Basil Blackwell, 1989); Edmund Blair Bolles, *Remembering and Forgetting: Inquiries into the Nature of Memory* (New York: Walker, 1988); Patrick H. Hutton, *History as an Art of Memory* (Hanover, N.H.: New England University Press, 1993); Jacques Le Goff, *Histoire et mémoire* (Paris: Gallimard, 1988); and James McConkey, ed., *The Anatomy of Memory: An Anthology* (New York: Oxford University Press,

1996). For a look at how an individual historian reflects on the problem of memory, see Henry May, *Coming to Terms: A Study in Memory and History* (Berkeley: University of California Press, 1987); and Cheryl Pearl Sucher, "History Is the Province of Memory," *Midstream* (April 1989): 53–56.

For a more psychologically oriented work, see Alan Baddeley, *Human Memory: Theory and Practice* (Boston: Allyn and Bacon, 1990). For a review of recent biological investigations of memory, see Israel Rosenfeld, *The Invention of Memory: A New View of the Brain* (New York: Basic, 1988). For a shorter, more focused overview of memory research on the biochemical level, see Philip Goelet, Vincent Castellucci, Samuel Schacher, and Eric Kandel, "The Long and the Short of Long-Term Memory: A Molecular Framework," *Nature* 322 (July 31, 1986): 419–22; and Mortimer Mishkin and Tim Appenzeler, "The Anatomy of Memory," *Scientific American*, June 1987, 80–89.

5. Oliver Sacks, "Making Up the Mind," *New York Review of Books*, April 8, 1993, 42.

6. Le Goff, *Histoire et mémoire*, 101.

7. Casey, *Remembering*, 258.

8. Yehuda Amichai, *Poems of Jerusalem* (New York: Harper and Row, 1977), 79. This ambivalent acceptance of the burden of memory comes through again in Amichai's poem "National Thoughts" (*Poems by Yehuda Amichai*, trans. Assia Guttman [New York: Harper and Row, 1969], 51). Here, too, the poet wrestles with his linguistic and cultural inheritance, while acknowledging that he cannot live or speak without it. For more poems that battle with the idea of remembrance, see Amichai, *V'lo al menat l'izkhor* (Not for the sake of memory) (Jerusalem: Schocken, 1971).

9. Bei Dao, "Huida" (The answer), in *Xinshi chao shiji* (New trends in poetry), ed. Yang Lian (Beijing: Beijing Daxue Chuban She, 1985), 13.

10. David Fine, "The Judeo-Confucian Tradition," *Points East* 10 (July 1995): 6.

11. Ibid.

12. Wm. Theodore de Bary, *The Trouble with Confucianism* (Cambridge: Harvard University Press, 1991).

13. Wm. Theodore de Bary, "Roundtable Discussion of *The Trouble with Confucianism*," *China Review International* 1 (spring 1994): 15.

14. Benjamin Schwartz, *The World of Thought in Ancient China* (Cambridge: Harvard University Press, 1985), 119.

15. Joseph Levenson, *Confucian China and Its Modern Fate* (Berkeley: University of California Press, 1968), 3:88.

16. For a fuller discussion of this essay and the legacy of Joseph Levenson more generally, see Maurice Meisner and Rhoads Murphey, eds., *The Mozartian Historian: Essays on the Works of Joseph R. Levenson* (Berkeley: University of California Press, 1976); and Vera Schwarcz, review of *The Mozartian Historian*, *History and Theory* 17(1978): 349–67.

17. Joseph R. Levenson, "The Choice of Jewish Identity," in *Mozartian Historian*, 106. For a further discussion of the centrality of Jewish questions in the sinology of Joseph Levenson, see Frederic Wakeman, foreword to Levenson's book *Revolution and Cosmopolitanism: The Western Stage and the Chinese Stages* (Berkeley: University of California Press, 1971), ix–xxi.

18. Angus McDonald, "The Historian's Quest," in *Mozartian Historian*, 78.

19. Joseph R. Levenson, "Will Sinology Do?" *Journal of Asian Studies* 23 (1964): 508.

20. For a fuller discussion of memory dilemmas under state socialism, see Rubie Watson, ed., *Memory, History, and Opposition* (Santa Fe, N.M.: School of American Research Press, 1994), 1–20, 87–104.

21. Walter Benjamin, *Reflections: Essays, Aphorisms, Autobiographical Writing*, trans. Edmund Jephcott, ed. and with an introduction by Peter Demetz (New York: Schocken, 1986), 26.

22. Walter Benjamin, "Theses on the Philosophy of History," in *Illuminations*, trans. Hannah Arendt (New York: Knopf, 1968), 263–64.

23. Joseph Needham, "Bridges," in *Science and Civilization in China*, ed. Needham, vol. 4, *Physics and Physical Technology* (Cambridge: Cambridge University Press, 1971), 147.

24. Derrick Beckett, *Bridges* (London: Paul Hamlyn, 1969), 27.

25. This is my translation of the Yang Shen poem that appears in Needham, *Science and Civilization*, 201.

26. For a fuller discussion of the connection between historical memory and the Talmud, see both the early work of Arsene Darmesteter, *The Talmud*, trans. Henrietta Szold (1897; reprint, Philadelphia: Jewish Publication Society, 1987), as well as the masterful, contemporary work by Rabbi Adin Steinsaltz, *The Talmud: The Steinsaltz Edition, A Reference Guide* (New York: Random House, 1989).

27. *Talmud Bavli* (Babylonian Talmud), "Masechet Bechorot," 55A. This translation follows Rabbi Dr. H. Freedman, trans. *English-Hebrew Edition of the Babylonian Talmud: Tractate Keddushin* (London: Soncino Press, 1960), 375.

28. *Talmud Bavli*, "Shabbath," 33B. This translation follows Rabbi Dr. H. Freedman, *Hebrew-English Edition of the Babylonian Talmud: Tractate Shabbath* (London: Soncino Press, 1972).

29. *Midrash Raba: Sefer Bereshit* (Jerusalem: Shlomo David, 1954), 584.

30. Quoted in J. D. Eisenstein's essay "Gesher" (Bridge), in *Ozar Yisrael Encyclopedia* (New York: Jewish Publications, 5669/1909), 3:320. For further discussion of Judah ben Avraham Bedersi, see *Encyclopedia Judaica*, 24 vols. (Jerusalem: Keter, 1971), 9:1308–09.

31. Arthur Green, *Tormented Master: A Life of Rabbi Nahman of Bratslav* (Birmingham: University of Alabama Press, 1979), 41–48.

32. For a further discussion of this passage from Rabbi Nachman of Bratslav's *Likutei Moharan*, see Shlomo Riskin, *The Passover Hagaddah* (New York: Ktav, 1983), 40.

33. Hou Renzhi, *Yanyuan shihua* (Anecdotes about Yanyuan) (Beijing: Beijing University Press, 1988), 105.

34. Ibid., 131.

35. Edwin T. Morris, *The Gardens of China: History, Art and Meaning* (New York: Scribner's, 1983), xi.

36. Crane, "The Bridge," *The Complete Poems*, 45.

37. Abraham Joshua Heschel, *Israel: An Echo of Eternity* (New York: Knopf, 1969), 128.

CHAPTER 1: HOW TO MAKE TIME REAL

1. Eudora Welty, *The Optimist's Daughter* (New York: Random House, 1977), 78.

2. I am indebted to Dana Kline and Joanne Rudof of the Fortunoff Video Archives for Holocaust Testimonies at Yale University for introducing to me the video testimonies of Jewish survivors from Cluj, Romania, as well as those who went through Shanghai, China.

3. Judith Miller, *One by One by One: Facing the Holocaust* (New York: Simon and Schuster, 1990), 287.

4. Clara Clairborne Park, "The Mother of the Muses: In Praise of Memory," in *The Anatomy of Memory: An Anthology,* ed. James McConkey, 173–79.

5. Le Goff, *Histoire et mémoire,* 104.

6. Casey, *Remembering,* 18–20. A similar discussion of resistance to memory in post-enlightenment thought is found in the work of Pierre Janet (a pioneer of modern psychology before Freud), *L'Evolution de la mémoire et de le notion du temps* (Paris: Presse Universitaire, 1928), 185.

7. George Allan, *The Importance of the Past: A Meditation on the Authority of Tradition* (Albany: State University of New York Press, 1986), 12.

8. Nancy Huston, "A Tongue Called Mother," *Raritan* 9 (winter 1990): 99.

9. I am grateful to Nancy Huston for sharing with me the French version, which was the first draft of her essay on mother tongues, as well as the account of her struggles with "mothering" in both English and French.

10. See the poem by Meredith Stricker, "Anya nyelv," which she dedicated to her mother, who was forced to surrender her Hungarian mother tongue after the Holocaust. The work begins with the decoding of words that describe mothering, such as *anya* (meaning "mother") and *meh* ("bee" or "womb") (Deborah Keenan and Roseann Lloyd, *Looking for Home: Women Writing about Exile* [Minneapolis: Milkweed, 1990], 24–25).

11. Blaga Dimitrova, *Because the Sea Is Black,* trans. Niko Boris and H. McHugh (Middletown: Wesleyan University Press, 1989), 23.

12. Dan Pagis, "Autobiography," in *Points of Departure,* trans. Stephen Mitchell (Philadelphia: Jewish Publication Society, 1981), 21. For a further discussion of the autobiographical themes in the work of Dan Pagis, see Sidra deKoven Ezrahi, "Dan Pagis and the Prosaics of Memory," in *Holocaust Remembrance: The Shapes of Memory,* ed. Geoffrey Hartman (London: Basil Blackwell, 1994), 121–33.

13. Lu Xun, "Kuang ren ri ji" (A madman's diary), in *Lu Xun quan ji* (Selected works of Lu Xun) (Beijing: Renmin Chubanshe, 1980), 1 : 24.

14. Ibid., 1 : 12.

15. Lu Xun, "Inscribed in a Copy of *Wandering,*" in *Selected Poems,* trans. W. F. Jenner (Beijing: Foreign Languages Press, 1982), 71.

16. Lu Xun, "In Memory of Wei Suyuan," in *Selected Works,* trans. Gladis Yang and Yang Xianyi (Beijing: Foreign Languages Press, 1980).

17. Aharon Appelfeld, "Words and Images," video interview by Professor Yigal Schwartz, December 1992.

18. Zhang Dainian, preface to *Suoyi* (Remembering as such) (Beijing: Zhonguo Wenshi Chuban she, 1993), iv.

19. For further discussion of this process, see the introduction to Vera Schwarcz, *Time for Telling Truth Is Running Out: Conversations with Zhang Shenfu* (New Haven: Yale University Press, 1992), 1–23. For Zhang Shenfu's own views on historical memory, see his *Suoyi* (Remembering as such) (Beijing: Zhonguo Wenshi Chubanshe, 1993).

20. Ibid., 18.

21. Marilyn A. Levine, "Transcending the Barriers: Zhang Ruoming and André Gide," *Studies in Chinese History* (spring 1990): 39.

22. Ibid., 46.

23. Vera Schwarcz, "Mingled Voices: On Writing My Father's Memoirs," *Columbia* 17 (fall 1991): 120–37.

24. Ibid., 125.

25. Nietzsche's metaphor for public history—"Mr. Hellishnoise"—comes from *Thus Spake Zarathustra* and is discussed further in Vera Schwarcz, "Memory and Commemoration: The Dilemma of Chinese Intellectuals," *Wilson Quarterly* (October 1989): 120–29.

26. Isaiah 56:5. This translation of *yad vashem* as "memorial" comes from the *Jerusalem Bible* (Jerusalem: Koren, 1969), 529.

27. Yehuda Amichai, "Travels of the Last Benjamin of Tudela," in *The Selected Poetry of Yehuda Amichai*, trans. Chana Block and Stephen Mitchell (New York: Harper and Row, 1986), 68–69.

28. Miriam Novitch, "Un Grand Poète: Itzhak Katznelson," introduction to Itzhak Katznelson, *Le Chant du peuple juif massacré* (Lohamei Hagetaot, Israel: Ghetto Fighters Kibbutz, 1983), 12.

29. David G. Roskies, *Against the Apocalypse: Responses to Catastrophe in Modern Jewish Culture* (Cambridge: Harvard University Press, 1984), 208–10.

30. Ibid., 296–97. For a further discussion of the lamentation narrative in Holocaust writings, see Sidra Ezrahi, "The Holocaust Writer and the Lamentation Tradition: Responses to Catastrophe in Jewish Literature," in *Confronting the Holocaust: The Impact of Elie Wiesel*, ed. Alvin Rosenfeld and Irving Greenberg (Bloomington: Indiana University Press, 1978).

31. Novitch, "Un Grand Poète," 21.

32. Henri Maspero, "The Mythology of Modern China," in *Asiatic Mythology*, ed. J. Hockin (New York: Crescent, 1972), 252–384.

33. Benjamin Blech, *The Secrets of Hebrew Words* (Northvale, N.J.: Jason Aronson, 1991), 86.

34. Yu Guangzhong, "Wangquan" (River of forgetting), in *Yu Guangzhong shixuan* (Selected poems of Yu Guangzhong) (Hong Kong: Hongfan Shudian, 1981), 256.

35. Zhang Xianliang, *Getting Used to Dying*, trans. M. Avery (New York: HarperCollins, 1991), 44.

36. Dr. Adrienne K. Holocaust Testimony (HVT-199), Fortunoff Video Archives for Holocaust Testimonies, Yale University Library (hereinafter cited as FVA), June 4, 1987, 50: 29–51:32.

37. Ibid., 52:11–53:40.

38. Appelfeld, *Words and Images*.

39. Ibid.: "Ani mistaber she ahava . . . ani mistaber she ahava ve omek, hem lo dvarim shovim, hem dvarim shonim."

40. Lucille Clifton, "i am accused of tending to the past," in *quilting: poems, 1987–1990* (Brockport, N.Y.: BOA, 1991), 7.

CHAPTER 2: THE BRIDGE OF WORDS

1. Yehuda Amichai, "Love Song," in *Amen*, trans. Ted Hughes (New York: Harper and Row, 1977), 48. This English-language collection was the basis of Fu Hao's translation of Amichai's poetry into Chinese. I am indebted to Amichai for bringing Fu Hao's work to my attention and for helping me get in touch with this Chinese poet in Beijing. For a Hebrew version of this poem, see Yehuda Amichai, *Shirei ahava* (Love poems) (Jerusalem: Shocken, 1981), 57.

2. Yehuda Amichai, "Qing ge" (Love song), trans. Fu Hao, *Waiguo wenxue* (Foreign literature), no. 109 (January 1991): 71. This translation and an expanded introduction to Amichai's work was published in book form: Fu Hao, *Yelusaleng zhi ge* (Songs of Jerusalem) (Beijing: Zhonguo Shehui Chubanshe, 1993). In Hebrew, the last lines of this "Love Song" read as follows: "B'aretz boeret zot/Milim tzrichot leshamesh tzel" (Amichai, *Shirei ahava*, 57).

3. To Chinese readers, this intimacy with the conflagrations of history becomes even more familiar, because Fu Hao inserts *mi* (rice) as the middle character in the transliteration of the name of Yehuda Amichai (*A-Mi-Hai*). The Jewish poet thereby becomes palatable, almost like native fare.

4. Gaston Bachelard, *The Poetics of Reverie*, trans. David Russell (New York: Orion, 1969), 29.

5. Fu Hao, "Bellows," manuscript, courtesy of the author.

6. Cynthia Ozick, *Memory and Metaphor: Essays* (New York: Alfred A. Knopf, 1989), 268.

7. Ibid.

8. *Hua Ying Si Shu* (The four classics in Chinese and English) (Shanghai: Commercial Press, 1924), 218.

9. James J. Y. Liu, *Language—Paradox—Poetics: A Chinese Perspective* (Princeton: Princeton University Press, 1988), 14.

10. Blech, *Secrets of Hebrew Words*, ix. The same idea—of a world-creating word—comes up in Psalm 33, where the poet acclaims: "For he spoke and it came to be./He commanded and it stood firm" (*Jerusalem Bible*, 741).

11. Rabbi Adin Steinsaltz, "The Letters of the Ten Utterances," *Wellsprings* (fall 1993/5754): 10.

12. Scott Corbett, *Bridges* (New York: Four Winds Press, 1978), 14.

13. I am indebted to Rabbi Ilyse Kramer of Wesleyan University for bringing this connection between "memory" and "merit" to my attention. The specific reference to the sechar/ merit of women comes from the Talmud, tractate "Shemot Rabbah," and is cited in Reuben Alcalay, *The Complete Hebrew-English Dictionary* (Jerusalem: Massada, 1963), 2619.

14. This passage from the *Analects* (with a slightly different translation given here) is discussed in Stephen Owen, *Remembrances: The Experience of the Past in Classical Chinese Literature* (Cambridge: Harvard University Press, 1986), 13–16.

15. *Hua Ying Si Shu*, 59.

16. For an excellent discussion of the post-Han usages of hao gu, see Wang Gongwu, "Loving the Ancients in China," in *Who Owns the Past*, ed. Isabel McBryde (Melbourne: University Publications, 1985), 175–95.

17. *The Pentateuch and Rashi's Commentary* (Brooklyn: S.S. & R. Publishing, 1950), 1:118.

18. The concept of Torah as *mashal hakadmoni* ("proverb of the ancients") is discussed by Rashi in his commentary upon Exodus 21:13 (*The Pentateuch and Rashi's Commentary*, 2:235).

19. For a full discussion of the literal and metaphorical meanings of zakhor in the Hebrew Bible, see Brevard Childs, *Memory and Tradition in Israel* (Naperville, Ill.: Alec Alenson, 1962), 18. Using Childs's painstakingly lexographic study, Yosef Yerushalmi expanded the discussion of Jewish cultural memory in his work, *Zachor: Jewish History and Jewish Memory* (Seattle: University of Washington Press, 1982). Yerushalmi's book is an analysis of the relationship between history and memory, especially as it affects the modern Jewish historian. Above all, it speaks to the author's own struggle to produce critical historiography in the face of a tradition that gave the past over to communal, religious concerns.

The very first reference in the Bible that includes the zayin-kaf-resh root appears in Genesis 1 : 27. In this passage, the word created out of this radical is not "memory" but "male," as in the passage: "And God created Adam (the earthling) in His own image, in the image of God He created him, male and female [zakhar ve nekevah] he created them."

20. Rabbi Ephraim Friedman, *Etched in Our Memories* (Chicago: CIS Publishers, 1993), vi.

21. Ibid., 12.

22. Berel Lang, "Holocaust Memory and Revenge: The Presence of the Past," *Jewish Social Studies* 3 (1996): 2–20.

23. Yerushalmi, *Zachor*, 44.

24. Ozick, *Memory and Metaphor*, 279.

25. Ibid.

26. Karl Lashley's pioneering paper "In Search of an Engram" is discussed in the context of current neurobiological research on memory by George Johnson, "Memory: Learning How It Works," *New York Times Magazine*, August 9, 1987, 18–19. Lashley's research is also addressed critically by Sacks, "Making Up the Mind," 41–44.

27. Anne De Coursey Clapp, *The Painting of T'ang Yin* (Chicago: University of Chicago Press, 1991), 67–68.

28. Pei-yi Wu, "Memories of K'ai-Feng," *New Literary History* 25 (winter 1994): 23.

29. Ibid., 26.

30. Wu-chi Liu and Irving Yucheng Lo, eds., *Sunflower Splendor: Three Thousand Years of Chinese Poetry* (New York: Anchor, 1975), 589.

31. This poem (in a slightly different translation) is discussed in Michael Fuller, *The Road to East Slope: The Development of Su Shi's Poetic Voice* (Stanford: Stanford University Press, 1990), 296.

32. Wang Huizu, *Bingta menghen lu* (Traces from a sickbed) (Shanghai: Commercial Press, 1928), 3.

33. Hosea 14 : 7, *Jerusalem Bible*, 683; "veyiferechu kagefen, zichro keyain Levanon."

34. Both the Rashi and the Kimchi commentaries on Hosea are discussed in A. Cohen, *The Soncino Chumash: The Five Books of Moses with Haphtoroth* (London: Soncino Press, 1979), 193.

35. *Machzor for Rosh Hashannah*, trans. Rabbi Nissen Mangel (Brooklyn: Merkos L'Inyonei Chinuchi, 5750/1990), 134–36.

36. The Hebrew original of this poem appears in T. Carmi, ed., *Hebrew Verse* (New York: Penguin, 1981), 333. For help in this translation of Halevi's poem, I am indebted to Professor Howard Needler of the College of Letters at Wesleyan University.

37. Half a century before Judah Halevi, the well-known poet Solomon Ibn Gabirol (1022–55) also developed the theme of dreams. Drawing upon the biblical tradition of Joseph (who also appealed for divine help to interpret the reveries of Pharaoh), Ibn Gabirol wrote: "I put my trust in You, like one who has / dreamt an obscure dream and places / his trust in the interpreter. All I ask is / that You listen to my plea" (Carmi, *Hebrew Verse*, 315).

38. A slightly different translation of the Chinese original of this poem is discussed in Fuller, *The Road to East Slope*, 98–99.

39. For a Western writer's informed evocation of the distinctively Chinese metaphor of hong zhao, see Almah James Johnston, *The Footprints of the Pheasant in the Snow* (Portland, Me.:

Anthuensen Press, 1978). This work is a memoir of the writer's experiences as a teacher of English at Yenching University in Beijing in the 1930s.

CHAPTER 3: BURNING SNOW

1. John Felstiner, Paul Celan: Poet, Survivor, Jew (New Haven: Yale University Press, 1996), 3–10.
2. Ibid., 21.
3. Childs, Memory and Tradition, 66.
4. Pierre Ryckmans, "The Chinese Attitude toward the Past," Papers on Far Eastern History 39 (March 1989): 1–16.
5. Childs, Memory and Tradition, 21–22.
6. Liu and Lo, Sunflower Splendor, 564.
7. Ibid., 166.
8. Ibid., 170.
9. Carmi, Hebrew Verse, 308–09.
10. Ibid., 315.
11. Jerusalem Bible, 793–94.
12. David Rosenberg, A Poet's Bible (New York: Hyperion, 1991), 46.
13. "Galileo Galilei," in Dictionary of Scientific Biography, ed. Charles C. Gallespie (New York: Scribner and Sons, 1972), 5:239.
14. Ci Jiwei, Dialectic of the Chinese Revolution (Stanford: Stanford University Press, 1994), 70. For a further discussion of state-sponsored amnesia in China, see Geremie Barmé, "History for the Masses," in Using the Past to Serve the Present, ed. Jonathan Unger (Armonk, N.Y.: M. E. Sharpe, 1993), 239–59.
15. Ibid., 80.
16. Nien Cheng, Life and Death in Shanghai (New York: Penguin, 1986), 202–05.
17. Gertrud Koch, "The Angel of Forgetfulness and the Black Box of Facticity," History and Memory 3:1 (spring 1991): 130.
18. Adolf Rudnicki, Ascent to Heaven, trans. H. C. Stevens (London: Dennis Dobson, 1951), 23.
19. André Neher, "Shaddai: The God of the Broken Arch (A Theological Approach to the Holocaust)," in Confronting the Holocaust, ed. Alvin H. Rosenfeld and Irving Greenberg (Bloomington: Indiana University Press, 1978), 158.
20. Primo Levi, The Drowned and the Saved (New York: Summit, 1986), 23.
21. Aliki Barnstone and Willis Barnstone, eds., A Book of Women Poets from Antiquity to Now (New York: Schocken, 1992), 377. For a further discussion of poetry's role as a bulwark against historical amnesia, see Carolyn Forché, Against Forgetting: Twentieth-Century Poetry of Witness (New York: Norton, 1993).
22. Jean Amery, At the Mind's Limits (New York: Schocken, 1986), 19–20.
23. Bei Dao, Notes from the City of the Sun: Poems by Bei Dao, ed. Bonnie McDougall, East Asian Papers, no. 34 (Ithaca: Cornell University Press, 1983), 38.
24. Ibid., 39.
25. For a thoughtful comparison of the literature produced by Chinese and Jewish survivors, see Sheng-mei Ma, "Contrasting Two Survival Literatures: On the Jewish Holocaust and the Chinese Cultural Revolution," Holocaust and Genocidal Studies 2:1 (1987): 81–93.
26. Felstiner, Paul Celan, 114–15.

27. Paul Celan, "The Lock Gate," in *The Poems of Paul Celan*, trans. Michael Hamburger (New York: Persea, 1988), 169.

28. Chang Shiang-hua, *A Chinese Woman in Iowa* (Boston: Cheng and Tsui, 1992), 31–33.

29. Yehuda Amichai, *Even a Fist Was Once an Open Palm with Fingers*, trans. Barbara Harshav and Benjamin Harshav (New York: Harper Perennial, 1991), 84.

CHAPTER 4: NOTES IN THE WALL

1. For a further discussion of Dan Pagis's poetry of "silence," see Sidra DeKoven Ezrahi, "Conversation in the Cemetery: Dan Pagis and the Prosaics of Memory," in Hartman, *Holocaust Remembrance*, 121–33.

2. Hartman, "Introduction: Darkness Visible," *Holocaust Remembrance*, 19.

3. Ibid., 15.

4. Javier Roiz, "Les espacios publicos internos," in *El experimento moderno* (Madrid: Editorial Trotta, 1992), 65–71.

5. Ibid., 27.

6. Rubie S. Watson, "Memory, History and Opposition under State Socialism: An Introduction," in Watson, *Memory, History and Opposition*, 7.

7. Schwarcz, "Memory and Commemoration," 127.

8. This conversation with Yang Zaidao took place at the 1989 conference commemorating the seventieth anniversary of the May Fourth Movement of 1919. During the crackdown that followed the student demonstration of 1989, I used a pseudonym for Yang in writing about his experiences. Subsequently, I was informed that he wanted his real name used; as a result, the record of our conversations appears more openly here.

9. Ibid.

10. Maurice Halbwachs, *The Collective Memory*, trans. Francis Ditter and Vida Yazdi Ditter (New York: Harper and Row, 1980).

11. Mary Douglas, *How Institutions Think* (Syracuse: Syracuse University Press, 1986), 70, 76.

12. Elie Barnavi, ed. *A Historical Atlas of the Jewish People* (London: Hutchinson, 1992), 33.

13. Arthur Waldron, *The Great Wall of China* (Cambridge: Cambridge University Press, 1990), 208–09.

14. Lu Xun, "A Curse on the Great Wall," in *Selected Works*, 2 : 167. For a discussion of Lu Xun's critical assessment of Chinese tradition see Vera Schwarcz, "A Curse on the Great Wall: The Problem of Enlightenment in Modern China," *Theory and Society* 13 (1984): 455–70. For a discussion of the negative impact of Lu Xun's iconoclasm, see Lin Yusheng, *The Crisis of Chinese Consciousness* (Madison: University of Wisconsin Press, 1979).

15. Edward Casey, "Commemoration and Perdurance in the Analects," *Philosophy East and West* 34 : 4 (October 1984): 391.

16. This quote from Nietzsche's "On the Use and Disadvantage of History for Life" is discussed in David Krell, *Of Memory, Reminiscences and Writing* (Bloomington: Indiana University Press, 1990), 78.

17. Owen, *Remembrances*, 14. In traditional China, no aspect of a prominent individual's life was immune from this urge to monumentalize its significance. The pervasive practice of *liezhuan* (inspirational biographies) was one way in which personal memory became translated into the idiom of public recollection. Whether dwelling on virtuous widows

(who refused to remarry in honor of their husband's memory) or high-minded officials (who spoke for public concerns in the presence of autocratic rulers), Chinese historiography insisted on teaching future generations by carefully editing the past.

18. For a fuller discussion of traditional Chinese historiography and its uses as a repository of moral value, see Yves Chevrier, "La Servante-maîtresse: Condition de la référence à l'histoire dans l'espace intellectuel chinois," Extreme-Orient/Extreme-Occident, no. 9 (1987): 119–44.

19. Sima Qian's letter to Ren An is translated in de Bary, Sources of Chinese Civilizations (New York: Columbia University Press, 1960), 1:223–25. This letter is discussed in James Liu, Language—Paradox—Poetics, 125.

20. Owen, Remembrances, 135.

21. W. Andrew Achenbach, "Public History: Past, Present and Prospects," American Historical Review 92:5 (December 1987): 1165. For a further discussion of public history in China, see W. J. F. Jenner, The Tyranny of History: The Roots of China's Crisis (New York: Penguin, 1992).

22. Amos Funkenstein, "Collective Memory and Historical Consciousness," History and Memory 2:1 (spring–summer 1990): 12.

23. Encyclopedia Judaica, 11:871–72.

24. This passage from the work of Shelemoh bar Shimshon is translated and discussed in Yerushalmi, Zachor, 38–40.

25. Ibid., 43.

26. Ismar Schorsch, "History as Consolation," in From Text to Context: The Turn to History in Modern Judaism (Hanover, N.H.: Brandeis University Press, 1994), 334–44.

27. The Kaifeng Memorial Book and its implications for the preservation of Jewish identity are discussed in Donald Daniel Leslie, The Survival of the Chinese Jews: The Jewish Community of Kaifeng (Leiden: E. J. Brill, 1972).

28. Ibid., 94.

29. Jack Kugelmass and Jonathan Boyarin, From a Ruined Garden: The Memorial Books of Polish Jewry (New York: Schocken, 1983).

30. Ba Jin, "Wen ge bowuguan" (A cultural revolution museum), in Suigan lu (Random reflections) (Beijing: Shenghuo, Dushu, Xinzhi, 1987), 823. For a further discussion of this text, see Pa Kin, Pour un musée de la Révolution Culturelle, trans. Angel Pino (Paris: Bleu de Chine, 1996), 113–20.

31. Zhou Ming, ed. Lishi zai zheli chensi (History has brought us to these reflections) (Beijing: Huaxia Chubanshe, 1986). This is a four-volume collection of Cultural Revolution memoirs detailing the daily experiences of students as well as older intellectuals—both those who were Red Guards and those who were their victims. For another personal account and historical analysis of the year of Red Terror (1966–76), see Yu Guangyuan, Wenge zhongde wo (Myself, during the Cultural Revolution) (Shanghai: Yuandong Chubanshe, 1995).

32. Nien Cheng, Life and Death in Shanghai, 10.

33. Wu Tianwei, "Zhungguo de 'huojie'?" (Is there a Chinese 'Holocaust'?), Jiujiu xuekan (Continental Review) 1:4 (summer 1987): 107–110.

34. For a fuller description of the "loyalty dances" and the spiritual humiliation these dances brought upon intellectuals castigated as "enemies of the people," see Yue Daiyun and Carolyn Wakeman, To the Storm (Berkeley: University of California Press, 1985).

35. Sun Longji, "The Deep Structure of Chinese Culture," in Barmé and Minford, Seeds of Fire, 32.

36. For a thoughtful analysis of Jewish identity among survivors who hid as Gentiles or actually worked for the Nazis, see Kenneth Jacobson, Embattled Selves (New York: Atlantic Monthly Press, 1994).

37. Jean Amery, At the Mind's Limits, 15, 19.

38. Art Spigelman, Maus (New York: Pantheon, 1985).

39. Elizabeth J. Perry and Li Xin, "Revolutionary Rudeness: The Language of Red Guards and Rebel Workers in China's Cultural Revolution," Indiana East Asian Working Papers, no. 2 (July 1993): 7.

40. This excerpt from Zheng Yi's Red Memorial is translated and discussed in Liu Binyan, "An Unnatural Disaster," New York Review of Books, April 8, 1993, 3.

41. Li Zehou, "Houji" (Postface), Pipan zhexue de pipan (The critique of critical philosophy) (Beijing: Renmin Chubanshe, 1979).

42. Ma Sheng-mei, "Contrasting Survival Literatures: On the Jewish Holocaust and the Chinese Cultural Revolution," Holocaust and Genocide Studies (1987): 47–92.

43. Theodor Adorno, "Commitment," in the Essential Frankfurt School Reader, ed. Andrew Avato and Eike Gebhardt (New York: Continuum, 1982), 313.

44. Tom L. Freudenheim, "Art from the Concentration Camps," in Spiritual Resistance, 1940– 1945, ed. Freudenheim (New York: Union of American Hebrew Congregations, 1981), 33–38.

45. David Koening, "After the Holocaust, No Poetry," in Blood to Remember: American Poets on the Holocaust, ed. Charles Fishman (Lubbock: Texas Tech University Press, 1991), 42.

46. Quoted in Miller, One by One by One, 262.

47. Levenson, Confucian China, 3:106.

48. Kostya Perutz-Kennedy, "To the Holocaust Museum," Jewish Currents (April 1995): 6–7.

49. Philip Gourevitch, "Behold Now Behemoth: The Holocaust Memorial Museum—One More American Theme Park," Harper's, July 1993, 55.

50. Ibid.

51. Edward Norden, "Yes and No to the Holocaust Museums," Commentary (August 1993), 27–28.

52. This excerpt from Shimon Huberband's writings "Kiddush Hashem" (Sanctification of the Name) is quoted and discussed by Elie Wiesel in his essay "Praising His Name in the Fire," New York Times Book Review, January 17, 1988, 11.

53. Bei Dao "Zou xiang dongtian" (Head for winter), in City of the Sun, McDougall, 76–77, 117.

54. Qian Zhongshu, preface to Yang Jiang, Six Chapters from My Life "Downunder," trans. Howard Goldblatt (Hong Kong: Chinese University Press, 1984), iv.

55. Primo Levi, The Drowned and the Saved (New York: Summit, 1986), 31, 34.

56. Ci Jiwei, Dialectic of the Chinese Revolution (Stanford: Stanford University Press, 1994), 76.

57. Xu Youyu, "Wenge Bowuguan?" (A cultural revolution museum?). *Qingnian Baokan Shijie* (Youth Periodicals Panorama) (January 1996): 10–12.

58. Dan Pagis, "Instructions for Crossing the Border," in *Points of Departure*, 27.

CHAPTER 5: LIGHT PASSERSBY

1. Personal correspondence, Rabbi Joseph Schachter, October 19, 1993.

2. Nadine Fresco, "La Diaspora de cendres," *Nouvelle Psychanalyse*, no. 24 (1981): 207. A similar obsession with ashes, but on the theoretical level of language possibilities after the Holocaust, is at the core of Jacques Derrida's *Cinders*, trans. and ed. Ned Lukacher (Lincoln: University of Nebraska Press, 1991).

3. "A Harom 17 Es" (The three 17s), a poem written in Hungarian by Willy Mund on January 17, 1981, on the occasion of the birthday of three friends from Cluj who were all born around January 17. I am greatly indebted to Mr. Mund for sharing his poems and his memories with me and also for the deep affection and commitment he has shown toward my parents. Often, when those closest to me were silent about the pain of the past, I found a willing, sensitive memorialist in this family friend.

4. Philip Kuberski, *The Persistence of Memory: Organism, Myth, Text* (Berkeley: University of California Press, 1992), 18–19.

5. Dori Laub, "Bearing Witness," in *Testimony: Crises of Witnessing in Literature, Psychoanalysis and History*, ed. Shoshana Feldman and Dori Laub (New York: Routledge, 1992), 57. For a further discussion of oral history studies of the Holocaust, see Lawrence L. Langer, *Holocaust Testimonies: The Ruins of Memory* (New Haven: Yale University Press, 1991); and Jacobson, *Embattled Selves*.

6. Li Weiqing, *Shanghai xiangtuzhi* (Shanghai local gazetteer) item 153 (Shanghai: n.p., 1907), quoted and discussed in Bryna Goodman, *Native Place, City and Nation: Regional Networks and Identities in Shanghai* (Berkeley: University of California Press, 1995), 12.

7. For a personal recollection of the extensive Jewish community networks in Shanghai, see the memoirs of Rabbi Avrohom Horofe, an eminent physician who ministered to both the physical and spiritual needs of Jewish refugees in China: *Sefer Hatoldos Reb Avrohom Horofe* (The generations of Rabbi Avrohom Horofe) (Brooklyn: M. A. Seligson, 1990). Other historical studies, notably David Kranzler, *Japanese, Nazis and Jews: The Jewish Refugee Community of Shanghai, 1938–1945* (New York: Yeshiva University Press, 1976), and Marvin Tokayer, *The Fugu Plan* (New York: Paddington Press, 1979), explore the details of the flight from Europe and of the Jewish ghetto in Shanghai with much insight. For a more recent memoir, see Evelyn Pike Rubin, *Ghetto Shanghai* (New York: Shengold, 1993).

8. For a fuller history of the Mirrer Yeshiva in Poland, see Samuel K. Mirsky, *Jewish Institutions of Higher Learning in Europe: Their Development and Destruction* (New York: Ogen, 1965), 87–132.

9. Interview with Rabbi Anschel Wainhaus, July 24, 1991. I was guided to Rabbi Wainhaus's home by his son, who lives in Connecticut, and by the archivist of the Fortunoff Video Archives. This particularly painful moment does not come up in the video testimony for the Yale Archives: Anschel W. Holocaust Testimony (HVT-612), FVA. I was able to touch upon it briefly only because Rabbi Wainhaus's son, Rabbi Alvin Wainhaus, was kind enough to speak with me before the interview in Borough Park. It was the son who first broke the silence surrounding the loss of his father's brother.

10. Interview with Rabbi Solomon Schwartzman, January 29, 1992. The return home from the army is also vividly recalled in Rabbi Solomon Schwartzman's video testimony for the New York Holocaust Museum, recorded on Novemember 27, 1990.

11. Interview with Rabbi Shimon Goldman, February 23, 1992. I am indebted to Rabbi Solomon Schwartzman and to Dr. Lawrence Harris for helping me locate Rabbi Goldman in Crown Heights. This enabled me to hear the distinctive voice of a Hassidic student who journeyed to China with the remnants of the Lubavitch Yeshiva.

12. The Pentateuch and Rashi's Commentary, 1 : 245.

13. Interview with Dr. Robert Sokal, February 28, 1992. I am indebted to Hannah Sokal Holmes, Dr. Sokal's daughter, and to her husband, Professor Oliver Holmes, for arranging this interview in their own home.

14. Kathe K. Holocaust Testimony (HVT-292), FVA, 10 : 32–10 : 47. For a further discussion of German-Jewish refugees in Shanghai, see Françoise Kreissler, L'action culturelle allemande en Chine (Paris: Editions de la Maison des Sciences de l'Homme, 1989), 272–94.

15. Ibid., 20 : 50–20 : 61.

16. For a fuller discussion of the Chinese experience in wartime Shanghai, see Tao Juyin, Gudao jianwen (Records of life on Lonely Island) (Shanghai: Remnin Chubanshe, 1979). "Lonely Island" is the name used by patriotic Chinese intellectuals when referring to Japanese-occupied Shanghai.

17. Kranzler, Japanese, Nazis and Jews, 614.

18. Interview with Anschel Wainhaus, July 24, 1991. See also Abraham Kotsuji, From Tokyo to Jerusalem (New York: Bernard Geis, 1964).

19. Ibid.

20. Interview with Robert Sokal, February 28, 1992.

21. Rabbi Shimon Goldman has recorded his recollections of the Amnshenover Rebbe in China in "Amod Ohr" (A pillar of light), Kfar Chabad (November 13, 1991), 22–24.

22. A Polish journalist quoted in Kranzler, Japanese, Nazis and Jews, 434. Tractate Gittin, which opens with a lengthy discussion of the laws of divorce in foreign lands was of particular significance to Jewish refugees who could readily identify with earlier periods of exile and the need to preserve Jewish law in inhospitable lands.

23. Interview with Anschel Wainhaus, July 24, 1991.

24. Dr. Moshe Carmilly-Weinberger, Memorial Volume for the Jews of Cluj-Kolosvar (New York: Memorial Foundation for Jewish Culture, 1970), 303.

25. Zheng Zhenduo, Zhijiu sanji (Reminiscences of life in hibernation) (Shanghai: Renmin Chubanshe, 1951), 32.

26. Carmilly-Weinberger, Memorial Volume, 294.

27. Dr. Adrienne K. Holocaust Testimony (HVT-199), FVA, 3 : 20–3 : 28.

28. Ibid. (HVT-931), 7 : 47–9 : 23.

29. Ibid. (HVT-199), 34 : 50—36 : 49.

30. Ibid., 36 : 50–37 : 30.

31. Ibid., 37 : 40–38 : 10.

32. Ibid., 38 : 14–38 : 29.

33. Ibid., 58 : 14–60 : 08.

34. Personal correspondence from Katherine Savin, June 25, 1994.

35. Interview with Willy Mund, June 25, 1993.

36. Rosita K. Holocaust Testimony (HVT-77), FVA, 1 : 14–1 : 48.

37. Ibid., 4 : 20–5 : 03.

38. Peter Cooley, "Under Heaven," in The Astonished Hours, ed. Cooley (Pittsburgh: Carnegie Mellon University Press, 1992), 60.

39. Elmer Savin, "Encounters Dictated by Fate," manuscript on deposit at Yad Vashem, Jerusalem, 112.

40. Ibid., 3.

41. Anschel W. Holocaust Testimony (HVT-612), FVA, 22 : 13–23 : 10.

42. Dr. Adrienne K. Holocaust Testimony (HVT-199), FVA, 44 : 54–45 : 10.

43. Ibid., 1 : 20 : 20-1:21 : 04.

44. Ibid., 1 : 24 : 21–1 : 28 : 10.

45. Ibid., 30 : 07–30 : 20.

46. Ibid., 39 : 12–40 : 08.

47. James Young, The Texture of Memory: Holocaust Memorials and Meaning (New Haven: Yale University Press, 1994).

48. Interview about the Cluj monument conveyed to me in a letter by Professor Ladislau Gyemant, director of the Dr. Moshe Carmilly-Weinberger Institute for Judaism and Jewish History at the Babes-Bolyai University in Cluj. The words of the poem by Louis Aragon on the steps of the monument in Cluj are "The dead don't sleep / They did not choose this stone / Helplessness overwhelms the effort to comprehend their names / Memory of the crimes, implacable / the only prayer they ask of us."

49. Raul Sorban, "Nine Jewish Artists Victims of the Holocaust in Northern Transylvania," 2 Studia Judaica (Cluj-Napoca, 1993): 53.

50. Willy Mund, "Marcika," unpublished poem, March 7, 1982.

51. Wu-chi Liu and Irving Yucheng Lo, K'uei Yeh Chi (Sunflower splendor) (Bloomington: Indiana University Press, 1976), 132. This is my own translation from the original Chinese and differs slightly from Daniel Bryant's version in Sunflower Splendor.

CHAPTER 6: THE MASTER'S TEARS

1. For a fuller discussion of the historical and literary context of Meng Jiao, see Stephen Owen, Tang Poetry: Han Yu and Meng Chiao (New Haven: Yale University Press, 1989).

2. I am indebted to Professor Yu Yingshi of Princeton University, who helped me locate sources for personal and public memory in traditional China. It was Professor Yu who first drew my attention to this passage from the late third-century Daoist classic Jin Shu.

3. Han Yu, "Song Meng Dongye Lu" (A dedication in honor of Meng Dongye), quoted in Qian Zhongshu, "Poetry as a Vehicle of Grief," Renditions (spring–autumn 1984), 29.

4. Ibid., 32.

5. Blech, Secrets of Hebrew Words, 86.

6. Anna Akhmatova, "Lot's Wife," in A Book of Women Poets, ed. Barnstone and Barnstone, trans. Richard Wilbur, (New York: Schocken Books, 1992), 373.

7. This passage from Elie Wiesel's Les Chants des morts is discussed further in Vera Schwarcz, Long Road Home: A China Journal (New Haven: Yale University Press, 1984), 173–75.

8. Elie Wiesel, Discours d'Oslo (Paris: Bernard Grasset, 1987), 28–29. For a further discussion

of the role of memory in Jewish historical consciousness, see Jean Halpérin and Georges Lévitte, ed., *Mémoire et histoire: Colloque des intellectuels juifs* (Paris: Editions Denoël, 1986).

9. Primo Levi, *Shema: Collected Poems of Primo Levi*, trans. R. Feldman and Brian Swann (New York: Menard Press, 1990), 21.

10. Ibid.

11. Eugene Rosenstock-Husey, *Out of Revolution: Autobiography of Western Man* (New York: Four Wells Press, 1964), 742.

12. Carolyn Steedman, "Why Clio Doesn't Care," in *Feminists Revision History*, ed. Anne Louise Shapiro (New Brunswick: Rutgers University Press, 1994), 92.

13. Graham Swift, *Waterland* (New York: Poseidon Press, 1983), 53.

14. Pagis, *Points of Departure*, 27.

15. Adrienne Matyas Krausz, M.D., letter of January 11, 1974 (courtesy of Katherine Savin); original text in German.

16. Vera Schwarcz, "Wiedergutmachung," *Hobo Jungle 7* (spring 1990): 71.

17. Arthur Kleinman and Joan Kleinman, "The Appeal of Experience, The Discovery of Images: Cultural Appropriations of Suffering in Our Time," *Daedalus* (winter 1996): 18–19.

18. Conrad Mehler, M.D., letter of March 25, 1974 (courtesy of Katherine Savin), 1; original text in German.

19. Ibid., 4.

20. Ibid.

21. Mehler, letter of November 11, 1974 (courtesy of Katherine Savin), emphasis added; original text in German.

22. Nadine Fresco, "Une langue gutturale," in *Un Allemand né de la dernière guerre*, ed. Lothar Baier (Paris: Genre Humain, 1988), 139–49.

23. Casey, *Remembering*, 201.

24. Nadine Fresco, "La Diaspora des cendres," 212.

25. Yu Kuang-chung, "Nostalgia," in *The Isle Full of Noises: Modern Chinese Poetry from Taiwan*, ed. and trans. Dominic Cheung (New York: Columbia University Press, 1987), 51–52.

26. Qian Zhongshu, "Poetry as a Vehicle for Grief," 21.

27. Ibid. For a fuller discussion of Qian Zhongshu's role in articulating historical trauma, see Vera Schwarcz, "The Pane of Sorrow: Public Uses of Personal Grief in Modern China," *Daedalus* (winter 1996): 119–48.

28. The contemporary Chinese literary critic Chen Kun also emphasizes the value of memory. A victim of the Cultural Revolution, Chen (like Qian Zhongshu) alludes to its madness obliquely. In *Xifang xiandaipai wenxue yanjiu* (Research on modernism in Western literature) (Beijing: Beijing Daxue Chubanshe, 1981), he describes the solace of memory: "Lessons from history are waiting attention. . . . But when such occasions turn up [people] would persevere in their self-righteousness and would not remember anything about history. Tumu said when he referred to the Chin dynasty: 'Chin people did not have time to grieve for themselves. Their descendants did. The descendants grieved but did not learn. Later generations were made to grieve for the descendants again.' What a piece of lament was this ancient remark" (312).

29. This discussion of the text of "Threshold" is based on the opening performance at La MaMa on June 14, 1989. For a more detailed analysis of the performance, see Vera

Schwarcz, "No Solace from Lethe: History, Memory and Identity in Modern China," *Daedalus* (spring 1991): 88–112.

30. For a thoughtful discussion of the relationship of exile to memory, see Leon Grinberg and Rebecca Grinberg, *Psychoanalytic Perspectives on Migration and Exile* (New Haven: Yale University Press, 1989). According to the Grinbergs, who have studied exiles from Latin America and Eastern Europe, humanity as a whole is marked by a movement out of a native place toward another, often alien world. This movement, according to the Grinbergs, is part of a universal desire to reach forbidden zones of foreign knowledge.

31. Schwarcz, "No Solace from Lethe," 90.

32. This report by Elizabeth Loftus to the American Psychological Association appears in the *Chronicle of Higher Education* (September 15, 1989), 4.

33. Charles S. Maier, "A Surfeit of Memory? Reflections on History, Melancholy and Denial," *History and Memory* 5 : 2 (fall–winter 1993): 136–51.

34. Ibid., 150.

35. Rosenstock-Husey, *Out of Revolution*, 696. For a further critique of the optimism embodied in the historian's craft, see Morton Smith, *Hope and History: An Exploration* (New York: Harper and Row, 1980).

36. Quoted in W. Andrew Achenbach, "Public History's Past, Present and Prospects," *American Historical Review* 92 : 5 (December 1987): 1170.

37. Sigmund Freud, "Remembering, Repeating and Working Through," in *Collected Works*, trans. James Strachey, vol. 22 (New York: International Universities Press, 1973), 196. For a fuller discussion of Freud's essay and its significance for contemporary memory studies, see Casey, *Remembering*, 305.

38. Peter Loewenberg, "Why Psychoanalysis Needs the Social Scientist and the Historian," in *Psycho/History: Readings in the Method of Psychology, Psychoanalysis, and History*, ed. Geoffrey Cocks and Travis L. Crosby (New Haven: Yale University Press, 1987), 30–45.

39. Dori Laub, "Bearing Witness," 56.

40. Arthur Kleinman and Joan Kleinman, "How Bodies Remember: Social Memory and Bodily Experience of Criticism, Resistance and Delegitimation Following China's Cultural Revolution," *New Literary History* 25 : 1 (winter 1994): 42.

41. Ibid., 43.

42. Burton Watson, *Ssu Ma Ch'ien: Grand Historian of China* (New York: Columbia University Press, 1958), 126.

43. Kugelmass and Boyarin, *From a Ruined Garden*, 110–45.

44. Dr. Mozes Carmilly-Weinberger, "Sirt Az Isten" (God also cried), *Memorial Volume*, 1.

45. Ibid., 2.

46. Ibid., 9.

47. Maya Angelou, *On the Pulse of the Morning* (New York: Random House, 1993), 7.

CONCLUSION

1. Andrei Codrescu, "Notes of a Native Son," *The Nation* (December 12, 1994): 719.

2. For a discussion of the Chinese ideograph for survival (*ren*) and the Hebrew expression for "tradition" (*masoret*), see the introduction of this volume.

3. Neher, "Shaddai," 151.

4. Ibid., 153.

5. Le Goff, *Histoire et mémoire*, 99. For a further discussion of the dilemmas of "professional specialists in memory" in the Chinese context, see Joshua A. Fogel, "Mendacity and Veracity in the Recent Chinese Communist Memoir Literature," *CCP Research Newsletter*, no. 1 (fall 1988): 31–34.

6. Jean-Philippe Antoine, "The Art of Memory and Its Relation to the Unconscious," *Comparative Civilizations Review* (spring 1988): 18.

7. Vera Schwarcz, "To Use Refuse," *Ibis* 1 (1995): 9.

8. *The Road through Theresienstadt: Peter Ginz (1928–1944), Chava Pressburger* (Jerusalem: Yad Vashem Martyrs' and Heroes' Remembrance Authority Art Museum, 1984), 6.

9. For a fuller discussion of Chen Yifei's painting, see Joan Lebold Cohen, *The New Chinese Painting, 1949–1986* (New York: Abrams, 1987), 99–101.

10. David Fine, "The Judeo-Confucian Tradition," 4–5.

11. Lyman Van Slyke, *Yangtze: Nature, History and the River* (Reading, Mass.: Addison-Wesley, 1988).

12. Vera Schwarcz, "Trouble in the Ontological Waters," *Blue Unicorn* (fall 1992): 10–11.

13. Yu Kuang-chung, "Memorial Day," in *Acres of Barbed Wire* (Taipei: Mei Ya, 1971), 12.

14. "My Memory Fails Me," *New York Times*, September 15, 1988, 33.

15. This English excerpt from Mahmoud Darwish's poem "Song of Stones" appeared in an article entitled "Palestinian Poem Unnerves Israelis," *New York Times*, April 4, 1991, 22.

16. Walter P. Zenner, " 'We Are the Jews of . . . ': The Symbolic Encounter of Diaspora Chinese with Jews," *Points East* 8 : 2 (June 1993): 1–3.

17. Lynn Pan, *Sons of the Yellow Emperor* (New York: Kodansha International, 1994), 129.

18. Zenner, "We Are the Jews of," 1.

19. For a fuller discussion of this illustration and its historical context, see Vera Schwarcz, "Who Can See a Miracle? The Language of Jewish Memory in Shanghai," in *The Jews of China*, ed. Jonathan Goldstein (New York: M. E. Sharpe, 1998).

20. *Pirkei-Avot: Ethics of the Fathers*, trans. and with a commentary by Rabbi Meir Zolowitz (New York: Artscroll, 1984), chap. 1: 12, 13.

Bibliography

Achenbach, W. Andrew. "Public History's Past, Present, and Prospects." *American Historical Review* 92:5 (December 1987): 1163–70.

Adorno, Theodore. "Commitment." In *The Essential Frankfurt School Reader*, edited by Andrew Avato and Eike Gebhardt. New York: Continuum, 1982.

Dr. Adrienne K. Holocaust Testimony (HVT-199, HVT-913), Fortunoff Video Archives for Holocaust Testimonies, Yale University Library.

Alcalay, Reuben. *The Complete Hebrew-English Dictionary.* Jerusalem: Massada, 1963.

Allan, George. *The Importance of the Past: A Meditation on the Authority of Tradition.* Albany: State University of New York Press, 1986.

Amery, Jean. *At the Mind's Limits: Contemplations by a Survivor on Auschwitz and Its Realities.* New York: Schocken, 1986.

Amichai, Yehuda. *Amen.* Translated by Ted Hughes. New York: Harper and Row, 1977.

———. *Even a Fist Was Once an Open Palm with Fingers.* Selected and translated by Barbara Harshav and Benjamin Harshav. New York: Harper Perennial, 1991.

———. *Poems of Jerusalem.* Translated by the author and Ted Hughes. New York: Harper and Row, 1977.

———. *Poems of Yehuda Amichai.* Translated by Assia Gutman. New York: Harper and Row, 1968.

———. *The Selected Poetry of Yehuda Amichai.* Translated by Chana Bloch and Stephen Mitchell. New York: Harper and Row, 1986.

———. *Shirei ahava* (Love poems). Jerusalem: Schocken, 1981.

———. *V'lo al menat l'izkhor* (Not for the sake of memory). Jerusalem: Schocken, 1971.

Angelou, Maya. *On the Pulse of the Morning.* New York: Random House, 1993.

Anschel W. Holocaust Testimony (HVT-612), Fortunoff Video Archives for Holocaust Testimonies, Yale University Library.

Antoine, Jean-Philippe. "The Art of Memory and Its Relation to the Unconscious." *Comparative
Civilizations Review* (spring 1988): 12–29.

Appelfeld, Aharon. *Words and Images.* Video interview by Professor Yigal Schwartz, December
1992.

Auerhahn, Nanette C., and Dori Laub. "Annihilation and Restoration: Post-Traumatic
Memory as a Pathway and Obstacle to Recovery." *International Review of Psycho-Analysis* 11
(1984): 327–43.

Ba Jin. *Suigan lu* (Random reflections). Beijing: Shenghuo, Dushu, Xinzhi, 1986.

Bachelord, Gaston. *The Poetics of Reverie.* Translated by D. Russell. New York: Orion Press,
1969.

Baddeley, Alan. *Human Memory: Theory and Practice.* Boston: Allyn and Bacon, 1990.

Baier, Lothar. *Un Allemand né de la dernière guerre.* Paris: Genre Humain, 1988.

Barmé, Geremie, and John Minford, eds. *Seeds of Fire: Chinese Voices of Conscience.* London: Hill
and Wang, 1988.

Barnavi, Elie, ed. *A Historical Atlas of the Jewish People.* London: Hutchinson, 1992.

Barnstone, Aliki, and William Barnstone, eds. *A Book of Women Poets from Antiquity to Now.* New
York: Schocken, 1992.

Beckett, Derrick. *Bridges.* London: Paul Hamlyn, 1969.

Bei Dao. *Notes from the City of the Sun: Poems by Bei Dao.* Edited by Bonnie McDougall. East Asian
Papers, no. 34. Ithaca: Cornell University Press, 1983.

Beijing Daxue jinian Mao Zedong bainian lunji (Beijing University commemorates the hundredth anniversary of Mao Zedong). Beijing: Beijing Daxue Chubanshe, 1993.

Ben-Dasan, Isaiah. *The Japanese and the Jews.* Translated by R. L. Gage. New York: Weather Hill,
1970.

Benjamin, Walter. *Illuminations.* Translated by Hannah Arendt. New York: Knopf, 1968.

————. *Reflections: Essays, Aphorisms, Autobiographical Writings.* Translated by Edmund Jephcott,
with an introduction by Peter Dememtz. New York: Schocken, 1986.

Bernstein, Louis, and Raphael Yankelevitch. *Pinkhos Churgin: Vision and Legacy.* Ramat-Gan, Israel:
Bar-Ilan University Press, 1987.

Blech, Benjamin. *The Secrets of Hebrew Words.* Northvale, N.J.: Jason Aronson, 1991.

Bolle, Edmund Blair. *Remembering and Forgetting: Inquiring into the Nature of Memory.* New York:
Walker, 1988.

Borowsky, Tadeusz. *This Way for the Gas, Ladies and Gentlemen.* Translated by B. Vedder. New York:
Viking, 1959.

Bower, Bruce. "Memory Maps: Where the Action Is." *Science News* 130:20 (November 15,
1986): 41–43.

Brodsky, Joseph. *Less than One: Selected Essays.* New York: Farrar, Straus and Giroux, 1986.

Broner, E. M. *The Telling.* San Francisco: HarperCollins, 1993.

Brown, Carolyn T., ed. *Psycho-Sinology: The Universe of Dreams in Chinese Culture.* Washington, D.C.:
Woodrow Wilson International Center for Scholars, 1988.

Bryant, Daniel, ed. *Sunflower Splendor: Three Thousand Years of Chinese Poetry.* Garden City, N.Y.: Anchor, 1975.

Buruma, Ian. *The Wages of Guilt: Memories of War in Germany and Japan.* New York: Farrar, Straus and Giroux, 1994.

Butler, Thomas, ed. *Memory: History, Culture and the Mind.* New York: Basil Blackwell, 1989.

Carmi, T., ed. *Hebrew Verse.* New York: Penguin, 1981.

Carmilly-Weinberger, Dr. Mozes. *The Memorial Volume for the Jews of Cluj/Kolosvar.* New York: Memorial Foundation for Jewish Culture, 1970.

Casey, Edward. *Remembering: A Phenomenological Study.* Bloomington: Indiana University Press, 1987.

———. "Commemoration and Perdurance in the Analects." *Philosophy East and West* 34 : 4 (October 1984): 387–98.

Celan, Paul. *The Poems of Paul Celan.* Translated by Michael Hamburger. New York: Persea, 1988.

Chang Shiang-hua. *A Chinese Woman in Iowa.* Boston: Cheng and Tsui, 1992.

Chen Kun. *Xifang xiandaipai wenxue yanjiu.* (Research on modernism in Western culture). Beijing: Beijing Daxue Chubanshe, 1981.

Cheng Nien. *Life and Death in Shanghai.* New York: Penguin, 1987.

Cheng Peikai. *Tiananmen dubai* (Tiananmen soliloquy). Hong Kong: n.p., 1991.

Chesneaux, Jean. *Pasts and Futures: Or What Is History For?* London: Thames and Hudson, 1976.

Cheung, Dominic, ed. *The Isle Full of Noises: Modern Chinese Poetry from Taiwan.* New York: Columbia University Press, 1987.

Chevrier, Yves. "La Servante-maîtresse: Condition de la référence à l'histoire dans l'espace intellectuel chinois." *Extreme-Orient/Extreme-Occident*, no. 9 (1987): 119–44.

Childs, Brevard. *Memory and Tradition in Israel.* Naperville, Ill.: Alec Alenson, 1962.

Chow Tse-tsung. *Wen-Lin: Studies in Chinese Humanities.* Hong Kong: N.T.T. Chinese Language Center, 1989.

Ci Jiwei. *Dialectic of the Chinese Revolution.* Stanford: Stanford University Press, 1994.

Clapp, Anne De Coursey. *The Painting of T'ang Yin.* Chicago: University of Chicago Press, 1991.

Clifton, Lucille. *quilting: poems, 1987–1990.* Brockport, N.Y.: BOA, 1991.

Cocks, Geoffrey, and Travis L. Crosby, eds. *Psycho/History: Readings in the Method of Psychology, Psychoanalysis, and History.* New Haven: Yale University Press, 1987.

Codrescu, Andrei. *Belligerence.* Minneapolis: Coffee House Press, 1991.

Cohen, Avraham. *The Soncino Chumash: The Five Books of Moses with Haphtoroth.* London: Soncino Press, 1979.

Cohen, Joan Lebold. *The New Chinese Painting, 1949–1986.* New York: Abrams, 1987.

Cooley, Peter. *The Astonished Hours.* Pittsburgh: Carnegie Mellon University Press, 1992.

Corbett, Scott. *Bridges.* New York: Four Winds Press, 1978.

Crane, Hart. *The Complete Poems and Selected Letters and Prose of Hart Crane.* Edited by B. Weber. New York: Liveright, 1966.

Darmesteter, Aresene. *The Talmud.* Translated by Henrietta Szold. 1897. Reprint, Philadelphia: Jewish Publication Society, 1987.

Darwish, Mahmoud. "The Peace Speech." *Jerusalem Post*, February 16, 1994.

de Bary, Wm. Theodore. "A Roundtable Discussion of *The Trouble with Confucianism.*" *China Review International* 1 : 1 (spring 1994): 1–28.

———. *Sources of Chinese Civilization.* 2 vols. New York: Columbia University Press, 1960.

————. The Trouble with Confucianism. Cambridge: Harvard University Press, 1991.

Derrida, Jacques. Cinders. Translated by N. Lukacher. Lincoln: University of Nebraska Press, 1991.

Des Pres, Terrence. The Survivor: Anatomy of Life in the Death Camps. New York: Washington Square Press, 1976.

Descharnes, Robert, ed. The World of Salvador Dali. Lausanne: Maurice Busenhart, 1962.

Dimitrova, Blaga. Because the Sea Is Black. Translated by Niko Boris and H. McHugh. Middletown: Wesleyan University Press, 1989.

Douglas, Mary. How Institutions Think. Syracuse: Syracuse University Press, 1986.

Durrant, Stephen. The Cloudy Mirror: Tension and Conflict in the Writings of Sima Qian. Albany: State University of New York Press, 1995.

Edelman, Gerald M. Bright Air, Brilliant Fire: On the Matter of the Mind. New York: Basic, 1993.

Ellman, Richard, ed. The New Oxford Book of American Verse. New York: Oxford University Press, 1976.

Encyclopedia Judaica. 24 vols. Jerusalem: Keter, 1971.

Feldman, Shoshana, and Dori Laub, eds. Testimony: Crises of Witnessing in Literature, Psychoanalysis and History. New York: Routledge, 1992.

Felstiner, John. "The Mother Tongue of Paul Celan." Orim 3 : 11 (autumn 1986): 23–35.

————. Paul Celan: Poet, Survivor, Jew. New Haven: Yale University Press, 1995.

Fine, David J. "The Judeo-Confucian Tradition." Points East 10: 2 (July 1995): 1–6.

Fishman, Charles, ed. Blood to Remember: American Poets on the Holocaust. Lubbock: Texas Tech University Press, 1991.

Fogel, Joshua A. "Mendacity and Veracity in the Recent Chinese Communist Memoir Literature." CCP Research Newsletter, no. 1 (fall 1988): 31–34.

Forché, Carolyn, ed. Against Forgetting: Twentieth-Century Poetry of Witness. New York: Norton, 1993.

Freedman, H., trans. Hebrew-English Edition of the Babylonian Talmud: Shabbath. London: Soncino Press, 1972.

————. Hebrew-English Edition of the Babylonian Talmud: Tractate Keddushin. London: Soncino Press, 1966.

Fresco, Nadine. "La Diaspora de cendres." Nouvelle Psychoanalyse, no. 24 (1981): 197–228.

Freud, Sigmund. "New Introductory Lectures in Psychoanalysis," in Collected Works, trans. James Strachey, vol. 22. New York: International Universities Press, 1973.

Freudenheim, Tom L., ed. Spiritual Resistance, 1940–1945. New York: Union of American Hebrew Congregations, 1981.

Friedman, Rabbi Ephraim. Etched in Our Memories. Chicago: CIS, 1993.

Fu Hao. "Bellows." Typescript.

————. "Qingge" (Love song). Waiguo Wenxue (Foreign literature) 109 (January 1991): 70–71.

————. Yelusaleng zhi ge (Songs of Jerusalem). Beijing: Zhongguo Shehui Chubanshe, 1993.

Fuller, Michael. The Road to East Slope: The Development of Su Shi's Poetic Voice. Stanford: Stanford University Press, 1990.

Funkenstein, Amos. "Collective Memory and Historical Consciousness." History and Memory 1 : 2 (spring–summer 1990): 10–21.

Galeano, Eduardo. *Memory of Fire: Genesis*. Translated by Cedric Belfrage. New York: Pantheon, 1985.

Gallespie, Charles C., ed. *Dictionary of Scientific Biography*. New York: Scribner and Sons, 1972.

Gao, Mobo C. F. "Memoirs and Interpretations of the Cultural Revolution." *Bulletin of Concerned Asian Scholars* 27 : 2 (summer 1995): 49–57.

Gardner, Charles S. *Chinese Traditional Historiography*. Cambridge: Harvard University Press, 1938.

Gay, Peter. *Freud for Historians*. New York: Oxford University Press, 1985.

Gilbert, Martin. *The Holocaust: A History of the Jews of Europe during the Second World War*. New York: Henry Holt, 1985.

Goelet, Philip, ed. "The Long and the Short of Long-Term Memory: A Molecular Framework." *Nature* 322 (July 31, 1986): 419–22.

Goldman, Merle. "Left-Wing Criticism of the Pai-hua Movement." In *Reflections on the May Fourth Movement*, edited by B. Schwartz. Cambridge: Harvard East Asian Monographs, 1972.

Goldman, Rabbi Shimon. "Amod Ohr" (A Pillar of Light). *Kfar Chabad*, November 13, 1991, 22–24.

Goldstein, Jonathan, ed. *The Jews of China*. New York: M. E. Sharpe, 1998.

Goodman, Bryna. *Native Place, City and Nation: Regional Networks and Identities in Shanghai*. Berkeley: University of California Press, 1995.

Gourevitch, Philip. "Behold Now Behemoth: The Holocaust Memorial Museum—One More American Theme Park." *Harper's*, July 1993, 48–59.

Green, Arthur. *Tormented Master: A Life of Rabbi Nahman of Bratslav*. Birmingham: University of Alabama Press, 1979.

Grinberg, Leon, and Rebecca Grinberg. *Psychoanalytic Perspectives on Migration and Exile*. New Haven: Yale University Press, 1989.

Halbwachs, Maurice. *The Collective Memory*. Translated by Francis Ditter and Vita Yazdi Ditter. New York: Harper and Row, 1980.

Halpérin, Jean, and Georges Lévitte, eds. *Mémoire et histoire: Colloque des intellectuels juifs*. Paris: Editions Denoël, 1986.

Hartman, Geoffrey, ed. *Bittburg in Moral and Political Perspective*. Bloomington: Indiana University Press, 1986.

———. *Holocaust Remembrance: The Shapes of Memory*. London: Basil Blackwell, 1994.

Hertz, J. H., ed. *The Pentateuch and Haftorahs*. London: Soncino Press, 1971.

Heschel, Abraham Joshua. *Israel: An Echo of Eternity*. New York: Knopf, 1969.

Hong Ye. *Shaoyuan yuanlu kao* (The records of Shao Yuan Garden). Taipei: Harvard-Yenching Institute Sinological Index Series, 1966.

Horofe, Rabbi Avrohom. *Sefer Hatoldos Reb Avrohom Horofe* (The generations of Rabbi Avrohom Horofe). Brooklyn: M. A. Seligson, 1990.

Horowitz, Edward. *How the Hebrew Language Grew*. Jerusalem: Kitav, 1960.

Hou Renzhi. *Yanyuan shihua* (Anecdotes about Yanyuan Garden). Beijing: Beijing University Press, 1988.

Hua Ying Si Shu (The four classics in Chinese and English). Shanghai: Commercial Press, 1924.

Huberband, Shimon. *Kiddush Hashem*. New York: Kitav, 1987.

Huston, Nancy. "A Tongue Called Mother." *Raritan* 9 (winter 1990): 87–102.

Hutton, Patrick H. *History as an Art of Memory*. Hanover, N.H.: University Press of New England, 1993.

Ibn Gabirol, Solomon. *Selected Religious Poems by Solomon Ibn Gabirol*. Translated by I. Zangwill. New York: Arno Press, 1973.

Jacobson, Kenneth. *Embattled Selves*. New York: Atlantic Monthly Press, 1994.

Janet, Pierre. *L'Evolution de la mémoire et de le notion du temps*. Paris: Presse Universitaire, 1928.

Jenner, W. J. F. *The Tyranny of History: The Roots of China's Crisis*. New York: Penguin, 1992.

The Jerusalem Bible. Jerusalem: Koren, 1969.

Ji Xianlin. *Huai jiu ji* (A collection of remembrances). Beijing: Beijing Daxue Chubanshe, 1996.

————. "Ta shixian le shengming de jiazhi" (He came to know the true value of life). In *Zhu Guanqian jinian ji* (Essays in memory of Zhu Guanqian). Anhui: Jiaoyu Chubanshe, 1987.

————. "Youtairen baikequanshu xu yi" (Introduction to the *Encyclopedia Judaica*). In *Youtairen baikequanshu* (Encyclopedia Judaica), edited by Xu Xin. Shanghai: Renmin Chubanshe, 1993.

Johnson, George. "Memory: Learning How It Works," *New York Times Magazine*, August 9, 1987.

Johnston, Almah James. *The Footprints of the Pheasant in the Snow*. Portland, Me.: Antheunsen Press, 1978.

Kafka, Franz. *I Am a Memory Come Alive: Autobiographical Writings*. Edited by Nahum Glazer. New York: Schocken, 1974.

Kathe K. Holocaust Testimony (HVT-292), Fortunoff Video Archives for Holocaust Testimonies, Yale University Library.

Katz, Steven. "The Shoah and Historical Memory." *Harvard Divinity Bulletin* 24 : 4 (1995): 4–7.

Katznelson, Itzhak. *Le Chant du peuple juif massacré*. Translated by Miriam Novitch. Lohamei Hagetaot, Israel: Ghetto Fighters Kibbutz, 1983.

Keenan, Deborah, and Roseann Lloyd, eds. *Looking For Home: Women Writing about Exile*. Minneapolis: Milkweed, 1990.

Kleinman, Arthur. *The Illness Narratives*. New York: Basic, 1988.

Kleinman, Arthur, and Joan Kleinman. "The Appeal of Experience, The Dismay of Image: Cultural Appropriations of Suffering." *Daedalus* (winter 1996): 1–22.

————. "How Bodies Remember: Social Memory and Bodily Experience of Criticism, Resistance and Delegitimation Following China's Cultural Revolution." *New Literary History* 25 : 1 (winter 1994): 27–48.

Koch, Gertrud. "The Angel of Forgetfulness and the Black Box of Facticity." *History and Memory* 3 : 1 (spring 1991): 42–56.

Kotsuji, Abraham. *From Tokyo to Jerusalem*. New York: Bernard Geis, 1964.

Krall, Hanna. *Shielding the Flame*. New York: Henry Holt, 1977.

Kranzler, David. *Japanese, Nazis and Jews: The Jewish Refugee Community of Shanghai, 1938–1945*. New York: Yeshiva University Press, 1976.

Kreissler, Françoise. *L'action culturelle allemande en Chine*. Paris: Editions de la Maison des Sciences de l'Homme, 1989.

Krell, David. *Of Memory, Reminiscences and Writing*. Bloomington: Indiana University Press, 1990.

Kuberski, Philip. *The Persistence of Memory: Organism, Myth, Text*. Berkeley: University of California Press, 1992.

Kugelmass, Jack, and Jonathan Boyarin. *From a Ruined Garden: The Memorial Books of Polish Jewry*. New York: Schocken, 1983.

Kumin, Maxine. *The Retrieval System.* New York: Viking, 1978.

Lang, Berel. "Holocaust Memory and Revenge: The Presence of the Past." *Jewish Social Studies* 3 (1996): 2–20.

Laub, Dori. "Art and Trauma." *International Journal of Psychoanalysis* 76 (December 1995): 991–1005.

———. "Knowing and Not Knowing the Holocaust." *Psychoanalytic Inquiry* 5 : 5 (1985): 1–8.

Le Goff, Jacques. *Histoire et mémoire.* Paris: Gallimard, 1988.

Leslie, Donald Daniel. *The Survival of the Chinese Jews: The Jewish Community of Kaifeng.* Leiden: E. J. Brill, 1972.

Levenson, Joseph R. *Confucian China and Its Modern Fate.* 3 vols. Berkeley: University of California Press, 1968.

———. "The Genesis of 'Confucian China and Its Modern Fate.'" In *The Historians' Workshop*, edited by L. P. Curtis. New York: Columbia University Press, 1970.

———. *Revolution and Cosmopolitanism: The Western Stage and the Chinese Stages.* Berkeley: University of California Press, 1971.

———. "Will Sinology Do?" *Journal of Asian Studies* 23 (1964): 507–22.

Levi, Primo. *The Drowned and the Saved.* Translated by R. Rosenthal. New York: Summit, 1986.

———. *Shema: Collected Poems of Primo Levi.* Translated by R. Feldman and Brian Swann. New York: Menard Press, 1974.

Levine, Marilyn Avra. "Transcending the Barriers: Zhang Ruoming and André Gide." *Chinese Studies in History* (spring 1990): 36–44.

Li Weiqing. *Shanghai xiantuzhi* (Local gazetteer of Shanghai). Shanghai: Commercial Press, 1907.

Li Zehou. *Pipan zhexue de pipan* (The critique of critical philosophy). Beijing: Renmin Chubanshe, 1979.

Lin Yusheng. *The Crisis of Chinese Consciousness.* Madison: University of Wisconsin Press, 1979.

Liu Binyan. "An Unnatural Disaster." *New York Review of Books*, April 8, 1993, 3–5.

Liu, James J. Y. *Language—Paradox—Poetics: A Chinese Perspective.* Princeton: Princeton University Press, 1988.

Liu, Wu-chi, and Irving Yucheng Lo, eds. *K'uei Yeh Chi* (Sunflower splendor). Bloomington: Indiana University Press, 1976. Originally published as *Sunflower Splendor: Three Thousand Years of Chinese Poetry.* New York: Anchor, 1975.

Lowenthal, Marvin, ed. and trans. *The Memoirs of Gluckel of Hameln.* New York: Schocken, 1977.

Lu Xun. *Selected Works*, translated by G. Yang and Yang Xian-yi. Beijing: Foreign Languages Press, 1980.

———. *Lu Xun quan ji* (Selected works of Lu Xun). Beijing: Renmin Chubanshe, 1980.

———. *Selected Poems.* Translated by W. T. F. Jenner. Beijing: Foreign Languages Press, 1982.

Ma Sheng-mei. "Contrasting Two Survival Literatures: On the Jewish Holocaust and the Chinese Cultural Revolution." *Holocaust and Genocidal Studies* 2 : 1 (1987): 81–93.

Machzor for Rosh Hashannah. Translated by Rabbi Nissen Mangel. Brooklyn: Merkos L'Inyonei Chinuchi, 5750/1990.

Mahler, Raphael. *Hassidism and the Jewish Enlightenment.* Translated by Eugene Orenstein. Philadelphia: Jewish Publication Society, 1985.

Maier, Charles S. "A Surfeit of Memory? Reflections on History, Melancholy, and Denial." *History and Memory* 5 : 2 (fall–winter 1993): 136–51.

Maspero, Henri. "The Mythology of Modern China." In *Asiatic Mythology*, edited by J. Hockin. New York: Crescent, 1972.

May, Henry F. *Coming to Terms: A Study in Memory and History*. Berkeley: University of California Press, 1987.

McConkey, James. *The Anatomy of Memory: An Anthology*. New York: Oxford University Press, 1996.

Meisner, Maurice, and Rhoads Murphy, eds. *The Mozartian Historian: Essays on the Works of Joseph R. Levenson*. Berkeley: University of California Press, 1976.

Midrash Raba: Sefer Bereshit. Jerusalem: Shlomo David, 1954.

Miller, Judith. *One by One by One: Facing the Holocaust*. New York: Simon and Schuster, 1990.

Mirsky, Samuel K. *Jewish Institutions of Higher Learning in Europe: Their Development and Destruction*. New York: Ogen, 1965.

Mishkin, Mortimer, and Tim Appenzeler. "The Anatomy of Memory." *Scientific American* 286 (June 1987): 80–89.

Moore, Charles A., ed. *The Chinese Mind*. Honolulu: East-West Center Press, 1967.

Morris, Edwin T. *The Gardens of China: History, Art and Meaning*. New York: Scribner's, 1983.

Needham, Joseph, ed. *Science and Civilization in China*, vol. 4, *Physics and Physical Technology*. Cambridge: Cambridge University Press, 1971.

Nora, Pierre, ed. *Les Lieux de mémoire*. Paris: Gallimard, 1984.

Norden, Edward. "Yes and No to the Holocaust Museums." *Commentary* 96 (August 1993): 23–30.

Owen, Stephen. *The Poetry of the Early Tang*. New Haven: Yale University Press, 1977.

———. *Remembrances: The Experience of the Past in Classical Chinese Literature*. Cambridge: Harvard University Press, 1986.

———. *Tang Poetry: Han Yu and Meng Chiao*. New Haven: Yale University Press, 1989.

Ozick, Cynthia. *Memory and Metaphor: Essays*. New York: Knopf, 1989.

Pa Kin. *Pour un museé de la Révolution Culturelle*. Translated by Angel Pino. Paris: Bleu de Chine, 1996.

Pagis, Dan. *Points of Departure*. Translated by Stephen Mitchell. Philadelphia: Jewish Publication Society, 1981.

"Palestinian Poem Unnerves Israelis." *New York Times*, April 4, 1991.

The Pentateuch and Rashi's Commentary. 5 vols. Brooklyn: S. S. & R. Publishing, 1950.

Perry, Elizabeth J., and Li Xin. "Revolutionary Rudeness: The Language of Red Guards and Rebel Workers in China's Cultural Revolution." *Indiana East Asian Working Papers* (July 1993): 1–17.

Perutz-Kennedy, Kostya. "To the Holocaust Museum." *Jewish Currents* (April 1995): 4–7.

Pirkei-Avot: Ethics of the Fathers. Translated and with a commentary by Rabbi Meir Zolowitz. New York: Artscroll, 1984.

Qian Zhongshu. "Poetry as Vehicle of Grief." *Renditions* (spring–autumn 1984): 20–27.

Riskin, Shlomo. *The Passover Hagaddah*. New York: Kitav, 1983.

Roiz, Javier. *El experimento moderno*. Madrid: Editorial Trotta, 1992.

Rosenberg, David. *A Poet's Bible*. New York: Hyperion, 1991.

Rosenfeld, Alvin. *A Double Dying: Reflections on Holocaust Literature*. Bloomington: Indiana University Press, 1980.

Rosenfeld, Alvin, and Irving Greenberg, eds. *Confronting the Holocaust: The Impact of Elie Wiesel.* Bloomington: Indiana University Press, 1978.

Rosenfeld, Israel. *The Invention of Memory: A New View of the Brain.* New York: Basic, 1988.

Rosenstock-Husey, Eugene. *Out of Revolution: The Autobiography of Western Man.* New York: Four Wells Press, 1964.

Rosita K. Holocaust Testimony (HVT-77), Fortunoff Video Archives for Holocaust Testimonies, Yale University Library.

Roskies, David G. *Against the Apocalypse: Responses to Catastrophe in Modern Jewish Culture.* Cambridge: Harvard University Press, 1984.

Rubin, Evelyn Pike. *Ghetto Shanghai.* New York: Shengold, 1933.

Rudnicki, Adolf. *Ascent to Heaven.* Translated by H. C. Stevens. London: Dennis Dobson, 1951.

Ryckmans, Pierre. "The Chinese Attitude toward the Past." *Papers on Far Eastern History* 39 (March 1989): 1–16.

Sacks, Oliver. "Making Up the Mind." *New York Review of Books,* April 8, 1993, 41–44.

Savin, Elmer. "Encounters Dictated by Fate." Manuscript on deposit at Yad Vashem, Jerusalem.

Schorsch, Ismar. *From Text to Context: The Turn to History in Modern Judaism.* Hanover, N.H.: Brandeis University Press, 1994.

Schwarcz, Vera. *The Chinese Enlightenment: The Legacy of the May Fourth Movement in Modern China.* Berkeley: University of California Press, 1986.

———. "A Curse on the Great Wall." *Theory and Society* 13 (1984): 455–70.

———. "Di er ci shijie dazhan: zai bowuguan de guangzhao zhi wai" (World War II: Beyond the museum lights). *Dong Fang* (Orient) 5 (fall 1995): 4–8.

———. *Long Road Home: A China Journal.* New Haven: Yale University Press, 1984.

———. "Memory, Commemoration, and the Plight of China's Intellectuals." *Wilson Quarterly* 13 (October 1989): 120–29.

———. "Mingled Voices: On Writing My Father's Memoirs." *Columbia* 17 (fall 1991): 120–37.

———. "No Solace from Lethe: History, Memory and Identity in Modern China." *Daedalus* (spring 1991): 85–112.

———. "The Pane of Suffering: Public Uses of Personal Grief in Modern China." *Daedalus* (winter 1996): 119–48.

———. Review of *The Mozartian Historian: Essays on the Works of Joseph R. Levenson,* edited by Maurice Meisner and Rhoads Murphey. *History and Theory* 17:3 (1978): 349–67.

———. *Time for Telling Truth Is Running Out: Conversations with Zhang Shenfu.* New Haven: Yale University Press, 1992.

———. "Wiedergutmachung." *Hobo Jungle,* no. 7 (spring 1990): 71.

Schwartz, Benjamin. *The World of Thought in Ancient China.* Cambridge: Harvard University Press, 1985.

Schwartzman, Rabbi Solomon. Video testimony, November 27, 1990. New York Holocaust Museum.

Shushan, Ibn. *Ha Milon Hahadash* (The new dictionary). Jerusalem: Kiviyut, 1980.

Siu, Helen F., and Zelda Stern. *Mao's Harvest: Voices from China's New Generation.* New York: Oxford University Press, 1983.

Smith, Morton. *Hope and History: An Exploration.* New York: Harper and Row, 1980.

Sorban, Raul. "Nine Jewish Artists Victims of the Holocaust in Northern Transylvania." *Studia Judaica* (1993): 48–58.

Spigelman, Art. *Maus*. New York: Pantheon, 1985.

Steedman, Carolyn. "Why Clio Doesn't Care." In *Feminists Revision History*, edited by Anne Louise Shapiro. New Brunswick: Rutgers University Press, 1994.

Steinsaltz, Rabbi Adin. "The Letters of the Ten Utterances." *Wellsprings* (fall 1993/5754): 9–12.

Steinsaltz, Rabbi Adin, ed. *The Talmud: The Steinsaltz Edition: A Reference Guide*. New York: Random House, 1989.

Sucher, Cheryl Pearl. "History Is the Province of Memory." *Midstream* (April 1989): 53–56.

Swift, Graham. *Waterland*. New York: Poseidon Press, 1991.

Tao Juyin. *Gudao jianwen* (Records of life on Lonely Island). Shanghai: Renmin Chubanshe, 1979.

Tokayer, Marvin. *The Fugu Plan*. New York: Paddington Press, 1979.

Tornopolsky, Noga. "Murdering Memory in Argentina." *New York Times*, December 15, 1994.

Tu Wei-ming. *Centrality and Commonality: An Essay on Confucian Righteousness*. Albany: State University of New York Press, 1989.

Unger, Jonathan, ed. *Using the Past to Serve the Present*. Armonk, N.Y.: M. E. Sharpe, 1993.

Van Slyke, Lyman. *Yangtze: Nature, History and the River*. Reading, Mass.: Addison-Wesley, 1988.

Wakeman, Frederic. "Roundtable Discussion of *The Trouble with Confucianism*." *China Review International* 1 : 1 (spring 1994): 22–26.

Waldron, Arthur. *The Great Wall of China*. Cambridge: Cambridge University Press, 1990.

Wang Gongwu. "Loving the Ancients in China." In *Who Owns the Past?: Papers from the Annual Symposium of the Australian Academy of the Humanities*, edited by Isabel McBryde. New York: Oxford University Press, 1985.

Wang Huizu. *Bingta menghen lu* (Traces from a sickbed). Shanghai: Commercial Press, 1928.

Watson, Burton. *Ssu Ma Ch'ien: A Grand Historian of China*. New York: Columbia University Press, 1963.

Watson, Rubie S., ed. *Memory, History, and Opposition under State Socialism*. Santa Fe: School of America Research Press, 1994.

Welty, Eudora. *The Optimist's Daughter*. New York: Random House, 1977.

Wiesel, Elie. *Les Chants des Morts*. Paris: Bernard Grasset, 1965.

———. *Discours d'Oslo*. Paris: Bernard Grasset, 1987.

———. "Praising His Name in the Fire." *New York Times Book Review*, January 17, 1988, 10–11.

Wu Pei-yi. *The Confucian's Progress: Autobiographical Writings in China*. Princeton: Princeton University Press, 1990.

———. "Memories of K'ai-Feng." *New Literary History* 25 : 1 (winter 1994): 20–34.

Wu Tianwei. "Zhongguo de 'huojie'?" (Is there a Chinese 'Holocaust'?). *Jiujiu xuekan* (Continental Review) 1 : 4 (summer 1987): 105–17.

Xu Xin, ed. *Youtairen baikequanshu* (Encyclopedia Judaica). Shanghai: Renmin Chubanshe, 1993.

Xu Youyu. "Wenge Bowuguan?" (A cultural revolution museum?). *Qingnian Baokan Shijie* (Youth Periodicals Panorama) (January 1996): 10–12.

Yang Jiang, *Six Chapters from My Life "Downunder."* Translated by Howard Goldblatt. Seattle: University of Washington Press, 1983.

Yang Lian, ed. *Xinshi chao shiji* (New trends in poetry). Vol. 1. Beijing: Beijing Daxue Chubanshe, 1985.

Yerushalmi, Yosef. *Zachor: Jewish History and Jewish Memory*. Seattle: University of Washington Press, 1982.

Yeshurun, Helit, ed. *International Poets' Festival*. Jerusalem: Mishkenot Sha'ananim, 1995.

Young, James E. *The Texture of Memory: Holocaust Memorials and Meaning*. New Haven· Yale University Press, 1994.

Yu Guangyuan. *Wenge zhongde wo* (Myself, during the Cultural Revolution). Shanghai: Yuandong Chubanshe, 1995).

Yu Guangzhong. *Yu Guangzhong shixuan* (Selected poems of Yu Guangzhong). Hong Kong: Hongfan Shudian, 1981.

Yu Kuang-chung. *Acres of Barbed Wire*. Taipei: Mei Ya, 1971.

Yue, Daiyun, and Carolyn Wakeman. *To the Storm*. Berkeley: University of California Press, 1985.

Zenner, Walter P. " 'We're the Jews of . . . ': The Symbolic Encounter of Diaspora Chinese with Jews." *Points East* 8 : 2 (June 1993): 1–3.

Zhang Dainian. Preface to *Suoyi* (Remembering as such). Beijing: Zhonguo Wenshi Chubanshe, 1993.

Zhang Shenfu. *Suoyi* (Remembering as such). Beijing: Zhonguo Wenshi Chubanshe, 1993.

Zhang Xianliang. *Getting Used to Dying*. Translated by A. Avery. New York: HarperCollins, 1991.

Zheng Zhenduo. *Zhijiu sanji* (Reminiscences of life in hibernation). Shanghai: Renmin Chubanshe, 1951.

Zhong Zhiyun, ed. *Zhongwen da cidian* (An encyclopedic dictionary of the Chinese language). Taipei: Zhong Gongchuban Bu, 1973.

Zhou Ming, ed. *Lishi zai zheli chensi* (History has brought us to this reflection). Beijing: Huaxia Chubanshe, 1986.

Index

DS 113 .S377 1998
Schwarcz, Vera
Chinese and Jewish Cultural
Memory.

DATE DUE

#47-0108 Peel Off Pressure Sensitive